What
SUCCESSFUL
Science Teachers Do

What
SUCCESSFUL
Science Teachers Do

75 Research-Based Strategies

Neal A. Glasgow ● Michele Cheyne ● Randy K. Yerrick

Foreword by Page Keeley

Skyhorse Publishing

Copyright © 2010 by Corwin Press.

First Skyhorse Publishing edition 2017

Skyhorse Publishing books may be purchased in bulk at special discounts for sales promotion, corporate gifts, fund-raising, or educational purposes. Special editions can also be created to specifications. For details, contact the Special Sales Department, Sky Pony Press, 307 West 36th Street, 11th Floor, New York, NY 10018 or info@skyhorsepublishing.com.

Skyhorse® and Skyhorse Publishing® are registered trademark of Skyhorse Publishing, Inc.®, a Delaware corporation.

Visit our website at www.skyhorsepublishing.com.

10 9 8 7 6 5 4 3 2 1

Library of Congress Cataloging-in-Publication Data is available on file.

Cover design by Michael Dubowe

Print ISBN: 978-1-63450-726-4
Ebook ISBN: 978-1-63450-725-7

Printed in the United States of America

Contents

Foreword

In the fifteen years since standards became the centerpiece of science education reform, schools and teachers have engaged in a flurry of activity around standards. Developing and aligning curriculum and assessment with standards, mapping curriculum, and supporting implementation of a standards-based curriculum have been at the forefront of reform efforts in schools across the nation. While these are important efforts in ensuring all students have an opportunity to achieve science literacy, they do not go far enough. The missing link seems to be a focus on instruction. While some districts have targeted instruction through generic tools and strategies designed to improve general pedagogy, science teachers face many pedagogical challenges unique to the discipline of science. It is this special pedagogical content knowledge (PCK) that distinguishes good science teachers from great science teachers and transforms science classrooms into places where students can excel in science.

With this book, *What Successful Science Teachers Do: 75 Research-Based Strategies*, teachers now have a comprehensive resource they can use to continually hone their practice and transform good teaching into great teaching. It is through effective instruction—the interface between the student, curriculum, and assessment—that the vision of standards-based reform truly comes to life. This is a much-needed, timely resource. President Barack Obama and his education secretary, Arne Duncan, have started talking quite a lot about great teaching, resulting in one of the largest competitive teacher effectiveness programs: Race to the Top. States must try to identify great teachers, figure out how they got that way, and then create more of them.

A few years ago I read a highly regarded management book, *From Good to Great: Why Some Companies Make the Leap . . . and Others Don't* (Collins, 2001), that described how some companies go from being average to soaring toward greatness. Greatness was defined as being several times better than average over a sustained period of time. One of the most important lessons I learned from this book—equally applicable to a business or a school—is to critically examine what works best for others and to strive to understand, implement, and evaluate similar practices in your own context. This is also much of the premise behind Race to the Top. In other words, consider giving up the "same old, same old" strategies that don't seem to be effective in moving students toward important learning goals in favor of considering research-based strategies that have been shown to work in classrooms.

However, in order to use research-based strategies, teachers must have access to the research in a ready-to-use, teacher-friendly format. That is exactly the kind of access that *What Successful Science Teachers Do* provides so well. The 75 strategies in the text, based on clear summaries of current research, cover a range of contextual considerations science teachers face in their daily interactions with students including inquiry-based instructional methods, collaborative teaching and learning, utilizing technology for student and teacher learning, assessment, culturally responsive teaching, gender issues, science and language literacy, and family connections.

One of the goals I focused on during my term as the 63rd President of the National Science Teachers Association (NSTA) was to identify strategies to help bridge the gap between research and practice. To my delight and amazement, this was a goal that resonated not only with the NSTA Research Division, but especially with practitioners in the field, both teachers and those who work to support teachers. One of the effective ways to do this is by making research more accessible to teachers through publications geared toward practitioners. Clearly teachers, science specialists, professional developers, preservice teachers, faculty and all who support science education have shifted from a reliance on individual bias and opinion to supporting the wisdom of their instructional decisions with the empirical evidence that comes from research. Furthermore, school administrators are increasingly asking the question "What research do you have to support this practice?" Finally, here is a well-researched book that can provide evidence on effective actions science teachers can take and the requisite classroom conditions necessary to facilitate learning for all students. Not only does it provide a summary of the research; most important, it provides teachers with the practical suggestions for applying the research findings, including caveats to be aware of when using research-based strategies in your own context.

In addition to the wealth of valuable information in this book, I find the format to be particularly appealing to practitioners. In 2008 Corwin published the best-seller *Science Formative Assessment: 75 Practical Strategies for Linking Assessment, Instruction, and Learning* (Keeley, 2008). As the author of this book and a professional developer who has worked with thousands of teachers and many school districts throughout the U.S., the comment I repeatedly hear is how teacher friendly the format is. One can pick a single strategy, focus on it, evaluate its success, and gradually increase one's repertoire of effective strategies by adding new ones. The format helps users easily understand the purpose of the strategy, the research behind it, and its implementation considerations. It moves teachers away from selecting a strategy because it looks interesting or might be fun for students, to being purposeful in their selection of strategies. And the most important comment I hear is that building a school culture where these 75 formative assessment strategies are being used across classrooms is transforming teaching and learning. Many professional learning communities are using the book to examine and link strategies to their goals for student achievement. I'm excited to see a similar format in Glasgow, Cheyne, and Yerrick's book that is sure to elicit the same reaction from educators. As a matter of fact, one of the questions I often get is "Can you do a similar book that focuses on instructional strategies?" Well, the simple answer is that there is no need for me to do so! This book serves that very purpose and is a wonderful companion to *Science Formative Assessment*. After all, instruction and assessment are two sides of the same coin—you can't have one without the other. They are inextricably linked and complement each other.

I especially want to thank the authors for furthering the important goal of bridging the gap between research and practice and providing another resource to move the work of science professional learning communities forward. As experienced educators and researchers, the authors are well-attuned to the reality of schools and teaching. They do not present their ideas as remote armchair theorists but rather as educators who respect and understand K–12 teaching and learning. They do not provide you with a bag of tricks or abstract theories, but rather a well-thought-out set of research-based principles and strategies for you to consider. Becoming a great science teacher is a lifelong, continuous process. Whether you are new to teaching, a veteran teacher, or one who works with teachers and future teachers, this book is sure to become your well-worn, dog-eared companion as you strive to be a GREAT teacher or teacher educator.

Page Keeley, Maine Mathematics and Science Alliance
Past-President of the National Science Teachers Association

Sources

Collins, J. (2001). *From good to great: Why some companies make the leap . . . and others don't*. New York: HarperCollins.

Keeley, P. (2008). *Science formative assessment: 75 practical strategies for linking assessment, instruction, and learning*. Thousand Oaks, CA: Corwin.

Preface

Two decades after science became the favored child of American education—with hundreds of millions of Federal dollars at its disposal and a clear-cut mandate to assure national security and lead American society into the technological age—biology, chemistry, and physics are once again fighting for their place in American schools.

Edward B. Fisk, April 1979
The New York Times

American students will move from the middle of the top—from the middle to the top of the pack in science and math over the next decade—for we know that the nation that out-educates us today will out-compete us tomorrow. And I don't intend to have us out-educated. We can't start soon enough.

President Barack Obama, April 2009
Presentation to the National Academy of Sciences

When *Sputnik*'s first "beeps" reached the earth on October 4, 1957, a sense of concern and paranoia swept over the United States as the Soviets had beaten the Americans into space. That concern sparked a refocusing of resources and a much-needed revolution in science education, scientific inquiry, and the development of intellectual and cognitive capacity in the United States. Since that burst of enthusiasm over 50 years ago, science education slowly has been taken over by new national demands and shifts of emphasis. The stature of science, science education, and scientific reasoning has been diminished in the classroom, and the cumulative effect of this resonates through science learning outcomes for generations of students. This is reflected in international assessments and choices students make for their careers. The good news is that President

Barack Obama is now calling for a revival of the *Sputnik*-era focus and a renewed commitment to the sciences and science education.

This leaves 21st-century science educators in a challenging position. Concerns about science education are becoming especially focused and rising to a level in Congress and federal agencies rarely seen since the *Sputnik* era. Science again matters, and we have reasons to be optimistic! We now have the attention of policy makers at the highest level. We must prepare and be ready to do our part. We need to reinvent ourselves as science teachers and developers of instruction.

Science, as practiced, is a beautiful example of an eloquent process of how humans strive to understand and define their world. However, in the classroom, underlying concepts, clear definitions, and simple answers and explanations are hidden in complex and tangled intellectual structures and curricular details. Textbook content and general science curriculum are often very far removed from the ways in which science is actually conducted and utilized today. The unifying concept, collectively called the nature of science, is often missing or hidden within the day-to-day details. Much of the time, we teachers haphazardly meander through a maze of different topics, under the banner of "coverage."

Where can teachers look for guidance and validation for their instruction and choices? For overall views, the National Academy of Sciences, the American Association for the Advancement of Science, and the National Science Teachers Association are three of the main organizations involved with science education. Fortunately, many of their policy positions and standards are in alignment.

Each subdiscipline in the sciences also has a range of professional organizations providing direction as to what to teach and how to teach. States also have governmental departments that deal with specific frameworks, scope and sequences, textbook adoptions, and a range of administrative tasks. Many of these look to the three main science organizations as a source of guidance when constructing their own documents.

Our overall aim in writing this book is to look for common ground and to search science education research for instructional, curricular, general education, and community-based strategies that unite the goals of all of those involved in facilitating science literacy. We were guided by seven central learning and teaching goals that we feel come close to defining what science literacy is:

1. Mastery of subject matter

2. Mastery and understanding of scientific reasoning

3. Understanding of the nature of science

4. Understanding the complexity of real empirical work, experimental design, and validity assessment

5. Mastering practical procedural and scientific process skills

6. Promotion and mastery of teamwork

7. Generating interest and motivating curiosity in science

Reflecting on these goals, especially the seventh goal related to curiosity, we recognize that many intangible factors resonate deeply with students as they form their views of science and decide the role science will play in their lives. School practices sometimes diminish curiosity from the important goal it should be. Curiosity is a quality that serves the sciences well and is a key element in what makes a science-literate person either a citizen consumer or a practitioner of science. A curious student is one we all want to have and foster in our classrooms, especially in the science classroom. We want to nurture curiosity and revive it in those who have lost it. With curiosity, soul, and passion, knowledge and skills can become extraordinary.

Students usually come to us seeking mastery over procedures, materials, processes, and content. Early in a career, teaching to these goals is enough. But we serve our students best once we introduce the deeper, more complex, and very personal engagement that produces the greatest worth over the long periods of time. Science is much more than procedures, materials, processes, and content. Teaching students how to think is more important than what to think. This may not always make professional sense in the age of standardized tests, but it makes lots of sense for future thoughtful citizens and decision makers. This is why we keep curiosity and scientific reasoning as themes in the back of our minds when writing.

Barnett and Kitto (2004) describe a research-practice gap in science and math education that they attribute to teachers having little interest in or use for the academic products of educational researchers. We have tried to fill that gap by closely examining the national standards and the academic research. We then filter that information through our own classroom, school, and community experiences to produce summaries, reflections, ideas, and curricular and instructional strategies that will help teachers move beyond simple "coverage" focused instruction. In this way, immersion in science will yield students who are curious, motivated, and ambitious, in addition to literate, with content mastery capable of higher levels of scientific reasoning and inquiry.

Source

Barnett, J, & Kitto, R. (2004). Mind the gap: A proposal for science, mathematics, and technology education. *Canadian Journal of Science, Mathematics and Technology Education, 4*(4), 529–535.

Acknowledgments

Corwin gratefully acknowledges the contributions of the following reviewers:

Deanna Brunlinger, Teacher
Elkhorn Area School District
Elkhorn, WI

Randy Cook, Chemistry/
   Physics Instructor
Tri County Area Schools
Howard City, MI

Susan B. Koba, Retired Science
   Education Consultant
Omaha Public Schools
Omaha, NE

Loukea Kovanis-Wilson,
   Chemistry Instructor
Clarkston High School
Clarkston, MI

J-Petrina Puhl, Science Teacher
Robert McQueen High School
Reno, NV

Maria Mesires, Seventh-Grade
   Life Science Teacher
Case Middle School
Watertown, NY

Toni B. Ramey, Science Teacher
Mobile County School System
Mobile, AL

Sara Stewart, Project Facilitator,
   Curriculum and Professional
   Development
Clark County School District
Las Vegas, NV

About the Authors

Neal A. Glasgow has been involved in education on many levels for many years. His experience includes serving as a secondary school science and art teacher both in California and New York, as a university biotechnology teaching laboratory director and laboratory technician, and as an educational consultant and frequent speaker on many educational topics. He is the author or coauthor of 11 books on education: *What Successful Schools Do to Involve Families: 55 Partnership Strategies* (2009); *What Successful Teachers Do: 101 Research-Based Classroom Strategies for New and Veteran Teachers, Second Edition* (2009); *What Successful Literacy Teachers Do: 70 Research-Based Strategies for Teachers, Reading Coaches, and Instructional Planners* (2007): *What Successful Teachers Do in Diverse Classrooms: 71 Research-Based Strategies for New and Veteran Teachers* (2006); *What Successful Teachers Do in Inclusive Classrooms: 60 Research-Based Strategies That Help Special Learners* (2005); *What Successful Mentors Do: 81 Researched-Based Strategies for New Teacher Induction, Training, and Support* (2004); *What Successful Teachers Do: 91 Research-Based Strategies for New and Veteran Teachers* (2003); *Tips for Science Teachers: Research-Based Strategies to Help Students Learn* (2001); *New Curriculum for New Times: A Guide to Student-Centered, Problem-Based Learning* (1997); *Doing Science: Innovative Curriculum Beyond the Textbook for the Life Sciences* (1997); and *Taking the Classroom to the Community: A Guidebook* (1996).

Michele Cheyne is a clinical faculty member in science education at the University of Pittsburgh, where she teaches a variety of courses in the secondary science teacher preparation program. She also supervises preservice teachers during their clinical experiences and works closely with inservice teachers. She has worked with Pittsburgh Public Schools on several projects and provides professional development for professional laboratory training programs. She has worked with the Interstate New Teachers Assessment and Support Consortium in Washington, DC, as a member of the committee that wrote the 2001 document *Model Standards for Licensing General and Special Education Teachers of Students With Disabilities: A Resource for State Dialogue.* She taught high school biology and chemistry for 11 years in Milwaukee Public Schools (MPS) prior to moving to Pittsburgh. While teaching in MPS, she also served as a department chair, hosted a multitude of preservice teachers, and cotaught with several special education teachers in inclusive settings. She also taught science methods courses at the University of Wisconsin-Milwaukee for both future science teachers and for future special education teachers.

Randy K. Yerrick is a professor of science education and associate dean of educational technology at the State University of New York at Buffalo. He began his career as a chemistry, physics, and math teacher in Michigan schools before becoming a full-time researcher in science education. Dr. Yerrick's research focuses on implementing contemporary visions of science inquiry in lower track classrooms where students share a strong history of failure and antisocial school behaviors. He has conducted ethnographies and critical autoethnographies in a variety of diverse teaching contexts as he continues to examine unresolved school issues of equity and diversity promoted by the continuous practice of tracking in science. He has also received recognition as an Apple Distinguished Educator, a group of innovative educators representing over 20 countries who integrate technology into classroom instruction in a 21st-century global learning community. Examples of his work can be found at http://gse.buffalo.edu/about/directory/faculty/yerrick and http://web.me.com/ubscience/.

Introduction

Science is not formal logic—it needs the free play of the mind in as great a degree as any other creative art. It is true that this is a gift that can hardly be taught, but its growth can be encouraged in those who already posses it.

Max Born (1882–1970)
German physicist, Nobel Prize, 1954

I do not know what I may appear to the world; but to myself I seem to have been only like a boy playing on the seashore, and diverting myself in now and then finding of a smoother pebble or a prettier shell than ordinary, whilst the great ocean of truth lay all undiscovered before me.

Sir Isaac Newton (1642–1727)
English physicist, mathematician

The two quotes above help set the tone for this book. We want to inspire teachers to recognize that there is so much more to science education than lectures and textbooks. To completely immerse students in science, we all need to foster basic human qualities. As you can already see, we have a particular instructional bias regarding science education, and we begin this introduction by discussing seven underlying assumptions we hold as important.

First, we welcome the establishment of a common framework for what teachers and students at various grade levels should be able to do and know in the science classroom. Science education reform is a complicated and often hotly debated field that has been around for over 100 years. Epistemological beliefs on the value of science knowledge for society at large and what science literacy should mean continue to manifest themselves as the "latest" reform. However, unlike other periods in the history of science education, there is now some unity in goals and standards. That is the good news. The National Science Education Standards (NSES), published by the National Research Council (NRC, 1996), gives teachers and everyone else a document that comes very near national consensus on what every K–12 student should be expected to know and be able to do in the area of science. Furthermore, it explains what guidance and reforms in professional development, teaching and learning assessment, curriculum design, and the pedagogy need to be addressed for teachers to be able to deliver a quality science education.

Most state departments of education have used the NSES in forming their own guidelines for science education. The state standards have then trickled down to regional and local efforts. They are used for structuring teacher education, textbook adoption, and assessments.

In addition, earlier, in 1993, the American Association for the Advancement of Science (AAAS) released *Benchmarks for Science Literacy*. Similar to the NSES, the document attempted to define the science content that students should be able to know and do before graduation. The original document did not address standards for assessment, professional development, and pedagogy; however, subsequent publications from the AAAS/Project 2061 have attempted to cover these topics. According to the NRC, there is a 90% overlap between the two in science content.

On the more practical and the professional development side, the National Science Teachers Association (NSTA) was founded in 1944 and is an organization committed to promoting excellence and innovation in science teaching and learning. The NSTA is focused on implementing many of the goals and guidelines identified by the AAAS and NRC documents. We support their strategic plan, which identifies four critical goals that guide their efforts:

- Engage all teachers of science continually to improve science education.
- Improve student learning by supporting and enhancing science teaching.
- Advocate for the importance of science, both science literacy and the development of scientific expertise.
- Enhance science education through research-based policy and practice.

We embrace the NSES and revisit them often. They come nearest to capturing the nature and spirit of the way science is known, conducted, and utilized outside the classroom. They also promote instructional strategies that can best characterize a form of science that relates in reflective ways to the concerns, interests, and activities of scientifically literate citizens as they go about their everyday business. Science education needs to nurture two masters—educating current and future citizens, while at the same time training future career scientists. The current standards address and balance these goals.

Our second assumption relates to the reality of the 21st-century classroom. Diversity, in many forms, is more the rule than the exception. Differentiated instructional techniques are gradually moving into the mainstream classroom. Historically, special educators have been trained to differentiate instruction, to provide individualized instruction to each student on their caseloads. They create individual education programs (IEPs) based on their students' needs and align goals and objectives with grade-level curriculum and state standards as much as possible. On the other hand, general educators have been trained in teaching methods and content area subjects (English, mathematics, science, reading). They teach large groups of students; rarely is there time for individualized instruction. As a result of the No Child Left Behind Act (NCLB) and Individuals with Disabilities Education Improvement Act (IDEA), general educators are now being asked to "design materials and activities that can meet the needs of all students initially, rather than make modifications after the fact" (van Garderen & Whitaker, 2006). Differentiated instruction is becoming a model to help teachers change the way they teach. We embrace this instructional approach for the science classroom.

Third, we also embrace scientific inquiry as a curricular vehicle and instructional tool. National standards call for "real phenomena" as a part of an investigation, as opposed to secondhand science learning derived from teacher-talk and/or textbooks. Much of what is called hands-on inquiry today is nothing more than demonstrations or procedural-dominated lab experiences that just reinforce textbook concepts. While these techniques have their role in science education, they should not be confused with science inquiry. Scientific knowledge hasn't come easy. Students should know the context in which their book content was conceived and validated. Students should have the chance to role-play to foster their potential for science reasoning. This concept should not be excluded because of excessive immersion in learning about what scientists already know. Remember, coverage doesn't guaranty knowledge retention or usefulness. We want to engage students in the type of thinking that has evolved in science communities over human history and how it has shaped society and culture. There is a process, beyond the textbook, that structures exploration, experimentation, and the entire process of answering scientific questions. The goal is to establish confidence and trust in science and also engage students in the critical, ethical, and moral thinking and decision making regarding scientific knowledge as it filters through society in general. Scientific exploration and thinking has a grand history and has also influenced thinking in other disciplines. Over time, engaging students in true inquiry has been shown as a significant motivator in facilitating career choices in the sciences.

Fourth, we recognize that scientific discourse, collaboration, teamwork, scientific reasoning, and peer review and argumentation are the norm in all scientific endeavors. Teachers can bring some of these qualities to their instruction as they engage students in critical thinking. We believe opportunities for these experiences should be part of any curricular or pedagogical development.

Fifth, we need to align and pattern our assessment tools in more authentic ways. Once leaving school, people are assessed and evaluated using very different criteria than those found in most classroom assessments. Science is a performance-based discipline, and assessments and evaluations should reflect some of that. The problem is how do we assess students' knowledge and skills that are learned during inquiry-based instruction or laboratory experiences. If the adage that what is valuable is tested, then science assessments that do not require inquiry skills and reasoning could result in a reduction of laboratory and inquiry-based experiences, although the NSES promote these experiences as the core of any science program. Many state-mandated tests now de-value inquiry-based and laboratory skills and knowledge. We still have a ways to go to reach consensus about what goals and outcomes are appropriate for high school and college or university students within inquiry or laboratory experiences, especially for those who do not aspire to careers in science and research.

Sixth, we support general overall literacy goals, which should become part of every instructional strategy. We think that expository science writing, reading, and discourse are unique and often underrepresented in English classes. We embrace literacy as a general mandate, and it should be a part of every lesson plan and assessment.

Finally, we believe that science must be part of a student's personal life outside the classroom, and we need to engage students in science activities and critical thinking in everyday community settings and life in general.

In sum, our philosophy is to develop a learning community with high expectations for schools, teachers, and students, while simultaneously offering the appropriate support for students to meet the demands of challenging science instruction. Personal teaching standards should be constructed in such a way that all learners are challenged at a level that is appropriate for them.

Within these goals, objectives, and beliefs, we had choices to make regarding this book's organization. Our intent is to bring the reader methodologies based on educational research findings in science education. This book is not meant to be read as one would read a novel but rather used as an informational guide. Our objective is to focus on useful and practical educational research that translates into a range of choices and solutions to individual teaching and learning problems in science. Within these chapters we present a wide range of instructional strategies and suggestions, based on educational, psychological, sociological, and literacy studies. The strategies are based on research done with preservice, student, beginning, and experienced teachers. Occasionally, the research explores less traditional educational settings often called informal science. Furthermore, a few strategies examine the connections between the science classroom and the world of science, as it is practiced in academic and industry settings.

Although certain student groups, such as special education students, students within urban settings, and English language learners, are often separated for attention, we have chosen embedded strategies specific to these specialized groups into our more general instructional categories. Because of the heterogeneity in science classrooms today, instruction needs to be as cognitively open-ended as possible.

Within the nine chapters in this book, strategies are structured in a user-friendly format with the following elements:

- The Strategy: a simple, concise, or crisp statement of an instructional strategy
- What the Research Says: a brief discussion of the research that led to the strategy, providing the reader with a deeper understanding of the principle(s) discussed
- Classroom Applications: a description of how this teaching strategy can be used in instructional settings
- Precautions and Possible Pitfalls: caveats intended to help teachers avoid common difficulties before they occur
- Sources: provided so the reader may refer to the original research

We feel that all science teachers can benefit from these practical classroom, home, and community applications based on the research findings. Our hope is that our work can provide advice and support regarding many facets of teaching that can be especially troublesome yet fundamental to science teaching. The strategies provide reality-based suggestions to strengthen and support classroom theory and practical application.

We suggest that veteran teachers can benefit from the knowledge gained from the most recent research and reflect and refresh their philosophies and instruction. Given the critical need for teachers now and in the future, we, as a profession, cannot afford to have potentially good teachers leaving the profession because they don't feel supported, they're too overwhelmed, or they suffer from burnout.

It is our hope that this book may help new teachers to avoid the "baptism by fire" that many experience when they first start teaching. However, we recognize that as a beginning teacher, there may be strategies in this book that presumably don't apply. As in any new endeavor, there is a tendency of "not knowing what you don't know." We ask that you come back and revisit this book from time to time throughout the year. What may not be applicable the first time you read it may be of help at a later date.

Science teaching, and education in general, has never been more exciting or more challenging. Expectations for teachers, students, and schools continue to rise. The more resources teachers have at their fingertips to assist students along the educational journey, the better the outcome. Hopefully, teachers will find this book useful and practical in defining and enhancing their teaching skills.

Sources

American Association for the Advancement of Science. (1993). *Benchmarks for science literacy: Project 2061.* New York: Oxford University Press.

National Research Council. (1996). *National science education standards.* Washington, DC: National Academy Press.

van Garderen, D., & Whittaker, C. (2006). Planning differentiated, multicultural instruction for secondary inclusive classrooms. *Teaching Exceptional Children, 38*(3), 12–20.

1

General Science Instruction

> **Strategy 1: Encourage students to become more involved and interested in science.**

What the Research Says

 Roberts and Wassersug (2009) studied a hands-on summer research program for high school students that ran from 1958 to 1972. They wanted to examine whether the effects of exposure to original scientific research produced more career scientists. They compared participants in the first program with science students that only began their inquiry research at a college or university.

Their data indicate that students who are interested in science and have opportunities to participate in original research in high school are significantly more likely to both enter and maintain a career in science in comparison to students whose first research experience didn't occur until at a college or university.

It should be noted that Roberts and Wassersug (2009) acknowledge the possibility of bias in their study. Self-selection bias and a number of other variables influence who participates in high school research programs and moves on to careers in science. Their data might not apply to all high school students. However, they state that, to the best of their knowledge, they are the first to explore this question.

Classroom Applications

The Roberts and Wassersug (2009) research follows the thinking that a lifelong interest in science is more likely to develop in childhood. There are many programs in the United States that provide high school and middle school science students with opportunities to engage in science in research settings. Many of these occur in outreach programs offered by local colleges and universities. In addition, students can be encouraged to participate in informal science programs, as recommended in the National Science Teachers Association (NSTA) position statement below:

> NSTA recognizes and encourages the development of sustained links between the informal institutions and schools. Informal science education generally refers to programs and experiences developed outside the classroom by institutions and organizations that include
>
> - children's and natural history museums, science-technology centers, planetariums, zoos and aquaria, botanical gardens and arboreta, parks, nature centers and environmental education centers, and scientific research laboratories;
> - media, involving print, film, broadcast, and electronic forms; and
> - community-based organizations and projects, including youth organizations and community outreach services. (National Science Teachers Association, 2010)

A growing body of research documents the power of informal learning experiences to spark curiosity and engage interest in the sciences during school years and throughout a lifetime. Informal science education institutions have a long history of providing staff development for teachers and enrichment experiences for students and the public. Informal science education accommodates different learning styles and effectively serves the complete spectrum of learners: gifted, challenged, nontraditional, and second-language learners.

In addition to having students involved in outreach programs, many of these programs offer opportunities for teachers to participant in inservice experiences to help train them in bringing inquiry into the classroom and to engage students in inquiry activities. Once teachers feel comfortable with inquiry activities, they can design similar learning opportunities in their classes.

Also, in most communities, science is being conducted—weather stations, water quality studies, and other environmental investigations are routinely taking place. Connecting with water quality boards can sometimes bring these science experts into the classroom to help design and involve students in their research. You may even survey your students and find parents involved in science activities in their careers. Is drawing on such relationships out of the teaching paradigm? Recruiting mentors from outside the classroom community is very common these days and is a great source of "real world" experiences for students, especially in those schools not near college and university resources.

Precautions and Possible Pitfalls

Common sense tells us that there is a point at which younger children can't be expected to engage in more self-directed but guided inquiry or research. Scientific inquiry requires repetition in order to get an adequate sample size. It also requires experimental design and highly controlled data gathering. Research can be tedious, monotonous, and puzzling for younger students.

It should be noted that there is another side to the research, as Bloom and Weisberg (2007) concluded in their work on adult resistance to science. Frequently, such resistance has its origins in childhood for a range of different reasons and may include the student's classroom science experiences as a factor. Starting too young or forcing unmotivated students into programs might lead them to reject science as a potential career, as they reach their frustration point with the details of inquiry.

Sources

Bloom, P., & Weisberg, D. S. (2007). Childhood origins of adult resistance to science. *Science, 316,* 996–997. Retrieved March 1, 2010, from http://www.edge.org/3rd_culture/bloom07/bloom07_index.html

National Science Teachers Association. (2010). *NSTA Official Position Statement: Informal Science Education.* Retrieved March 1, 2010, from http://www.nsta.org/about/positions/informal.aspx

Roberts, L. & Wassersug, R. (2009). Does doing scientific research in high school correlate with students staying in science? A half-century retrospective study. *Research in Science Education, 39,* 251–256.

Strategy 2: Guide students to engage in science-appropriate discourse.

What the Research Says

Huang (2005) explored students' use of language in the process of making sense of genetics concepts. This study was conducted in a middle school with a diverse class of 25 students, and the specific study group was composed of average to high ability in terms of academic performance. Huang identified two distinct forms of classroom discourse. The student's first or primary discourse community comes in the form of informal experiences, social practices, and from family, friends, and community. The second type or secondary discourse community comes from science, the science classroom, and school instruction. Huang states that students need to manage these two different discourse communities and use them both to articulate their sense of scientific knowledge. Furthermore, teachers need to let students utilize both types of discourse to accurately gauge student comprehension and understanding.

Huang (2005) points out that all language plays an important role in developing and mediating a student's science learning by providing a system and method for thinking and developing understanding. This is in addition to the role of language for communicating ideas. The study highlights the fact that the academic language, as practiced in the school and science classroom, is often very different from the language utilized in the home and community. Sometimes the home or community environment nurtures the use of secondary or school language, and other times it doesn't.

Some students in the Huang (2005) study found themselves unable to participate actively in the dominant classroom academic culture and became alienated from the classroom community. These students decided instead to maintain their identity and solidarity with their way of talking and thinking. They did this for a variety of reasons, and many times it related to a social agenda they may have had within the class or within the school in general. Huang recommends that science instruction build a learning community in which students' use of language is recognized, and the border crossings between levels and rigor of discourses are facilitated in the process of learning and assessing science.

Brown and Ryoo (2008) also investigated language and student learning in classrooms. Specifically, they were interested in looking at the effect of separating the development of conceptual understanding and the development of language used to describe those ideas. The study was conducted with fifth-grade students. One half of the students were instructed using an approach that relied exclusively on scientific language. The experimental approach used everyday language prior to the introduction of scientific language.

Results of the study indicated that students in the experimental approach demonstrated overall greater improved conceptual understanding and language competence of science ideas. Students scored highest on post-test measures on questions assessing their conceptual understanding and struggled on questions assessing their use of scientific language. Brown and Ryoo (2008) highlight that result as evidence in support of separating the teaching of concepts and language. In further support of the everyday-language-first approach is the performance of the experimental group on questions utilizing scientific language. The experimental group dramatically outperformed the group that was instructed using scientific language only. This study lends support to the idea suggested in the National Science Education Standards (NRC, 1996) that students should experience phenomena and develop explanations prior to the introduction of scientific language. The conclusion to be drawn seems to be that providing opportunities for students to talk about scientific phenomena in everyday language, followed by carefully scaffolded development of scientific language should lead to both better conceptual understanding and ability to effectively use scientific language.

Classroom Applications

Teachers need to recognize that oral language is a window into understanding and thinking. They need to make science discourse available and accessible to students and mediate the conflicts that interfere in the use of scientific discourse. Teachers need to become skilled at "listening" for reasoning and understanding when students don't cross over into academic language. Teachers also need to listen for language that can provide them with opportunities to replace nonacademic language constructs with more appropriate academic science discourse.

Furthermore, students are often provided with definitions and descriptions of phenomena they will be studying prior to any investigation they will be undertaking. The assumption is that there is some critical basic knowledge necessary to carry out the investigation. Rarely is this the case. Take, for example, a situation of observing materials diffusing through a semi-permeable membrane:

- What is really *necessary* for the students to know beforehand in order for them to make observations of this particular system?
- Do they need to know a definition of "diffusion"?
- Do they need to know the definition of "semi-permeable membrane"?

Think instead of the discussion that might result if, in fact, they do not have this information but only have data that suggest that materials move from one side of a barrier to another side of a barrier:

- What sorts of explanations might students generate to explain the data they have collected?
- How does such a discussion differ from one that might result from an activity in which students already know what will happen—that materials will move from areas of higher concentration to areas of lower concentration?

The issue here is one of language, when to introduce language, and what it will do for both you and your students.

So what are some strategies that teachers can use to provide these hands-on experiences for students that do not rely on the use of term-heavy talk? Provide opportunities for students to describe and interact with materials in their own language. Formal and informal analysis of the patterns of discourse interaction characteristic of most classrooms has shown that, on average, teachers talk for more than two-thirds of the time. Furthermore, a few students contribute most of the answers, boys talk more than girls, and those sitting in the front and center of the class are more likely to contribute than those sitting at the back and sides (Alpert, 1987).

Recent attempts to reform teaching based on constructivist views of learning have called for teachers to ask fewer questions and for students to learn to state and justify their beliefs and argue constructively about reasons and evidence. Greater attention is now being paid to the ways in which meanings evolve as teachers and students mutually construct the unique discourse (with its roles, rules, and expectations) that characterizes each classroom. In this approach, teachers craft ways of using discourse as a method of formative assessment.

As interest in the constructivist nature of language developed, researchers, in a general sense, argued that a large part of the learning process is contained in the process of participating in classroom discourse. As students engage in the discourse, they acquire ways of talking and thinking that characterize a particular curriculum area. For example, to learn science is to become an increasingly expert participant in classroom discourse about the procedures, concepts, and use of evidence and argument that constitutes science. This approach is supported by the theories of the Russian psychologist Lev Vygotsky (1987) who argued that the higher mental processes are acquired through the internalization of the structures of social discourse. There is still a need, however, for detailed linguistic and ethnographic analyses of classroom discourse to provide independent evidence of how students' knowledge and beliefs are changed by their participation in the discourse.

Finally, teachers need to keep in mind that when working toward a pattern of science, appropriate discourse is always going to be a work in progress from year to year. Teaching and changing discourse patterns may best be done within a department as students move through their K–12 experience. This type of collaboration validates the work that each teacher puts into the effort.

Precautions and Potential Pitfalls

 In the world of science, clear communication is essential. It is a required job skill. Students need to be taught how to converse in appropriate ways in all disciplines. In the same class, some students need to learn to restrain themselves, while others need to be nurtured into discussions, questioning, and responses. It would be a mistake to believe that appropriate classroom discourse can't really be taught or doesn't warrant your instructional time. Protocols and structures need to be developed and scaffolds built to support all students. The goal of this strategy is to help you become aware of how discourse should be utilized as an instructional tool. The topic is too broad to cover it within the format of this text. However, a quick look into Amazon.com yielded five pages of books on various aspects of classroom discourse. For example, Randy R. Yerrick has written extensively on discourse in the K–12 science classroom; Michael Hale, Elizabeth City, and Thomas Farrell have written more general books on classroom discourse.

A class full of articulate students in a nurturing classroom environment helps create willing and curious learners. Building on the concept of appropriate discourse is far more enjoyable and rewarding for the teacher than a class of students without a voice or engaging in frustrating communication.

Sources

Alpert, B. R. (1987). Active, silent, and controlled discussions: Explaining variations in classroom conversation. *Teaching and Teacher Education, 3*(1), 29–40.

Brown, B. A., & Ryoo, K. (2008). Teaching science as a language: A "content-first" approach to science teaching. *Journal of Research in Science Teaching, 45*(5), 529–553.

Huang, H. (2005). Listening to the language of constructing science knowledge. *International Journal of Science and Mathematical Education, 4*, 391–415.

National Research Council. (1996). *National science education standards.* Washington, DC: National Academy Press.

Vygotsky, L. S. (1987). Thinking and speech. In *The Collected Works of L. S. Vygotsky, Vol. 1: Problems of General Psychology,* (Norris Minick, Trans.). New York: Plenum Press.

Strategy 3: Utilize graphic organizers in your classroom.

What the Research Says

Graphic organizers have been applied across a range of curriculum subject areas. Although reading is by far the most well-studied application, science, social studies, language arts, and math are additional content areas that are represented in the research base on graphic organizers (Hall & Strangman, 2005).

Structuring and restructuring knowledge into memorable and useful concepts requires slow and carefully structured change. As Radencich (1995) and Routman (1991) suggest for instructional methodology, it is important to take one step at a time and add one new component at a time in the process of change. To reduce a teacher's dependence on students' rote learning and memorization that often occurs during basic reading assignments, a *graphic organizer* is one component that should be considered (Kirylo & Millet, 2000). When graphic organizers are used effectively, both the teacher and the students expand their roles in the lesson.

In a concrete way, utilizing graphic organizers is an inexpensive literacy dynamic that taps into prior knowledge, cultivates active participation, and fosters an understanding of conceptual relationships, leading to a facilitation of comprehension. Loranger (1997) asserts that educators, including veteran teachers, are looking for more meaningful ways to strengthen reading comprehension and specific content instruction. Utilizing graphic organizers as a tool assists in fostering the goal of reading instruction and content retention and understanding, that is, for students to become independent readers and learners.

Classroom Applications

Traditional and electronic graphic organizers can help students organize ideas, convey complex concepts, progress through the steps of the writing process, and develop their mathematical and scientific thinking skills. You can address different learning styles by presenting information in a visual format that shows the connections between concepts.

Graphic organizers are one way for visual thinkers to arrange their ideas, which can be expressed in many ways. Graphic organizers have many names, including visual maps, mind mapping (see Strategy 9), and visual organizers. Although many students plan with paper and pencil, technology tools can be very helpful because they allow easy editing.

Graphic organizers convert complex and messy information collections into meaningful displays because they compress and focus. As students conduct their research, using graphic organizers does the following:

- Focuses the purpose
- Guides the gathering of data
- Shows what is gained
- Shows what is still missing

Graphic organizers make interpretation, understanding, and insight much easier. As students develop a report of their findings, a graphic organizer is an effective means of organizing their thoughts and conclusions.

Graphic organizers can be used in all phases of learning from brainstorming ideas to presenting findings. They can be used individually or in large groups. These tools are particularly useful in activities that require critical thinking skills. Ideas for when to implement graphical organizers include the following:

- To set the stage before beginning a new learning situation, address prior knowledge, develop background or essential learning, and guide thinking
- During a new learning situation, to categorize and/or organize information, raise questions for consideration, predict solutions or conclusions
- After a new learning situation, to confirm or reject prior knowledge, relate new information to what was already known, extend new learning to other situations; for example, some teachers like to create a class concept map to review at the end of a unit

For more specific examples of what graphic organizers look like and how they are created, visit the Center for Applied Special Technology Universal Design for Learning online at http://www.cast.org/publications/ncac/ncac_go.html.

Precautions and Potential Pitfalls

A big problem with graphic organizers is assessment. Some students may look at the graphic organizer as just another assignment and not authentically engage in its construction. There are a number of ways to avoid this. You could ask the students to exhibit their work in front of the class and explain it. Individuals and groups will feel a bit more pressure to authentically engage when they have an audience. You may also consider allowing access to their graphic organizers as part of an "open-book" style test. If students know that they need to rely on their graphic organizer on a test, they will be more motivated to do a good job.

You can also consider a graphic organizer as a formative assessment tool and use it to look for content misunderstandings or concept confusion. Also, rather than asking students to construct a graphic organizer to show their understanding of a section of the textbook, you could ask them to graphically organize the notes from a lecture. In this way, the graphic organizer will tell you how well the students understood the major points within a lecture or discussion.

Sources

Hall, T., & Strangman, N. (2005). *Graphic organizers*. National Center on Accessing the General Curriculum Publications. Retrieved March 23, 2005, from http://www.cast.org/publications/ncac/ncac_go.html

Kirylo, J. D., & Millet, C. P. (2000). Graphic organizers: an integral component to facilitate comprehension during basal reading instruction. *Reading Improvement, 37*(4), 179–186.

Loranger, A. L. (1997). Comprehension strategies instruction: Does it make a difference? *Reading Psychology: An International Quarterly, 18*(1), 31–68.

Radencich, M. C. (1995). *Administration and supervision of the reading/writing program.* Boston: Allyn & Bacon.

Routman, R. (1991). *Invitations: Changing as teachers and learners K–12.* Portsmouth, NH: Heinemann.

Strategy 4: Increase depth of coverage to improve student learning.

What the Research Says

Although the trend in education in the past decades has been shifting from science education for future scientists to science education for all (AAAS, 1989), there is still the need to prepare students for the rigors of college science courses. In doing so, many teachers make the assumption that providing students with the opportunity to come into contact with the broadest array of content possible will lay the firmest foundation for college. A study by Schwartz, Sadler, Sonnert, and Tai (2008) calls this assumption into question.

This study was based on a larger study, "Factors Influencing College Science Success" (Tai, Sadler, & Mintzes, 2006), which used surveys to collect data from students enrolled in 55 colleges and universities. The final sample size of the students in the analysis was 8,310 undergraduates. The survey asked students a variety of questions about their high school science experiences. In examining one of the questionnaires (in this case for biology), it shows that students were asked questions about the types of science classes they took, the level of the class (regular track or honors), the number of days and hours per week that the class met, the perceived level of difficulty of the course, the topics covered, the types of activities in which they engaged in class, and the way in which they engaged in tasks, among other questions. The survey consisted of 65 questions in all.

The dependent variable in the study was the grade reported for each student. Results of the study indicated that high school teachers who elect to pursue studying at least one topic in depth have students who show a positive performance on outcome measures in their introductory college science courses. Students who experience high school science classes in which a wide number of concepts are covered (breadth over depth) experience no advantage in physics and chemistry and are at a disadvantage in biology.

One interesting finding was that a group of students who reported their high school experience as being "depth present–breadth absent" were found to have a two-thirds–year advantage over their peers who viewed their experience as having breadth over depth. This observation has significant implications for curricular decisions of both individual teachers and curriculum leaders.

Classroom Applications

When deciding on a subject you would like to cover in more depth, it is best to chose a part of the curriculum that you know is problematic for the students. This is something the students will need more time to learn anyway, has broader implications in terms of future learning (connects to *big ideas* across disciplines and grade levels), and tracks across multiple standards. You can also help to appease those who may be nervous about the time you are spending by including opportunities for students to read, write, and do mathematics (all of which you can document in your lesson plans).

There are several ways you can plan meaningful opportunities for students to engage deeply in the content. You could try some inquiry-based activities that take more time. They ask more of the students cognitively, so they are a great way of getting them more engaged with the content. Other appropriate tools are extended investigations, computer simulations, research projects, and problem-based learning—all of which involve your students more actively in their own learning. By spending an increased amount of time going into greater depth in a least one subject in your curriculum, you will not only provide your students greater insight into that subject, you will also offer them an experience similar to what they will find in college.

Precautions and Potential Pitfalls

It is not always possible for individual teachers to deviate from the prescribed curriculum. In large school districts, decisions about curriculum scope and sequence are rarely made by individual teachers at the school level. In smaller districts, teachers may have more latitude. In either case, sharing research, such as the Schwartz et al. (2008) study, may help you to obtain the academic freedom to teach some content with more depth.

Sources

American Association for the Advancement of Science. (1989). *Project 2061: Science for all Americans.* Washington, DC: American Association for the Advancement of Science.

Schwartz, M. S., Sadler, P. M., Sonnert, G., & Tai, R. H. (2008, December 22). Depth versus breadth: How content coverage in high school science courses relates to later success in college science coursework. *Science Education.* Available at http://www.interscience.wiley.com

Tai, R. H., Sadler, P. M., & Mintzes, J. J. (2006). Factors influencing college science success. *Journal of College Science Teaching, 36*(1), 52–56.

Strategy 5: Foster self-efficacy and motivation in your students.

What the Research Says

Walker (2003) summarizes the major points of other authors and researchers since 1990 regarding the concepts of self-efficacy, which refers to people's belief in their capabilities to carry out actions required to reach a high level of achievement. She then reviews the steps teachers can take to promote self-efficacy in the teaching and learning environment. She explains responses teachers can choose to increase self-efficacy, which in turn increase performance in reading and writing. Her premise is that understanding students' motivation, particularly those exhibiting self-efficacy, can help educators better engage students in literacy activities because young people who are efficacious are more likely to work hard, to persist, and to seek help to complete challenging tasks they sometimes believe are beyond their ability.

Classroom Applications

You routinely hear students talk about disciplines they like and do well in and those in which they feel they have no abilities or skills. Math and science are common targets for these generalizations. To compound these notions, parents often excuse and validate their son's or daughter's self-critique based on their own past experiences with the subjects. Teachers of science and math need to understand the barriers they face in overcoming their students' self-fulfilling prophecies and barriers to learning.

Teachers can help their reluctant science and math students by analyzing and defining the traits of efficacious students. Individuals develop their academic self-efficacy in a number of ways. Most commonly, successful learning experiences that are somewhat challenging yet doable create a sense of accomplishment that may significantly foster self-efficacy. Second, a strong source of self-efficacy comes from positive verbal response from parents, teachers, or peers that reinforce the student's capacity for performing certain activities. For example, accurate positive self-attributions can be developed when teachers provide task-specific comments on student success and attribute that success to tasks that are learnable within the school environment. When faced with challenging activities, students with high self-efficacy apply metacognitive skills and strategies by asking themselves questions about concepts and content while checking their understanding.

Cultivating self-efficacy within a curricular framework is difficult. However, a number of authors (Zimmerman, Bandura, & Martinez-Pons, 1992; Schunk & Pajares, 2004) have suggested that self-efficacy can be cultivated in low-performing students. The following are four suggestions that are mentioned most frequently:

1. Giving students a choice within activities. Students should be challenged but not frustrated.

2. Encouraging and modeling strategic thinking about activities. Help individuals, groups, and classes "pre-think" and analyze activities, noting pitfalls and providing tips before beginning an activity.

3. Offering opportunities and tools for self-assessment. Provide students with your range of expectations at specific points during the activity, not just the final expectation.

4. Changing the assessment purpose and context. Part of the assessment process could be formative and part summative assessment.

To look at each of the these suggestions more closely, let us begin with incorporating a choice that asks students to make decisions about their interests and what they may already know about a task. When given a choice, students bring more effort to activities. Allowing a choice in literacy activities increases motivation and authentic engagement. Teachers can provide a choice of activities within the day-to-day educational environment by offering personal reading and writing time, inquiry-oriented activities, and collaborative discussions based on student interests. This is not a common strategy in the science classroom. However, when you think about the many science topics that can be explored from various reading perspectives, introducing a variety of readings about related topics and perspectives could be an interesting approach!

Second, the suggestion that teachers introduce thinking strategies arises because many less-than-successful students look at failure as products or factors beyond their control. They think that luck, the teacher's attitude toward them, and the rigor of the materials have more influence on outcome and products of learning than their own ability and effort. Often, they do not recognize or acknowledge the effective strategies they use. Their mistakes are looked at as a continuous or repeated stream of blunders that have little value for learning. Learning from failure is rarely an option for them; failure just reinforces a negative self-image. They read and write without using or learning alternative strategies. What they are really saying is, "I don't have strategies, and I don't know how to do it."

Because of these phenomena, science teachers need to teach instructional strategies such as monitoring of meaning, understanding, and elaboration. Teachers can help students deal with mistakes and use alternative strategies when students confront difficult or challenging curriculum. The most powerful, appropriate, and important strategies can be modeled by the instructor, and student strategies can be defined and recognized as legitimate coping strategies. Low-efficacious students need this type of help.

Related to how failure and success work in the lives of low-efficacious students is the notion of self-assessment. Many low-performing and/or low-efficacious students believe they are not up to doing many tasks; therefore, they assess their work and abilities negatively. Science literacy progress is very difficult for students to assess. Positive self-evaluation and assessment raise self-efficacy because students understand the complex relationships between performance and their strategy and the literacy processes. Teacher-produced rubrics and checklists, emphasizing the strategic steps within tasks, help support effective adoption of techniques and strategies. Specific checklists help students revisit and rethink their strategic actions and help students see clearly the connections between strategy and personal success. Defining and quantifying the steps in strategies and showing their connections to success cultivate self-efficacy and empower students. These assessment tools help students attribute their success to strategic actions. Checklists also allow students to evaluate how their general science literacy and learning strategies are progressing. The checklist and rubric strategy work well in both reading and writing activities.

Finally, changing the assessment context supports a learning notion rather than a performance orientation. Grades and learning are supposed to go hand in hand, yet grades today often create a sense of false security for teachers, students, and parents. Students often believe that grades equate to learning. Rather than focusing on grades, low-efficacious students should be focusing on what they are learning and what they can do. By utilizing both specifically designed portfolios, with carefully crafted requirements and student-led conferences with parents and teachers, assessment strategies can become learner rather than grade centered.

Within a portfolio, a form of authentic assessment, students can evaluate their success with instructional activities and also help measure progress over time. Parents, students, and teachers can collaboratively review the students' work and what students can do. The goals of assessment and evaluation are thus shifted from grade performance to specific learning goals that empower students and hopefully increase student efficacy. Past tasks are used to measure what students are learning, not to get better grades. Focus is on what they can do and how they are achieving their literacy goals.

By giving choices, providing learning literacy strategies, offering self-assessment strategies, and changing the focus of assessment, teachers can guide students through more positive learning environments within more rigorous curriculum. All of this contributes to increased ownership of learning, authentic engagement, and motivation and effort to continue to read and write, in turn enhancing self-efficacy.

Precautions and Potential Pitfalls

Another element to consider is that redesigning curriculum, assessment, and instructional strategies takes time and adds another layer of complexity. However, self-efficacy is one of those educational intangibles that can't be measured yet is one of the most important characteristics a teacher can enhance. Nothing is more satisfying than having a room full of empowered students! Please consider it a necessity during curricular development and not just another required mandate. Self-efficacy is a gift you can help your students open.

Source

Schunk, D. H., & Pajares, F. (2004). Self-efficacy in education revisited: Empirical and applied evidence. In D. M. McInerney, & S. Van Etten (Eds.), *Big theories revisited*, (pp. 115–138). Greenwich, CT: Information Age.

Walker, B. J. (2003). The cultivation of student self-efficacy in reading and writing. *Reading and Writing Quarterly, 19*, 173–187.

Zimmerman, B. J., Bandura, A., & Martinez-Pons, M. (1992). Self-motivation for academic attainment: The role of self-efficacy beliefs and personal goal setting. *American Educational Research Journal, 29*(3), 663–676.

 Strategy 6: Challenge your students with different levels of questioning.

What the Research Says

There is evidence that much of teaching amounts to "telling" or use of teacher talk, which students often find boring. Research suggests that when teachers do ask questions, most of them are at relatively low cognitive levels (e.g., identify, define, describe). When teachers ask a majority of low-level questions, student thinking is not challenged and does not reach as high a level as it does when students are asked mostly higher-level questions (e.g., predict, justify, evaluate) (Redfield & Rousseau, 1981).

Research was conducted to investigate what questions teachers asked and why they asked them. Thirty-six high school teachers from five schools, representing all subject areas, participated in the study. They were asked to give examples of the questions they asked, to explain how they used them, and to tell to whom the questions were addressed. These results, along with findings from previous research by Bloom (1956), Tisher (1970), and Smith and Meux (1970), led to a system of classifying types of questions teachers ask in the classroom (see the following).

Classroom Applications

Teachers use questioning strategies for a variety of reasons in their classrooms. Probing and challenging students with questions facilitates reasoning and thinking. There are many types of questions to use, as well as many to avoid. Learning science requires understanding, and when a topic that requires thought and deduction is being considered, it is usually good to probe students on their understanding. Questions should be formulated with respect to long-term learning goals and should be succinctly structured to guide students' development so that they can think like scientists and adopt scientific reasoning techniques. Questions can range from those that require low-level responses (e.g., recall of facts for definitions and descriptions), intermediate-level responses (e.g., classifying and comparing/contrasting), or high-level responses (e.g., predicting, evaluating, synthesizing) that may have no definite answer but require a judgment or prediction to be made. Further clarification of questions is as follows:

Cognitive Questions

1. *Recalling data, task procedures, values, or knowledge.* This category includes naming, classifying, reading out loud, providing known definitions, and observing. These are responses to low-level questions. For example, knowledge-only questions: "How many stages are there in meiosis?" or "What are the products of photosynthesis?"

2. *Making simple deductions usually based on data that have been provided.* This category includes comparing, giving simple descriptions and interpretations, and giving examples of principles. These are responses to intermediate-level questions. For example, "How does meiosis compare and contrast with mitosis?"

3. *Giving reasons, hypotheses, causes, or motives that were not specifically covered or taught in the instruction.* These are responses to high-level questions. For example, "What are possible explanations of global warming that are not in our book?" or "What are some of the hidden problems with 'green' energy production that people don't usually think about?"

4. *Solving problems, using sequences of reasoning.* These are also responses to high-level questions. For example, "What investigative steps would you take to solve that problem or answer that question? What order do they go in and why?"

5. *Evaluating one's own work, a topic, or a set of values.* These are also responses to high-level questions. For example, "Did I make any careless mistakes? How can I verify my answer?"

Speculative and Affective Questions

1. *Making speculations and intuitive guesses, offering creative ideas or approaches, and answering open-ended questions.* These have more than one right answer and permit a wide range of responses. For example, "Approximately how long will it take before the chemical reaction we're expecting takes place?" "How do you think we'll know if it worked?" "How else could we produce that reaction?"

2. *Expressing empathy and feelings.* For example, "How do you think she felt when the incubator hard boiled all of the eggs she was trying to hatch for her science project?"

Management Questions

Teachers also use questions to manage individuals, groups, or the entire class. This category includes checking that students understand a task, seeking compliance, controlling a situation, and directing students' attention. For example, "Which groups solved the problem? Which groups need help?"

There are many different questioning taxonomies teachers can consult to help them vary the types and levels of questions they ask. Teachers should spend most of their time questioning at intermediate and high levels. The following chart contains examples of intermediate- and high-level questions for teaching biology, chemistry, and physics.

Science Subject	Intermediate Estimate	Intermediate Synthesize	High Causality	High Verify
Biology	If two animals heterozygous for a single pair of genes mate and have 276 offspring, about how many will have the dominant phenotype?	What does research on environmental cues show about biochemical and neural control of reproductive behavior?	Under what conditions might you infer that the mutations were caused by X-rays?	How could you prove that those parents produce that probable composition of the F2 generation?

(Continued)

(Continued)

Science Subject	Intermediate Estimate	Intermediate Synthesize	High Causality	High Verify
Chemistry	About how long do you expect it to take for the reaction to occur?	What did those theories suggest about the structure of an atom?	What causes diffraction patterns?	How could you check to make sure that you have written the correct electron configuration for an atom?
Physics	Approximately what is the mass of that drop now?	How could you summarize what you learned about electric fields from that experiment?	Why do you get a shock when touching another person after walking on a synthetic rug?	How could you double-check the accuracy of your calculation of the electric field at the specified point in space?

Precautions and Possible Pitfalls

You can create questioning at all cognitive and intellectual levels. Answers can range from recalling general knowledge to analyzing complex ideas and synthesizing new theory. Teachers, even new teachers, know from their training and/or experience that questioning plays an important role in today's instruction. Because this instructional strategy can dominate discourse and because students are active and usually involved during the discussion, there are more chances for management problems to arise if teachers do not follow good questioning techniques. The following are some questioning strategies that minimize classroom management problems:

1. Write out some questions when planning the lesson.
2. Establish your expectations for student behavior before beginning the questioning period.
3. Call on a variety of students.
4. Cue students before asking the question.
5. Ask questions that are the appropriate level for each student.
6. Ask questions that elicit positive or correct responses.

7. Provide students with sufficient wait time after asking a question and before responding to their comments.

8. Vary the way students respond to questions.

9. Respond to every answer and correct errors.

10. Ask follow-up questions.

Even good questions can lose their value if they are overused. Avoid asking ambiguous questions and questions requiring only one word answers such as yes or no questions. Teachers need to consciously and deliberately decide at which intellectual level they want their students to work and develop their questions accordingly.

Sources

Bloom, B. S. (Ed.). (1956) *Taxonomy of educational objectives, the classification of educational goals—Handbook I: Cognitive domain.* New York: McKay.

Brown, G. A., & Edmondson, R. (1984). Asking questions. In *Classroom Teaching Skills,* E. C. Wragg (Ed.). New York: Nichols Publishing.

Redfield, D., & Rousseau, E. (1981). A meta-analysis of experimental research on teacher questioning behavior. *Review of Educational Research, 51*(2), 237–245.

Sigel, I. E., McGuillicudy-DeLisi, A. V., & Johnson, J. E. (1980). *Parental distancing beliefs and children's representational competence within the family context.* Princeton, NJ: Educational Testing Service.

Smith, B. O., & Meux, M. O. (1970). *A study of the logic of teaching.* Urbana: University of Illinois Press.

Tisher, R. P. A. (1970). *Study of verbal interaction in science classes and its association with pupils' understanding in science.* St. Lucia: R.P. Tisher University of Queensland Press.

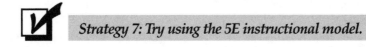

Strategy 7: Try using the 5E instructional model.

What the Research Says

The Biological Sciences Curriculum Study has been using the 5E Instructional Model (Engage, Explore, Explain, Elaborate, and Evaluate) as the basis for its curriculum materials since the late 1980s (Bybee et al., 2006). The 5E model, also referred to as the learning cycle, derives from the theory that learning is an active process in which new learning builds from currently held knowledge. Key are the connections learners make between what they currently know and what they are learning. Two things are important for the teacher. First, learning is an active process, which means that the students must be *doing* something and cannot just be sitting passively simply taking notes or completing a worksheet. Second, students come into each learning opportunity knowing *something* about what they are to learn. This prior knowledge, whether it be something they learned in or out of school, impacts how they experience whatever new activity in which they engage. In the seminal work, *How People Learn* (NRC, 1999), three key findings are identified, with implications for both teaching and learning:

1. "Students come to the classroom with preconceptions about how the world works. If their initial understanding is not engaged, they may fail to grasp the new concepts and information that are taught, or they may learn them for purposes of a test but revert to their preconceptions outside of the classroom" (p. 14). Students do not come to our classrooms as blank slates; rather, they have previous experiences and ideas about how the world around them works. These preconceptions are an amalgam of in-school and out-of-school ideas that may or may not have any basis in science. Some common misconceptions actually originate or are reinforced by school science (e.g., theories are guesses that can become laws, deoxygenated blood is blue, fingernails and hair continue to grow after death, the orbit of the earth is noticeably elliptical). If these prior conceptions are not engaged, students may not learn the new concepts or may learn "school science" only temporarily, as what they learn in school may not replace their previously held ideas.

An excellent example of how tenacious prior learning (or misconceptions) can be has been documented in the video *A Private Universe* (Harvard-Smithsonian Center for Astrophysics, 1987). In this video, recent graduates and faculty of Harvard University are interviewed and asked what astronomical phenomena cause the seasons. Those interviewed, including those who identity themselves as knowledgeable in science, overwhelmingly cannot answer this question correctly. In fact, the responses of these college graduates mirror those of ninth graders interviewed for the video. These same ninth graders cling to their misconceptions even *after* instruction.

2. "To develop competence in an area of inquiry, students must (a) have a deep foundation of factual knowledge, (b) understand facts and ideas in the context of a conceptual framework, and (c) organize knowledge in ways that facilitate retrieval and application" (NRC, 1999, p. 16). For example, just knowing the definitions of the component parts of photosynthesis is not enough; students need to see the big picture—how does it all fit together and to what end—to understand not only the individual components of photosynthesis but the process as well. Providing a structure for organizing new learning will aid in retrieval and use of newly learned content.

3. "A 'metacognitive' approach to instruction can help students learn to take control of their own learning by defining learning goals and monitoring their progress in achieving them" (p. 18). It should not be assumed that students will inherently be able to engage in self-talk

to monitor their own understanding. As with many other observed behaviors in the classroom, this skill will need to be taught to many students. But self-monitoring strategies can be learned by children of all ages, including children in primary grades.

Classroom Applications

In a review of the literature of research studies on the learning cycle, the 5E Instructional Model demonstrated effectiveness in increased subject matter mastery, increased sophistication in scientific reasoning, and greater student interest in science (Bybee et al., 2006). The 5E Instructional Model consists of five phases. The table below summarizes the phases and the types of activities in which the teacher and students might engage during each of the phases.

Phase	Teacher Actions	Student Actions
Engage	The teacher assesses the students' prior knowledge by engaging them in a task related to the new concept to be learned. The task should connect prior learning to new learning. This activity should provide an opportunity for students to talk about their prior experiences with the concept.	The students engage in a short activity or series of short activities. They make public their ideas about the concept they will be investigating.
Explore	The teacher provides a common activity, task, or series of activities and/or tasks in which the students engage. The tasks should provide students with the opportunity to collect data that will allow them to generate explanations for the phenomenon under investigation.	The students engage in the activities and/or tasks collecting and organizing their data.
Explain	The teacher leads a discussion around the students' data as they relate to the phenomenon in question. The teacher introduces vocabulary, ideas, concepts, and so on as necessary. The teacher and students may co-construct an explanation for the phenomenon under investigation.	The students share their data and tentative explanations for what they observed. They actively engage in the class discussion.
Elaborate	The teacher provides opportunities for the students to extend their understanding by providing new and/or related experiences for them to apply what they have learned.	The students engage in additional activities. These may be additional hands-on activities, or they may be virtual tasks, practice problems, writing prompts, and so on.

(Continued)

(Continued)

Phase	Teacher Actions	Student Actions
Evaluate	The teacher assesses the students' understanding of the concept through any appropriate manner.	Students demonstrate their conceptual understanding through an assessment.

The 5E Instructional Model is a great planning tool. It helps to start with a question or statement that identifies what exactly the focus of the investigation will be. Not everything should, or will work, with this format. Since it is more time-consuming to teach this way, think about content that is more conceptually difficult for the students and more open-ended. For example, the teacher could use the 5E Model to teach significant figures to students in chemistry and have them spend numerous days deriving the rules for whether those zeros are significant. However, they'll eventually come up with the same rules that are in the back of the book anyway, and they still need to *memorize* them. Learning them is not *conceptually* difficult, just a pain. So . . . don't spend the time using a learning cycle format for this. However, when you start to get into the *big ideas* in chemistry—that all matter is made up of particles and that they interact in predictable ways—you do need to spend more time grappling with some difficult concepts. You need to slow down. As a teacher, you need to know more about what ideas your students already hold because that information will impact how they interact with what you are asking them to learn. They need to spend more time "messing around" not only with stuff but also with ideas. You need to create not only the activities but also the time. The 5E Instructional Model helps to provide the structure for you to do just that.

Precautions and Potential Pitfalls

As with anything that might be new for students, it helps to explain to them what the ride might be like. Clear expectations, both academic and behavioral, help increase the likelihood for successful learning outcomes and reduce the likelihood for misbehaviors. Telling students that you expect a particular product to be turned in at the end of a certain time will prompt them to get right to work and greatly reduce wasted time.

Also, expect that things might take longer than you initially anticipated if this process is new for both you and your students. Organization is key to reduce the wasting of time. One tip is to get an activity's materials together ahead of time and place them in dishpans. Students then just need to retrieve a dishpan. This greatly reduces set-up time. It also makes clean-up easier because you can quickly see if everything is cleaned up as students are instructed to place all materials back in their dishpans (number dishpans to correspond to numbered lab stations). This dishpan method works well in settings where there may be no real lab space, as is the case in elementary schools and some middle schools or in high schools where teachers share classrooms, and material must be cleaned up after every class.

Sources

Bybee, R. W., Taylor, J. A., Gardner, A., Van Scotter, P., Powell, J. C., Westbrook, A., & Landes, N. (2006). *The BSCS 5E instructional model: Origins, effectiveness, and applications.* Retrieved April 6, 2009, from http://www.bscs.org

Harvard-Smithsonian Center for Astrophysics. (1987). *A private universe.* [Video]. Indianapolis, IN: Annenberg Media.

National Research Council. (1999). *How people learn: Brain, mind, experience, and school.* Washington, DC: National Academy Press.

Strategy 8: Support your students to engage effectively in disciplinary argumentation.

What the Research Says

Reform documents, including the Benchmarks for Scientific Literacy (AAAS, 1993) and the National Science Education Standards (NRC, 1996), advocate for the need to develop and support students' ability to engage in scientific argumentation as part of the process of inquiry. This involves, in part, students' demonstrating the conceptual understanding of scientific investigation, knowledge of the procedures and equipment required to conduct those investigations, and the ability to construct explanations as a result of those investigations (NRC, 1996).

Hamza and Wickman (2009) investigated the intellectual pieces students need in order to generate the types of explanations suggested by a reform curriculum. The students in this study worked with electrochemical cells and were engaged in five tasks involving the cells:

1. Using detailed instructions, set up a working electrochemical cell.

2. Observe the working electrochemical cell and the electric fan and/or light emitting diode.

3. Take voltage measurements.

4. Closely observe the copper and magnesium strips that were components of the cells.

5. Try to explain what they saw. (Hamza & Wickman, 2009, p. 7)

Results indicated students had gaps in two broad areas that Hamza and Wickman (2009) categorized as taxonomic interest and measurement interest. Issues related to taxonomic interest were those in which the students struggled connecting specific language or terminology to objects with which they were working. In addition to gaining a facility with the language necessary to maneuver in the particular setting, the students also needed to recognize both important and unimportant events with the materials with which they were working that could contribute to their explanations. As novices to particular situations with specific pieces of equipment, the students were unable to determine which of their observations were going to be important to incorporate into their explanations and which were essentially "noise." Hamza and Wickman looked at these as gaps "in the particulars" in the investigations that the students were carrying out.

Other results were related to issues around measurement and the students' uncertainty about the significance of the measurements that they were taking. Students demonstrated lack of understanding about what types of voltage readings were reasonable and struggled with understanding the relationship between voltage and time. Hamza and Wickman (2009) state that this study adds to the literature that describes students' use of reasoning in science.

Classroom Applications

The Hamza and Wickman (2009) study adds to our understanding of how our students can struggle with ideas that we might take for granted as relatively simple. The students in this study had issues with how to recognize and/or name particular things and/or events in the tasks in which they were engaged. In some cases, their inability to equate language that was printed in a procedure to what they were seeing hampered their ability to discuss what they were seeing and therefore to develop explanations.

Here is a tip for this situation. Make sure that students are familiar with the equipment with which they are working—what it is called, what it measures, in what units, essentially what information that piece of equipment will give them. Often, teachers provide a procedure for the students to follow and access to equipment but with little instruction as to how to use the equipment or what that equipment will actually tell them.

In other cases, the students did not know if particular observations were important or could be ignored because of their inexperience with electrochemical cells. They were unable to exclude "background noise" from that which was truly important. This suggests the need for some explicit discussions during investigations about what students might be doing and observing. The decision about when to have this discussion with your students will depend on their experiences with the phenomenon under study. This discussion could be conducted either with the whole class or in small groups. The exact format might be best determined by how many students are struggling with determining what observations need to be attended to.

The study also indicates that students can be confused around issues of measurement. It seems that students can collect empirical data with relative ease—but they have difficulty in interpreting what the data are telling them. Clearly, data interpretation is an important skill in science, not just in inquiry-based instruction. The teacher may need to build in more support for the students. Explicit discussions around what specific quantity a particular instrument measures, what that piece of information tells us at a particular point in time, and what a change in that measure might mean could lead to greater student understandings.

Precautions and Potential Pitfalls

Engaging in disciplinary argumentation is not easy and is not always successful (Hogan & Corey, 2001). One aspect of argumentation is identifying the necessary content students need to know in order to engage in disciplinary arguments. Even once we have done that, getting students to develop arguments is still difficult as this process is one with which they are generally unfamiliar. Letting students struggle can be frustrating for everyone. The temptation can be then to just tell the students the answers to the questions they are asking. You will need to decide just how much information to provide for the students and how much to scaffold in a whole-class versus small-group discussion. You want your students to have the tools necessary to get the job done, but it shouldn't be too easy. Academic rigor is important to maintain, yet you will see no progress if your students shut down and refuse to work. Only you can decide on just the right balance.

Sources

American Association for the Advancement of Science. (1993). *Benchmarks for science literacy: Project 2061.* New York: Oxford University Press.

Hamza, K. M., & Wickman, P.-O. (2009). Beyond explanations: What else do students need to know to understand science? *Science Education, Early View,* 1–24.

Hogan, K., & Corey, C. (2001). Viewing classrooms as cultural contexts for fostering scientific literacy. *Anthropology & Education Quarterly, 32*(2), 124–243.

National Research Council, (1996). *National science education standards.* Washington, DC: National Academy Press.

> ☑️ **Strategy 9: Utilize mind mapping to improve student achievement.**

What the Research Says

The research on mind maps and other visual tools that help learners to organize information indicates that these tools help students to build links between the concepts they are learning, something that teachers recognize as being particularly difficult for students of all ages and in all content areas. Mind maps also help students to recognize patterns among and between concepts, adopt a stance of multiple perspective taking, and better develop a capacity for reflection and revision of ideas based on critical feedback (Buzan, 2000; Hyerle, 1996).

Mind mapping is the forerunner to visual organizational tools such as concept maps, Vee diagrams, and other graphic organizers (see Strategy 3). Mind maps are generally seen to have a less formal structure than do concept maps. The structure is more weblike or may be thought of looking like tree branches. A mind map is often initiated by writing a word or idea in the center. Related words or ideas are added, like spokes on a bicycle or branches on a tree. Unlike concept maps, hierarchy is not an issue in the construction of mind maps. Students involved in mind-mapping activities are encouraged to brainstorm ideas, and the process encourages creativity. Students can distinguish between ideas using words or symbols and colors. Mind maps also generally just focus on one word or idea at a time. This is also quite different from concept maps that often are used to link concepts or ideas.

Research over the years has demonstrated that the use of various graphic organizers (concept maps, Vee maps, flow maps) results in largely positive outcomes for students in terms of enhancing achievement and learning in science (Anderson & Demetrius, 1993; Tsai, 1998; Westbrook, 1998). However, this research also brought to light limitations of these tools. Students often struggle with the use of the tool itself, as in the case of Vee maps (Esiobu & Soyibo, 1995).

Abi-El-Mona and Adb-El-Khalick (2008) conducted a study with eighth-grade students to determine if using mind maps influenced their achievement in science. Mind mapping was used as a learning tool, and the students received instruction on the construction and use of mind maps as part of their regular science instruction. A comparison group received instruction on a note-taking strategy. Students in the comparison group were allotted the same amount of class time to use note taking as their peers had to engage in mind mapping.

All students' understanding of the science content was then assessed using a framework consistent with the National Assessment of Educational Progress (NAEP). Essentially, students who received training in and constructed mind maps during a unit of instruction scored significantly higher than did a comparison group on measures of conceptual understanding and practical reasoning (Abi-El-Mona & Adb-El-Khalick, 2008). Interestingly, students' prior achievements in science had no impact on their learning gains. Students in all categories—basic, proficient, and advanced—all showed improvement in learning. This is significant in that often we see some students better able to benefit from particular strategies that are implemented in classrooms, although the greatest gains were demonstrated by those students identified as advanced.

Classroom Applications

 It is helpful to keep in mind the following when utilizing mind maps in the classroom. A mind map consists of five essential characteristics (see http://www.mindmapping.com):

- The main concept, idea, or core word is located in the center.
- The major related ideas radiate from this central point like branches from a tree or spokes from a wheel.
- The concept, idea, or word associated with the branch is printed on a line accompanying the branch for identification purposes.
- Ideas that are considered less important take a position of "twig" on the appropriate branch. All twigs on a branch are relevant to that branch but may only be loosely connected to other twigs.
- The branches form a connected nodal structure.

Mind mapping can be used for note taking, for finding out what students might already know about an idea or concept, or for having students represent what they have learned about an idea or concept.

The mind-mapping website (http://www.mindmapping.com) includes information on the theory behind mind mapping, as well as some limited information on mind maps and education. Examples of constructed mind maps and a section on software for mind mapping, including free software (see the "links" section), are also available. In addition to his books, Tony Buzan (2000) (often credited with developing mind mapping) also has videos on YouTube (http://www.youtube.com) on mind mapping.

Precautions and Potential Pitfalls

Students will initially need instruction on the construction and use of mind maps. While some students experience frustration with the constraints of concept maps, those same students are often more comfortable with the looser structure of mind maps. Construction of mind maps takes time, and materials are necessary. It is helpful to have large paper and colored pencils, crayons, and/or markers available for the students. Use of computerized software is another option. In this case, the necessary number of computers and either freeware or purchased software are required so that all of the students can actively participate. Students can construct mind maps collaboratively, but this generally works best if no more than two students work together at a time.

Sources

Abi-El-Mona, I., & Adb-El-Khalick, F. (2008). The influence of mind mapping on eight graders' science achievement. *School Science and Mathematics, 108*(7), 298–312.

Anderson, O. R., & Demetrius, O. J. (1993). A flowmap method of representing cognitive structure based on respondents' narrative using science content. *Journal of Research in Science Teaching, 30*(8), 953–969.

Buzan, T. (2000). The mind map book: How to use radiant thinking to maximize your brain's untapped potential. New York: Plume.

Esiobu, G. O., & Soyibo, K. (1995). Effects of concept and Vee mappings under the three learning modes on students' cognitive achievement in ecology and genetics. *Journal of Research in Science Teaching, 32*(9), 971–995.

Hyerle, D. (1996). *Visual tools for constructing knowledge.* Alexandria, VA: Association for Supervision and Curriculum Development.

Tsai, C. C. (1998). An analysis of Taiwanese eighth graders' science achievement, scientific epistemological beliefs, and cognitive structure outcomes after learning basic atomic theory. *International Journal of Science Education, 20*(4), 413–426.

Westbrook, S. L. (1998). Examining the conceptual organization of students in an integrated algebra and physical science class. *School Science and Mathematics, 98*(2), 84–92.

Strategy 10: Test students' ideas to facilitate reasoning skills.

What the Research Says

Rosalind Driver (1991) was a penultimate science educator and author and was known for her research with children's ideas. In her book *Pupil as Scientist?* Driver explored the differences between children's and experts' thinking and speaking about the world, arguing that students can and should be asked to explore their own ideas as a path for becoming more scientific. Karen Gallas (1995) has extended Driver's notions to include open discourse in "science circles," in which her first-grade students developed shared meaning and explored answers to questions such as "What is in blood?" and "Where do stars go during the day?" Her book is a profound contribution to what can be expected from the early childhood classrooms and the potential sophistication and pro-foundness of an inquiring learning community. Similarly, Eleanor Duckworth's (2007) *The Having of Wonderful Ideas* pushes this notion to other content areas to challenge teachers of all backgrounds and learning contexts to facilitate a learning environment where children's beliefs, thoughts, and experiences serve as the basis of topics of research and col-laborative investigation.

Classroom Applications

There are a variety of classroom applications for invoking a strategy of testing children's ideas as a venue for promoting inquiry. All of them are predicated on the practice of opening up at least a small but regu-lar part of the classroom discourse to students' uninterrupted talk. Gallas (1995) does this with her first graders by having them sit in a circle and ini-tiating questions emerging from the inquiring minds of young children. She then invites other children to critique, explore, confront, and test the beliefs and statements. What results is a rich and marvelous example of emerging discourse that is strikingly similar in many ways to what reforms call for in the form of *critical thinking* for more advanced grade levels.

In beginning a unit where advanced, conceptual development will be required by the end, it is a good idea to find out exactly how students think about the concept by asking open-ended questions at the beginning of the unit. One popular example is to ask the students questions like, "Why do we have seasons?" or "What causes moon phases?" These have been explored, and video examples of the results and strategies for addressing the responses have been created by the Annenberg Foundation's *A Private Universe* (Harvard-Smithsonian Center for Astrophysics, 1987). Teachers can have students discuss their thoughts in an clinical interview setting and create drawings that represent their answers to such questions that can then be used to select or design units to address children's thinking. Some units that have been developed for this strategy include McDermott's *Physics by Inquiry* (1996) series, which has been based upon such investigations of students' ideas.

Another strategy that can be used to explore students' thinking and application of conceptual models is to have them respond to a question such as "How do audio tapes store their information?" Students can form their solution to the problem and pose ways to test if they are correct. Students then explain their models on the board, attach their names to the idea, and pursue a course of investigation that is in direct competition to the other ideas on the board. After sufficient time has been spent in gath-ering data to support their ideas, the different research groups meet again at a round-table discussion and present their findings to competing groups. A more detailed discussion of using this kind of format can be found elsewhere in Yerrick (1999).

Mental models play a nontrivial role in how students understand what the teacher is trying to teach and in filtering selectively what they want to believe. As Ausubel (1968) and Driver (1991) have described, children's ideas are "amazingly tenacious" and resistant to change. The key to overcoming misconceptions is to have students commit themselves publicly to one specific position. There is too much opportunity in typical classrooms for children to back out, change their minds, or to say at the end, "Oh yeah. Well, that's what I meant." Children's names should be posted on the board alongside each model under investigation and specific contrasts made between ideas before investigations begin. This raises engagement and commitment to the task a quantum leap above the original level. Another key component in selecting the research teams is that the underpinnings for the personal theory must be adequately explored. Students may agree on the surface, but often their reasoning is different. It is essential to find out *why* students think what they do and what *evidence* or *procedures* they intend to use to prove their ideas to be correct.

Precautions and Possible Pitfalls

Competition is not a positive motivator for all students. Boys in particular favor this method of investigation, but there are also more collaborative ways to approach the close examination of proposed models. It also shouldn't be expected that students will instantly speak like experts simply because the reigns are removed. It took scientists over 200 years of close examination to figure out the mechanism for photosynthesis that is based on an abstract concept of electron capture reaction occurring in fractions of seconds at the center of the chloroplast magnesium. If one were to place children in a room and give them unlimited resources, they likely would not reach the same conclusion. Roth (1987) has argued that children may simply conclude that when plants die in a dark room that light is food for plants. This absurd example is meant to highlight that students will not stumble upon and discover necessarily the rigorous abstract concepts you may want to teach. However, by structuring classrooms around students' inquiries and real beliefs about the world, teachers can gain real insight into how children think and how to respond to children's thinking with curricular activities and assessments that help guide children into increasingly mature and sophisticated ways of thinking critically about their own ideas, as well as those of others.

Sources

Ausubel, D. (1968). *Educational psychology: A cognitive view.* New York: Holt.

Driver, R. (1991). *Pupil as scientist?* Philadelphia: Open University Press.

Duckworth, E. (2007). *The having of wonderful ideas and other essays on teaching and learning* (3rd ed.). New York: Teachers College Press.

Gallas, K. (1995). *Talking their way into science: Hearing children's questions and theories, responding with curricula.* New York: Teachers College Press.

Harvard-Smithsonian Center for Astrophysics. (1987). *A private universe.* [Video]. Indianapolis, IN: Annenberg Media.

McDermott, L. C., Shaffer, M. L., & the PEG. (1996). *Physics by inquiry.* New York: Wiley and Sons.

Roth, K. (1987). *Learning to be comfortable in the neighborhood of science.* Occasional Paper, Institute for Research on Teaching, Michigan State University.

Yerrick, R. (1999). Re-negotiating the discourse of lower track high school students. *Research in Science Education, 9,* 269–293.

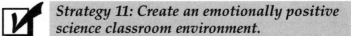

Strategy 11: Create an emotionally positive science classroom environment.

What the Research Says

Pellittera, Dealy, Frasano, and Kugler (2006) examined the construct of emotional intelligence (EI) as a framework for understanding the emotional processes that students with reading difficulties experience in the school or classroom context. Their research considers emotional factors and specific elements such as interpersonal interactions of peer groups, opportunities for developing emotional learning, and the dynamic affective-aesthetic responses of the individual students during the reading process. The article examines the underlying affective processes as they relate to cognition, motivation, and social functioning.

The authors state that a student's social and academic difficulties can be explained by the breakdown of these emotional processes. Students can experience difficulties in understanding social interaction with peers because of poor perception of emotional cues and failure to access emotional knowledge in school social situations. These factors affect performance in literacy instruction. Furthermore, the authors state that constructs related to emotional intelligence examined in reading disability literature are understood to impact a students' academic functioning.

From a human ecological perspective, Pellittera et al. describe the particular social-emotional and learning needs of students with reading disabilities that must be considered in creating an optimal personal learning environment fit. The authors list the systems that most directly impact the emotional dimensions of the student with reading disabilities:

- The psychological environment of the school and the classroom
- The policies that determine the student's class placement, curriculum, and activities
- The structure of the student's interpersonal peer relations

In their introduction, Pellittera et al. (2006) describe the research of Gredler (1997), who stated that "individuals tend to interpret stress reactions and tension as indicators of vulnerability to performance. . . . Therefore, the only way to alter personal efficacy is to reduce stress and negative emotional tendencies during a difficult task" (p. 290). They also list specific emotionally intelligent interventions and discuss their implementation in the school environment.

Classroom Applications

The overall culture of the school and the academic science classroom can produce an environment that is so emotionally stressful that certain students become emotionally paralyzed or so academically dysfunctional that achievement is the last thing they want to strive for. Their behavior turns inward, often aimed at protecting their self-esteem, managing tensions within the learning or teaching environment, and/or coping with the frustration of academic cognitive tasks. Many students with reading problems have experienced excessive failure and have negative reactions and emotions connected to academic triggers and the teacher's instructional efforts in the school setting.

A major goal of intervention regarding these factors is to create an emotionally positive science classroom environment that reduces the students' general anxieties and increases their positive associations with the school and classroom. The emotional environment of the school and the classroom are created by the interpersonal interactions between students and the adults within the setting. Teachers need to develop their own emotional awareness and begin to create a more intelligent classroom environment. Smiling, speaking in a pleasant tone of voice, and using encouraging words are some examples of beginning steps. Removing negative stresses should be a curricular priority for students challenged with reading problems. These students can still have a positive interaction with the sciences if teachers make it a point to foster inclusiveness for all students, especially those with reading problems.

On a different level, a more systemic intervention considers the emotional needs of the students when scheduling classes and class activities. In some counseling situations, placement of students can include selecting educational environments that buffer threats to self-esteem and foster a student's willingness to take risks. Teacher matching can also be considered. Teachers have a responsibility to set and monitor group dynamics and the emotional tone of the classroom interactions. When a teacher values empathy, emotional sensitivity, and self-awareness in a learning environment, he or she can alter peer group dynamics and derogatory behavior within a classroom. Peer rejection and a student's failure at social adjustments are associated with academic performance within literacy strategies.

In addition, peer or cross-age tutoring arrangements, pairing older struggling readers with younger struggling readers, often set up a positive dynamic for both participants. With preparation, such arrangements provide a sense of competence for the older student that improves self-esteem, self-efficacy, and a positive emotional experience regarding reading.

Individually, the written text needs to become a source of motivation to read and a positive stimulus with positive affective associations. This is the big goal. Science teachers need to help students become comfortable with not knowing all of the words rather than interpreting reading mistakes as a sign that they are always wrong. Science teachers also need to structure activities that are challenging yet still provide students with positive and successful experiences. From an emotional intelligence perspective, teachers can use reader-response activities to help the students examine their own emotions and develop the ability to reflect on their own responses to learning activities. In this way, reading sessions can be used as a vehicle for personal social insight and self-awareness. Furthermore, deciphering the text provides teaching and learning opportunities for young readers to begin to see themselves and their beliefs and feelings more clearly.

Planning for the emotion dynamics of the learning environment is essential. The emotional realm affects and influences the learning environment of struggling readers and learners in general. By becoming aware of and regulating the emotional reactions of students in literacy activities, science teachers can increase not only fluency and mechanics but also the motivation to engage reading materials both inside and outside the classroom. You just have to remember that every academic task has an emotional component for many students, and this needs to be mitigated.

Precautions and Potential Pitfalls

It's not unusual to find that underachieving older students are resistant to strategies you might employ. A few students have had so many negative experiences and interactions with teachers and peers that school has become a painful place. The many attempts teachers have made to "reach" them over the years may have hardened them. Chances are, many teachers have tried to reach out to them, and now they anticipate your efforts and are ready to resist. There are no easy answers for dealing with these students. Sometimes time and sincerity are the most effective qualities in building trust.

Sources

Gredler, M. E. (1997). *Learning and instruction: Theory into practice* (3rd ed.). Upper Saddle River, NJ: Merrill.

Pellittera, J., Dealy, M., Frasano, C., & Kugler, J. (2006). Emotionally intelligent interventions for students with reading disabilities. *Reading & Writing Quarterly, 22,* 155–171.

Strategy 12: Engage students who have a history of poor school achievement.

What the Research Says

Jeanne Oakes (1985) studied children who had been homogenously grouped according to historically poor school achievement. In her book *Keeping Track,* Oakes challenges the assumptions upon which these groupings are made. Two of these assumptions are (1) students feel better about themselves as learners when they are separated from other students and (2) students' abilities and potential to learn are visible through external behaviors.

Her research and the work of others comprise a cogent argument against the school practices of ability tracking. Should teachers find themselves in the position of teaching a group of students who have had collective histories of failure in school, they will likely observe a mélange of values, dispositions, and behaviors of a microculture that has been marginalized from the academic school culture. Too often, common knowledge would mandate that teachers should return to basics or provide a simpler curriculum. Instead, several studies suggest that trying alternative strategies to re-establish connections to the content through more real-world connections is a better solution (Calabrese-Barton, 1998, 2001; Hildebrand, 1998; Lee & Fradd, 1998; Yerrick, 1999, 2000).

Classroom communities can be transformed and children can be encouraged to think critically despite their histories of failure in any given subject if teachers turn their continued attention toward establishing a new learning community. One of the keys to long-term shifts in classroom discourse is remembering to structure in success for students.

Classroom Applications

Providing staged progression to students early on can build a community of success, increase buy-in of students into the process, and develop early expertise for peer learning. Each of these accomplishments will limit the demands on teachers who are trying to promote shifts in discursive practices. Many refer to this as reducing processing demands when promoting new approaches to teaching and learning. This may come in the form of using more common language instead of specific content vocabulary (see Strategy 2) or modification of the assigned task itself in order to help students progress quickly to desired outcomes.

Many science concepts are connected to students' prior knowledge that cuts across concepts and can become confusing for students learning to speak scientifically. When learning why objects slow down after they are pushed, students can be encouraged to debate, collect data, and engage in arguments about their experiments. However, these debates can quickly reach an impasse because of misconceptions of two different concepts: friction and inertia. If teachers carefully select the events that students experiment with and argue about, they can help students acquire ways of using data and constructing arguments to make specific conclusions, rather than raising the frustration levels when the confusion leads the students away from the point of learning to argue with evidence.

As teachers desire to bring English language learners into the complex discourse of open discussions (to which they may intentionally avoid contributing), teachers can focus the participation on particular aspects of this talk, structuring opportunities for success. For example, a teacher may set students up for success by setting the boundaries and inviting them to participate. The teacher could say, "Today, in this open discussion, we will be working on asking questions. A good question to the speaker might be phrased in this way: 'What evidence do you have for . . .?' or 'I am not sure I agree. Can you tell me more about . . . ?' Everyone practice this with the partner sitting next to you, and in five minutes, we'll put this into the discussion of _____ with the whole group."

Precautions and Possible Pitfalls

Teachers should not expect the culture of the classroom to change in the short term simply based upon good intentions. Changing norms of classroom discourse is not something that will happen in a week. It is a sometimes a long process but one that is well worth it.

There is a saying among teachers, "If I respect them, they'll respect me." This kind of respect may not be immediately evident as teachers in these contexts are working against sometimes years of socialization in this microculture. However, the results can be profound when students believe that their teachers are there as their advocates for learning and connections to the content and the lives of students are finally clear to marginalized students. What's more, it has also been observed among teachers of marginalized youth that once teachers have made that connection and established the norms of thoughts and behaviors in class, such students are "fiercely loyal" to their teachers and their causes.

Sources

Calabrese-Barton, A. (2001). Science education in urban settings: Seeking new ways of praxis through critical ethnography. *Journal of Research in Science Teaching, 38,* 899–917.

Calabrese-Barton, A. (1998). Teaching science with homeless children: Pedagogy, representation, and identity. *Journal of Research in Science Teaching, 35*, 379–394.

Hildebrand, G. M. (1998). Disrupting hegemonic writing practices in school science: Contesting the right way to write. *Journal of Research in Science Teaching, 35*, 345–362.

Lee, O., & Fradd, S. (1998). Science for all, including students from non-English-language backgrounds. *Educational Researcher, 27*, 12–21.

Oakes, J. (1985). *Keeping track: How schools structure inequality.* New Haven, CT: Yale University Press.

Yerrick, R. (2000). Lower track science students' argumentation and open inquiry instruction, *Journal of Research in Science Teaching, 37*, 807–838.

Yerrick, R. (1999). Re-negotiating the discourse of lower track high school students. *Research in Science Education, 9*, 269–293.

Strategy 13: Include students with special needs in student-centered instruction.

What the Research Says

With the enactment of the Individuals with Disabilities Education Act (IDEA) and No Child Left Behind, teachers are seeing more students with special needs, and students with significant disabilities, included in general education classrooms for significant portions of the school day. Statistics show that in the 2004–2005 school year, slightly over 50% of students with disabilities received 80% of their education in general education classrooms. For example, the percentage of students with disabilities being educated in general education classrooms increased from 8.4% in 1995 to 9.2% in 2004 (U.S. Department of Education, 2006).

Special education teachers may suggest direct instruction as the preferred method for many students with disabilities. This method of instruction is quite procedural and didactic—and appears to be the antithesis of the inquiry-based instruction that is advocated in the Benchmarks for Science Literacy (AAAS, 1993) and the National Science Education Standards (NRC, 1996). Direct instruction (often referred to in the literature as DI) is generally recognized as having six steps. Friend and Bursuck (2006) identify these steps to include the following:

1. A review and check of the previous day's work. This step involves reteaching if the students do not appear to have mastered the content from the day before.

2. New content is presented. Before this presentation is started, the teacher prefaces the instruction with a statement about the objectives

of the lesson and what the students are expected to learn. The new material is presented in small bits with adequate opportunity for examples and questions.

3. The teacher then engages the students in closely monitored practice. Practice occurs until the objectives of the lesson are met.

4. Reteaching occurs with individual students or the entire class as necessary.

5. Independent practice provides students the opportunity to increase speed and accuracy. Independent practice is monitored and student work is assessed.

6. Previously learned content is continually reviewed. Content with which students continue to struggle is retaught.

This type of didactic instruction can be differentiated from what we might call explicit teaching. Palmquist and Finley (1997) describe explicit teaching as the direct teaching of concepts or ideas, but they do not mean that this instruction must necessarily occur through a lecture format or in a way that aligns with the direct instruction methodology advocated by special educators. What explicit teaching does mean is that by the end of class, or at the end of a piece of instruction, all of the students should be able to walk away knowing exactly what it is they are expected to know. This is hardly something that teachers would object to as a result of instruction, especially as many students struggle with learning science.

In a review of the nature of science literature, Abd-El-Khalick and Lederman (2000) investigated the ways in which students learn about the nature of science. The studies indicated that students did not learn nature of science via curriculum in which the instruction of content was implicit. Rather, they found that explicit teaching was more effective at producing the desired learning outcomes. This has important implications for teaching in inclusive classrooms because students with special needs, in particular, may struggle with content if the connection between learning goals and the task is not explicit.

In a study conducted by Bay, Staver, Bryan, and Hale (1992), students in Grades 4 through 6 with mild disabilities (learning and behavioral disabilities) who were enrolled in general education science classes received either direct instruction or what the authors called discovery instruction. The authors' conception of discovery teaching is based on constructivist learning theory, which posits that students have an active role in constructing meaning in the world around them. The lessons in which the students engaged required that they ask questions, manipulate materials and collect data, and generate explanations. In this regard, the authors' use of the term "discovery" sounds much like the use of the term "inquiry" in the current science education literature.

Bay et al. found that on the post-test, both students with learning disabilities and those with behavioral disabilities in the discovery teaching condition outperformed a comparison group of students in the direct teaching condition. Both groups of students with disabilities also showed greater retention than did a similar group of peers in the direct teaching condition. Students' ability to generalize the scientific process was mixed, with students with learning disabilities in the discovery condition outperforming their similar peers in the direct teaching condition. Students with behavioral disabilities in the discovery condition, however, were not able to generalize quite as well as their peers in the direct teaching condition.

Mastropieri, Scruggs, and Magnusen (1999) reported in a study looking at activities-oriented curriculum that students with learning disabilities and mild cognitive disabilities learned successfully with the activities-oriented curriculum (with the appropriate accommodations), that students reported enjoying the hands-on curriculum more than a book-centered curriculum, and that students appeared more motivated and were more likely to actively engage in on-task classroom behaviors.

Overall, it appears that a growing body of research supports the learning of science through more hands-on, activity-oriented instruction. To this approach, Palmquist and Finley (1997) add that it is important to help the students understand the connection to what they might be observing and what they are being asked to come to understand conceptually. This is important for *all* students, not just students with special needs.

Classroom Applications

Students in classrooms tend to be heterogeneous in terms of previous science experiences. Even in elementary school, it seems like some students have had more experiences than others with science-like activities, whether it be with gardening at home, caring for family pets, exploring science museums, or other informal or formal experiences. Including students with disabilities can increase the spread of heterogeneity in terms of experiences and formal school science skills. For example, a chemistry teacher could get students in their final year of high school who had *never* been in any science classroom.

Involving students in a common hands-on experience to investigate in small groups is a great way to provide students with a phenomenon to discuss later as a whole class in a more structured setting. The students can be strategically grouped based on the specific strengths and areas of need—general and special education students working together. One teacher reports that some of her best data recorders were students with autism (a strength for a particular student), and some of her best reporters were students with learning disabilities (whereas recording data may not have been a strength). It can be easy to group strategically after a few weeks of getting to know your students. Groups may need to change depending on the task. Perceived deficits often become strengths, and students come to rely on one another. As part of the classroom environment, cooperation is key, and the success of all members of the group is essential.

The teacher using the student data can facilitate the explicit piece of the instruction. It is essential that the teacher have in mind the "take home message" that must be reached by the end of the lesson and that all of the students must understand. If just the activity alone is done and the teacher assumes the students will "get the point," the learning goals will be implicit and perhaps some of the students will get it. This is not what is effective based on the research. Unpacking what the students have done and/or observed at the end of the task explicitly helps ensure that the learning goals will be met. When the students leave class at the end of the period, they all need to have the same "take-home message."

Precautions and Potential Pitfalls

As with all types of activities, it is important to match the activity structure to the learning goals and objectives. The way in which we ask students to learn should align with what we want them to learn. And if students are engaged in activity structures that are new to them, instruction in the structure of the task will be needed to ensure success. Just make sure they know how to do what you are asking them to do. If they don't, take some time to teach them and model the behavior and/or skill so that they are successful. This is far less frustrating for everyone.

Students with special needs may require additional accommodations and/or modifications, depending on their specific disabilities. The great thing about this type of activity structure is that in many cases, the differentiation can be built into the lesson ahead of time, reducing the amount of work to be done accommodating and/or modifying after the fact or during instruction. Asking a special education teacher to assist in the process and to assist in the classroom is also very helpful if you are new to this process. Once you get to know your students, it becomes easier to think about differentiation as you develop the tasks. Thinking in advance about the strengths and areas of need of your students and keeping groups in mind makes everything run more smoothly.

Sources

Abd-El-Khalick, F., & Lederman, N. G. (2000). Improving science teachers' conception of nature of science: A critical review of the literature. *International Journal of Research in Science Teaching, 22,* 665–701.

American Association for the Advancement of Science. (1993). *Benchmarks for science literacy: Project 2061*. New York: Oxford University Press.

Bay, M., Staver, J. R., Bryan, T., & Hale, J. B. (1992). Science instruction for the mildly handicapped: Direct instruction versus discovery teaching. *Journal of Research in Science Teaching, 29*(6), 555–570.

Friend, M., & Bursuck, W. D. (2006). *Including students with special needs: A practical guide for classroom teachers*. Boston: Pearson.

Mastropieri, M. A., Scruggs, T. E., & Magnusen, M. (1999). Activities-oriented science instruction for students with disabilities. *Learning Disability Quarterly, 22*(4), 240–249.

National Research Council. (1996). *National science education standards*. Washington, DC: National Academy Press.

Palmquist, B. C., & Finley, F. N. (1997). Pre-service teachers' views of the nature of science during post-baccalaureate science teaching program. *Journal of Research in Science Teaching, 34*(6), 595–615.

U.S. Department of Education (2006). *Twenty-eighth annual report to congress on the implementation of the Individuals with Disabilities Education Act, 2006*. Washington, DC: Author. Retrieved May 25, 2009, from http://www2.ed.gov/about/reports/annual/osep/2006/parts-b-c/index.html

2

Scientific Inquiry and Laboratory Experience

Strategy 14: Engage your students in inquiry-based science.

What the Research Says

Barrow (2006) looks at the term "inquiry" and its historical context within the sciences. He describes how interpretations of inquiry have changed during the 20th century and how multiple meanings of the term have resulted in debate and confusion among teachers and also their students. Barrow goes on to make suggestions for preservice programs (both scientific methods and science courses). He further comments on professional development programs for veteran teachers and the general science educational community to help all stakeholders reach consensus about the nature of inquiry and scientific reasoning.

Classroom Applications

Inquiry-based learning has been of great influence in science education, especially since the publication of the U.S. National Science Education Standards (NRC, 1996). However, some educators have advocated a return to more traditional methods of teaching (i.e., lecture, reading, discussions) and assessment, mostly due to the types of high-stakes standardized assessment being used today. Others feel that inquiry is important in teaching students to understand scientific research, scientific investigation, reasoning, and learning in general.

Scientists use their background knowledge of principles, concepts, and theories, along with the scientific process skills, to construct explanations for natural phenomena to allow them to understand the natural world. This is known as "science inquiry." When students are learning using inquiry-based science, they use the same ideas as scientists do when they are conducting research. However, inquiry experiences for students can be difficult to structure within the classroom context. There are science teachers who would rather default to textbooks and lecture instructional strategies. Inquiry is often more complicated than more direct instruction.

It is our experience that many teachers of science do not have the opportunity during their own training to truly engage in scientific inquiry themselves. There is often a wide knowledge and experience gap between K–12 classroom teachers and those involved in "real-world" academic and industrial applications of science, especially involving the concept of scientific inquiry. In general, the science undergraduate experience likely won't engage students in the process of sophisticated inquiry. Self-directed inquiry skills are usually taught and mastered during a science major's graduate experience.

The National Science Education Standards (NRC, 1996) challenge educators to master the teaching strategies that support engaging students in the inquiry process. This is a definite change from the simplistic "processes of science" that have characterized discussions regarding inquiry for years. In fact, the authors of the standards indicate that developing the abilities and understandings of inquiry are essential components of the science content in the K–12 science curriculum. Many state standards and other science organization documents also support this position, although it is not always presented in such a straightforward manner as in the National Science Education Standards.

In the National Science Education Standards for science teaching, inquiry is highlighted as a way of achieving knowledge and understanding about the natural world. The fundamental abilities of inquiry specified by the NRC (1996) are to

1. identify questions and concepts that guide investigations (students formulate a testable hypothesis and an appropriate design to be used);

2. design and conduct scientific investigations (using major concepts, proper equipment, safety precautions, use of technologies, etc., where students must use evidence, apply logic, and construct an argument for their proposed explanations);

3. use appropriate technologies and mathematics to improve investigations and communications;

4. formulate and revise scientific explanations and models using logic and evidence (the students' inquiry should result in an explanation or a model);

5. recognize and analyze alternative explanations and models (reviewing current scientific understanding and evidence to determine which explanation of the model is best); and

6. communicate and defend a scientific argument (students should refine their skills with written and oral presentations that involve responding appropriately to critical comments from peers). (p. 113)

Accomplishing these six abilities requires K–12 teachers of science to provide multi-investigation opportunities for students. This type of investigation would not be just a "search for the right answer" laboratory experience that only reinforces content. When students practice inquiry, it helps them develop their critical thinking abilities and scientific reasoning, while developing a deeper understanding of science and how it is practiced (NRC, 2000).

The second domain of scientific inquiry is understanding about inquiry so that students will develop meaning about science and how scientists work. The six categories identified by the NRC (1996) are as follows:

1. Conceptual principles and knowledge that guide scientific inquiries

2. Investigations undertaken for a wide variety of reasons—to discover new aspects, explain new phenomena, test conclusions of previous investigations, or test predictions of theories

3. Use of technology to enhance the gathering and analysis of data to result in greater accuracy and precision of the data

4. Use of mathematics and its tools and models for improving the questions, gathering data, constructing explanations, and communicating results

5. Scientific explanations that follow accepted criteria of logically consistent explanation, follow rules of evidence, are open to question and modification, and are based upon historical and current science knowledge (p. 113)

The NRC (1996) recommends that science educators put less emphasis on the following:

1. Knowing scientific facts and information

2. Studying subject matter disciplines (physical, life, earth sciences) for their own sake

3. Engaging in activities that demonstrate and verify science content

4. Getting an answer

5. Involving individuals and groups of students in analyzing and synthesizing data without defending a conclusion

6. Privately communicating student ideas and conclusions to the teacher (p. 113)

Conversely, teachers should put more emphasis on the following:

1. Understanding scientific concepts and developing abilities of inquiry

2. Learning subject matter disciplines in the context of inquiry, technology, science in personal and social perspectives, and the history and nature of science

3. Engaging in activities that investigate and analyze science questions

4. Using evidence and strategies for developing or revising explanation

5. Creating groups of students and strategies for developing or revising an explanation

6. Publicly communicating student ideas and work to classmates (p. 113)

If you feel your background in inquiry is weak, there are many ways you can explore to learn more about inquiry and how to engage your students. First, many colleges and universities now have outreach programs to help teachers better understand science processes. While these programs might stress exploration in a specific content area, inquiry often becomes the backbone of the experience. Second, teachers can become proactive in recruiting scientists to help structure inquiry experiences for their students. These connections can occur both informally or formally through college and university outreach programs. Third, there are also many books and other resources available (e.g., Bently, Ebert, & Ebert, 2007; Llewellyn, 2001; Olson & Loucks-Horsley, 2007) that can be found in most online bookstores. This text also includes a section in

Chapter 6 that is focused on inquiry-based instruction. Finally, check out the National Science Education Standards (1996) at http://www.nap.edu/openbook.php?record_id=4962.

Precautions and Possible Pitfalls

⚠ Knowledge generated by science is a unique form of information. At its best, this knowledge is a product of thoughtful inquiry and has been validated through peer review. At its worst, knowledge should be weeded out, critiqued, and examined for the flaws in the methodology that produced it, as new information comes to light. Simply put, citizens need to know the role of science and how its knowledge base came to be and continues to evolve.

We assume that 95% of your students will not become part of the science community. However, their opinions of science and scientific knowledge will be sculpted by the science classrooms they inhabit, and their views of science will be dependant on the expertise of their teachers. Therefore, it is very important to somehow give them a clear understanding of how scientific inquiry works and is filtered and consumed throughout society and culture. This is as important as knowing about the scientific details found in the chapters of most science textbooks. Teachers simply have to find ways to engage students in thought about the inquiry process, either as philosophical content or as a scientific process.

Sources

Barrow, L. (2006). A brief history of inquiry: From Dewey to standards. *Journal of Science Teacher Education, 17*, 265–278.

Bently, M. L., Ebert, E. S. II, & Ebert, C. (2007). Teaching constructivist science, K–8: Nurturing natural investigators in the standards-based classroom. Thousand Oaks, CA: Corwin.

Llewellyn, D. (2007). *Inquire within: Implementing inquiry-based science standards in grades 3–8* (2nd. ed.). Thousand Oaks, CA: Corwin.

National Research Council. (2000). *Inquiry and the national science education standards: A guide for teaching and learning.* Washington, DC: National Academy Press.

National Research Council. (1996). *National science education standards.* Washington, DC: National Academy Press.

Olson, S., & Loucks-Horsley, S. (2007). *Inquiry and the national science education standards: A guide for teaching and learning.* Committee on the Development of an Addendum to the National Science Education Standards on Scientific Inquiry, National Research Council.

Strategy 15: Teach model-based inquiry over the scientific method.

What the Research Says

Wong and Hodson (2008) sought to identify the key features of the nature of science embedded in authentic inquiry. In their study, 13 well-established scientists responded to an open-ended questionnaire regarding the nature of science and participated in in-depth interviews focused on the nature of science from a curricular standpoint. The researchers found striking contrasts in the scientists' descriptions of their practice of science and the image of science and inquiry usually described in science curriculum, textbooks, and classrooms. Wong and Hodson felt the stories that these scientists tell offer considerable potential as teaching resources to enhance and enrich the typical science classroom's understanding of the nature of science and for the design of more effective laboratory and field work.

It was pointed out by a number of scientists in the study that the textbook notion of the "scientific method" or the scientific inquiry process is grossly oversimplified as presented in a linear fashion. For example, the participating high-energy physicist stated, "I don't do experiments. . . . The experiments in physics have become larger and larger in scale, especially in my specialty. It is difficult for scientists to deal with both theoretical and experimental issues at the same time" (Wong & Hodson, 2008, p. 117). He went on to say that Fermi was the last physicist to be both a theorist and an experimentalist, and the approach taken in scientific investigation can be flexible and depends on the particular circumstances. Some scientists develop experiments, while others use more naturalistic observations and studies, historical reconstructions, or computer simulations and/or modeling tools. All scientists in the Wong and Hodson study stated that creativity and imagination are also very important at all stages of scientific investigation—experimental planning and design, data collection, and data interpretation.

Furthermore, in a report based on a national observation survey, Weiss, Pasley, Smith, Banilower, and Heck (2003) reported students in U.S. math and science classrooms are often busy but engaged in tasks that require little understanding of content on their part. In some 55% of the observed lessons, students had limited to no intellectual engagement with the conceptual ideas necessary to understand the content represented in the lesson. How is this related to the discussion of the teaching of a universal scientific method?

The following four areas that emerge from the data by Wong and Hodson (2008) can be singled out for attention:

1. The current classroom understanding of the phrase "scientific method"

2. The definition and use of the word "experiment"

3. The role that creativity and imagination plays in science

4. Different perceptions of scientific "laws, models, theories and principles"

Wong and Hodson (2008) pointed out that the scientists in this study felt that context determined the method of inquiry in their field, yet many science teachers continue their belief in a common "scientific method" usually found in textbooks. This belief may be a simple solution to a curricular presentation and supports the few pages in the textbook devoted to the scientific method, but it creates an oversimplified version of "what scientists do." This notion usually results in a generic, all-purpose approach to laboratory activities and reports in which students are asked to emphasize each step in the scientific method.

Recent reform documents (AAAS, 1993; NRC, 1996, 2000) suggest that students should both learn about and learn through inquiry. These documents encourage engaging students in authentic science that asks them to pursue scientifically oriented questions, gather data, and give priority to evidence that is then used to generate explanations, evaluate these explanations based on the evidence, and then present and evaluate the explanations. Using the scientific method as an organizing framework for understanding the epistemic principles of inquiry-based science (that it is testable, revisable, explanatory, conjectural, and generative) seems not only limiting but also problematic (Windschitl, Thompson, & Braaten, 2008).

Duschl and Grandy (2008) discuss the idea of the scientific method and its basis in logical positivism. Their conclusion is that while the logical positivist position cannot be completely discarded, it must be supplemented if the conception of the scientific method that derives from it is to continue to be useful. Recent studies on how science is done indicate that science routinely involves model building, testing, and revision (Duschl & Grandy, 2008; Gierre, 1988). Duschl and Grandy (2008) identify five meanings for the term "model": mathematical description, physical comparison, representation, mental, or public. In this case, model does not necessarily refer to a physical object such as a Plasticine model of a root tip. Model is used here as a mental or cognitive representation of an explanatory concept. An example might be a model of planetary motion that would explain the observed seasons. Models can represent abstract concepts or those things that are inaccessible due to size or location.

Windschitl et al. (2008) suggest that using the scientific method as a framework for thinking about scientific processes is problematic in four ways:

1. When students frame questions within the paradigm of the scientific method, those questions are often based on what they might be interested in or what they might consider to be likely to be successful. These questions are often not grounded in any theoretical perspective or model. As such, the questions students choose to investigate are frequently *not* connected to the larger ideas that they are studying in class; they are essentially random. Thus, there is a troubling disconnect between the content that students should be learning and the activities in which they engage to support that learning.

2. Direct experimentation in a control-of-variables model is viewed as a sanctioned method of collecting data and conducting experiments. Indirect observation, field-based experiments, and use of historical data are seen as less desirable experimental methods even though they represent the primary ways of data collection in some of the science disciplines. This limited view of the ways in which scientists *do* science misrepresents the wide variety within the discipline itself.

3. Little opportunity exists for students to develop explanations based on data they do collect as they do not start from a theoretical perspective. Consider for a moment one of the examples provided by Winschitl et al.—that plants might grow better when provided soft drinks rather than water. Without some understanding of what nutrients are present in soft drinks and what things are necessary for plant growth, just what will the results of this experiment allow students to say? How will this further their understanding of plant anatomy and physiology, energy cycles, and so on?

4. While the scientific method is not always portrayed as linear, it often is. And although it may not be visualized in text as linear, it is frequently enacted in classrooms as linear. This can be useful considering the constraints of both time and curriculum. However, this distorts the way in which science is actually carried out (Latour, 1999).

Misunderstandings about the role of the scientific method and how it can and/or should help to guide scientific inquiry are present both in pre-service and inservice teachers (Winschitl et al., 2008). Participants in their study largely believed in a universal scientific method that could be used to direct experiments in which the ultimate goal was to prove or disprove a relationship between two variables. Participants also correctly held the view that hypotheses were predictions about potential outcomes. However, their understanding of the connection between outcomes (data) and the hypothesis was weak or nonexistent. These participants did not consider that data and hypotheses connect as part of a larger explanatory network. In thinking about the features of inquiry identified by the National Research Council (2000), many were absent in how the participants discussed the doing of science—principally, the part of inquiry that involved talk. Model-based inquiry has at its core the development of explanations based on evidence.

Classroom Applications

 Look in the introductory chapter of any middle or high school science textbook and you are likely to see a section on the scientific method. The exact number of steps may vary, but the scientific method is generally represented to look something like the following:

- Make an observation.
- Ask a question.
- Construct a hypothesis.
- Test the hypothesis.
- Draw a conclusion.

Numerous websites offering posters of the scientific method represent it as a series of four to six steps, often linear, sometimes iterative. In most cases, the end point is a theory or a law. Students frequently engage in a paper and pencil activity at the beginning of the year in which they match a particular description with a "step" in the scientific method as a way of demonstrating their understanding of the scientific process. However, the scientific method, as outlined in most textbooks, has little in common with how science is conducted in most real settings. As such, students develop an unrealistic image of science and the practice of authentic science.

What differentiates inquiry-based instruction from other forms is the emphasis on argumentation or the development of evidence-based explanations. In order for this to occur, Windschitl et al. (2008) recommend that the teacher begin by setting parameters. The teacher makes decisions about the content that is to be investigated, choosing content that has intellectual muscle in that it can link to other content and doesn't represent a curricular dead end. An additional consideration in choosing a phenomenon to investigate is that it should have a causal mechanism that the students will be able to understand.

The teacher then engages the students in the following activities:

1. *Organizing what is already known about the phenomenon under investigation.* The authors state that two principles must be kept in mind: the

phenomenon to be studied should be something of interest from the natural world, and the students must have experiences or resources so that they are able to develop a tentative model. This is similar to the type of thing that students might experience in any other inquiry-based activity, provided the task leads to the development of an explanatory model.

2. *Generating potential hypotheses to explain the phenomenon under investigation.* The question to be investigated must not only be testable, but it also must make sense when considering the phenomenon under study. In other words, the question should not appear random or arbitrary. The authors suggest considering the following questions when generating hypotheses:

- What aspects of our model do we want to test?
- Are there competing hypotheses that could both explain what we are observing?
- When we look at our tentative model and consider the question we want to ask, what would our models predict?
- How can we test our models in a way that generates better descriptions of how this phenomenon happens?
- Can we test our models in a way that helps us understand some process or thing that explains why the models work the way they are predicted to? (Windschitl, et al., 2008, p. 958)

3. *Gathering evidence.* Questions are posed and decisions are made about gathering data regarding the question that has been asked.

4. *Generating an argument using the evidence they have collected.* The students defend their arguments, as well as acknowledge the strengths of other arguments and the weaknesses of their own. Students also revise their explanations based on discussions with their peers.

Precautions and Potential Pitfalls

Teaching "the scientific method" may be required by some district and state curricula and may show up on state science assessments; therefore, teachers may still need to provide opportunities for students to come into contact with the canonical scientific method. A discussion of the strengths and limitations of the various ways of "doing" science may actually be of benefit to students and improve their understanding of the nature of science. This kind of discussion will, of course, take some time, and it will provide students the opportunity to learn using model-based inquiry.

Supporting argumentation and discourse in the classroom is not an easy thing to do. Students are accustomed to a question-and-answer format that is mediated through the teacher. Argumentation works best when students talk to each other with the teacher mediating. Teachers will need to model the types of things that students need to say in terms of the feedback they provide to the presentation of an explanation. The discussion needs to be explicit, with the teacher outlining clearly how a specific piece of evidence either supports or does not support a particular claim. This is a skill that both teachers and students will gain facility with over time.

Sources

American Association for the Advancement of Science. (1993). *Benchmarks for science literacy: Project 2061*. New York: Oxford University Press.

Duschl, R., & Grandy, R. (2008). Reconsidering the character and role of inquiry in school science: Framing the debates. In R. Duschl & R. Grandy (Eds.). *Teaching scientific inquiry: Recommendations for research and application* (pp. 1–37). Rotterdam: Sense Publishers.

Giere, R. N. (1988). *Explaining science: A cognitive approach.* Chicago: University of Chicago Press.

Latour, B. (1999). *Pandora's hope: Essay on the reality of science studies.* Cambridge, MA: Harvard University Press.

National Research Council. (2000). *Inquiry and the national science education standards: A guide for teaching and learning.* Washington, DC: National Academy Press.

National Research Council. (1996). *National science education standards.* Washington, DC: National Academy Press.

Weiss, I. R., Pasley, J. D., Smith, P. S., Banilower, E. R., & Heck, D. J. (2003). Looking inside the classroom: A study of K–12 mathematics and science education in the United States. Retrieved February 23, 2007, from http://www.horizon-research.com/reports/2003/insidetheclassroom/looking.php

Windschitl, M., Thompson, J., & Braaten, M. (2008). Beyond the scientific method: Model-based inquiry as a new paradigm of preferences for school science investigations. *Science Education, 92*(5), 941–967.

Wong, S. L., & Hodson, D. (2008). From the horse's mouth: What scientists say about scientific investigation and scientific knowledge. *Science Education, 93*(1), 109–130.

 Strategy 16: Use problem-based learning to introduce students to inquiry-based science.

What the Research Says

 Confronted with the many challenges put forth in the National Science Education Standards (NSES) (NRC, 1996), as well as with the pressures of meeting the demands for preparing students for standardized assessments, teachers are necessarily searching for strategies that will assist them in meeting multiple goals and agendas.

Science teachers must not only help their students in becoming proficient in the standards in science, but must also provide opportunities for students to develop competence across content standards, including those in technology. It can sometimes be difficult to provide students with adequate learning opportunities that involve inquiry as identified in the NSES:

- Identify questions and concepts that guide scientific investigations.
- Design and conduct scientific investigations.
- Use technology and mathematics to improve investigations and communications.
- Communicate and defend a scientific argument.

Problem-based learning (PBL) is one way to engage students more deeply in science content and develop students' abilities to participate in the activities of inquiry, as well as involve students in utilizing a variety of productivity and communication tools. A learner-centered instructional method based on real-world issues or problems, PBL was originally developed as a method for training doctors in medical school. The PBL model, developed by Howard Barrows in the 1970s (Savery & Duffy, 1995), is becoming more commonly used across learning contexts, and not just to replace lectures in the first two years of medical school. At its core is the construction of a learning environment in which the solution of a problem drives the learning. In the search to solve the problem, students learn the necessary content. At the heart of PBL is involving students in an ill-structured problem for which no single solution exists, but multiple problem-solving paths exist. Students do not have all of the information needed when they begin, and they gather information to solve the problem as part of the process (Chin & Chia, 2004). Uyeda, Madden, Brigham, Luft, and Washburne (2002) suggest that to maximize student motivation and learning, the problem should be authentic and be based on some past or present event that has relevance for the students.

Greenwald (2000) describes the specific steps in the PBL process as the following:

1. The students are presented with a scenario of an ill-defined problem. The students should not have enough prior knowledge to immediately solve the problem.

2. The students ask questions about what is interesting, what is problematic, and what it is they need to find out.

3. Students pursue finding out more about the problem. This involves exploring why the issue is problematic and what specifically makes it so.

4. Students map the problem finding, prioritizing the problem to show patterns and relationships between and among the ideas discussed in the previous step.

5. Once the students have decided on a course of action, they investigate the problem and collect the results of their investigations. These investigations may be research based or experimentally based.

6. Students analyze their result and relate it back to their initial thinking.

7. Students then generate potential solutions and communicate them to others orally and/or in writing.

Problems are introduced at the beginning of a unit of study, and the content students subsequently learn is in support of solving the problem. This approach is generally in the reverse order of more traditional teaching methodologies in which students are first taught content and then asked to apply what they know. In this problem-first approach, the problem is contextualized, and students have a better understanding of why they are being asked to learn specific content.

Classroom Applications

 Making the initial jump to include problem-based learning can seem intimidating. You can begin by looking at test and essay questions in exams, texts, and other materials. You can create problems or cases from these. A case doesn't need to be something that your students will spend the entire semester completing. Initially, you might want to think about something that might take your students just a few days to complete.

When designing a PBL activity, Grow and Plucker (2003) identify elements to consider:

- That the problem is authentic and that the scenario is introduced prior to any relevant instruction
- That the role of the teacher becomes more of facilitator
- That the students assume more responsibility for their own learning and are engaged in higher-level thinking while working in small groups
- That students are assessed in ways that are aligned with the way in which they are engaging with the content and not in traditional paper-and-pencil test

They also suggest some ideas for topics of investigation in physical science classrooms.

Uyeda et al. (2002) describe the process of problem construction as one of finding and preparing data with which the students will interact. If the problem the students will be working with is a real problem—for instance, that of over-population of white tail deer in a suburban community—then data will already exist. It will just be a matter of locating sources for the data. Local newspapers can be a good place to start. Government websites can also be useful. Utilizing the Internet will provide access to information your local or school library may not have.

Another great resource is the National Center for Case Study Teaching in Science at the State University of New York at Buffalo (http://library .buffalo.edu/libraries/projects/cases/case.html), which includes countless numbers of cases that have been submitted by educators from around the country. Some of the cases are more appropriate for college students in terms of both content and reading level. Others can be adapted to make them more appropriate for high school or middle school students.

The students need to work in groups. Anytime this happens, group membership needs to be carefully considered. Group size should be related to the nature of the problem—groups need to be large enough to accomplish all that needs to be done but not so large that some students will be idle. Generally, each group should have four to five members (see also Strategies 22 and 23).

It is really helpful to have access to the Internet. Bookmark the sites that the students are to use so they don't spend a lot of time searching sites that will not be helpful. You can even use a WebQuest program to lock in the sites so students won't go surfing in areas that are not productive. Finding these sites will take time on your part, but it greatly reduces the time it will take students to find useful information and ensures that they *will* find the information that you know will be useful. If you do not have access to a sufficient number of computers so that there are no more than two students to a computer (or you have no Internet access), you can print and make copies of information that otherwise would have been read on screen.

In addition to using computers for students to access information, computers are also helpful for students who are preparing information that they will present. Students can create graphs and charts, documents, and so on that are of presentation quality.

Precautions and Potential Pitfalls

This is a situation in which much of the teacher's work is done ahead of time. Designing the problem or case, locating appropriate resources, and anticipating issues are all aspects of PBL that you must consider in advance. Class time belongs to the students, and the teacher acts more as a facilitator. This change in roles may seem strange for all involved at first. Setting timelines and deadlines for students and requiring written products and progress reports will provide opportunities for you to assess the students' interim work and hold them accountable.

It can initially be time-consuming to develop cases that work well within your curriculum and that are appropriate for your students. Searching for cases that have been developed by others is certainly a place to start, and resources that are helpful in accomplishing this are provided in the previous section. Often, it is the time required to develop new activities that prevents already overtaxed teachers from implementing exciting changes in their classrooms.

It is also important to find cases that your students will find relevant and interesting. Developing a case on a topic of regional significance may do more to pique your students' interest than choosing a topic about which the students will have little personal experience.

Sources

Chin, C., & Chia, L. (2004). Problem-based learning: Using students' questions to drive knowledge construction. *Science Education, 88,* 707–727.

Greenwald, N. (2000). Learning from problems. *The Science Teacher, 67*(4), 28–32.

Grow, P. L., & Plucker, J. A. (2003). Good problems to have: Implementing problem-based learning without redesigning a curriculum. *The Science Teacher, 70*(9), 31–35.

National Research Council. (1996). *National science education standards.* Washington, DC: National Academy Press.

Savery, J. R., & Duffy, T. M. (1995). Problem based learning: An instructional model and its constructivist framework. *Educational Technology, 35,* 31–38.

Uyeda, S., Madden, J., Brigham, L. A., Luft, J. A., & Washburne, J. (2002). Solving authentic science problems: Problem-based learning connects science to the world beyond school. *The Science Teacher, 69*(1), 24–29.

Strategy 17: Implement inquiry-based instruction in low-track classes.

What the Research Says

Reform documents in science education advocate teaching both about and through inquiry (AAAS, 1993; NRC, 1996). States have written standards that incorporate the ideas regarding scientific inquiry into what students need to know and be able to do in science. Students across the country are now being assessed on these standards as part of the No Child Left Behind Act. While more and more students are experiencing inquiry-based instruction, this type of instruction is rare in lower-track classrooms. Far more common are instructional practices in which teachers tightly control the learning environment through lecture and the use of worksheets; potentially dangerous lab-based activities and involving students in more open-ended tasks that may appear to lack structure are avoided.

Randy Yerrick (2000) has conducted several long-term studies of students in lower-track classes in which they were involved in inquiry-based instruction. The students were required to generate questions, design experiments, and construct arguments as part of their normal course work. Yerrick was particularly interested in the nature of the discourse that resulted from the more authentic work in which the students were engaging in their general science course. The course represented a "last chance" for meeting graduation requirements for most of the students enrolled in the course. The students appeared to be typical of many in lower-track classes: They had a history of poor attendance, discipline problems, and failed classes. They were alienated from school, hostile, and uncooperative. The students would not appear, on the surface, to be the type of students with which to attempt to implement an inquiry-based curriculum.

Yerrick's (2000) experiences with his students were not without frustration. His students were accustomed to a typical interaction pattern in the classroom (teacher initiates a question, students responds, teacher evaluates the response), even though they might not participate enthusiastically. The instructional experience in which the students engaged was carefully scaffolded to develop the students' ability to the appropriate discourse of science. The students showed growth in their ability to understand the tentativeness of knowledge claims, use of evidence, and views regarding authority. As the discourse expectations changed and with instruction, students suggested more potential answers to the problem; these potential answers were more sophisticated and the students also suggested ways to test these proposed answers (Yerrick, 2000).

Prior to instruction, the students conflated observations with answers. At the end of the semester, the students demonstrated a more robust understanding of the role of data, how to collect data, what to do with data, and how to interpret data. Use of data as evidence is a key component of inquiry in the National Science Education Standards (Yerrick, 2000).

The view the students held regarding their own role in determining answers to problems in science also changed. Before the start of the semester, the students held little agency as learners. By the end of the semester, the students saw themselves as being capable of determining appropriate experiments and using results to make evidence-based decisions (Yerrick, 2000).

Classroom Applications

While this particular study by Yerrick (2000) detailed the learning of five students (due largely to issues of continuity of enrollment), the class itself was larger and all of the students participated in the inquiry-based curriculum. Challenges can certainly present themselves with large classes of students who may be unruly. It is entirely possible that students in lower-track classes have had minimal, if any, opportunity to engage in hands-on science during their school careers. Lower-track classes often do not have a lab period, or teachers may elect not to do labs with their lower-track students. In such cases, engaging in any type of group activity may be a novel experience. As with any new experience, teachers should make both academic and behavioral expectations explicit for the students.

It is also suggested that the first experiences be more structured and of shorter duration. Activities can be designed that last perhaps 30 minutes and have a fairly tightly defined procedure. The focus for the students in this first experience can be on what they *do* with the data—what claims the data might let them make, how the data serves as evidence, and what additional data might support their claim. This first activity can also be planned using benign materials to reduce the likelihood of injury.

Precautions and Potential Pitfalls

 As with all inquiry, the temptation may exist to just tell the students the answer if they get stuck or if they persist in asking for the "right" answer. In order for the students to get the most from inquiry-based instruction, it is necessary to work through the entire process, considering where they might get stuck and what types of interventions might be necessary to avoid just giving them the answer.

Sources

American Association for the Advancement of Science. (1993). *Benchmarks for science literacy: Project 2061.* New York: Oxford University Press.
National Research Council. (1996). *National science education standards.* Washington, DC: National Academy Press.
Yerrick, R. K. (2000). Lower-track science students' argumentation and open inquiry instruction. *Journal of Research in Science Teaching, 37*(8), 807–838.

 Strategy 18: Attain educational goals through laboratory experiences.

What the Research Says

Laboratory and research experiences have been a part of high school science experiences for 100 years, although educators and policy makers continue to debate the value of inquiry-based laboratory instruction. In an effort to clarify the role that laboratory instruction and inquiry currently play in American schools, the authors of

America's Lab Report: Investigations in High School Science reached the following conclusions (NRC, 2005, Executive Summary, pp. 2–9):

Conclusion 1. Researchers and educators do not agree on how to define high school science laboratories or on their purposes, hampering the accumulation of evidence that might guide improvements in laboratory education. Gaps in the research and in capturing the knowledge of expert science teachers make it difficult to reach precise conclusions on the best approaches to laboratory teaching and learning.

Conclusion 2. Four principles of instructional design can help laboratory experiences achieve their intended learning goals if (1) they are designed with clear learning outcomes in mind, (2) they are thoughtfully sequenced into the flow of classroom science instruction, (3) they are designed to integrate learning of science content with learning about the processes of science, and (4) they incorporate ongoing student reflection and discussion.

Conclusion 3. The quality of current laboratory experiences is poor for most students.

Conclusion 4. Improving high school science teachers' capacity to lead laboratory experiences effectively is critical to advancing the educational goals of these experiences. This would require major changes in undergraduate science education, including providing a range of effective laboratory experiences for future teachers and developing more comprehensive systems of support for teachers.

Conclusion 5. The organization and structure of most high schools impede teachers' and administrators' ongoing learning about science instruction and ability to implement quality laboratory experiences.

Conclusion 6. State science standards that are interpreted as encouraging the teaching of extensive lists of science topics in a given grade may discourage teachers from spending the time needed for effective laboratory learning.

Conclusion 7. Current large-scale assessments are not designed to accurately measure student attainment of the goals of laboratory experiences. Developing and implementing improved assessments to encourage effective laboratory teaching would require large investments of funds.

Classroom Applications

 While the strategies of lecture, reading, and discussion as instructional techniques work well in other disciplines, learning scientific reasoning, the nature of science, empirical work, and teamwork make much more sense in an inquiry laboratory context. You can accomplish many of your standards-based goals by carefully crafting and embedding inquiry-based laboratory experiences within your curriculum. That is, connect laboratory activities with other types of science learning such as lectures, readings, and discussion. The overall goal of this strategy is to have teachers move beyond traditional procedural-based laboratory experiences and begin, continue, and/or fine-tune inquiry, laboratory, or research activities in the science classroom as more effective learning and teaching pedagogy.

The authors of *America's Lab Report* (NRC, 2005) sum up this notion in the last chapter by stating that science is best experienced as a process in addition to its content. Science process centers on direct interactions with the natural world aimed at explaining natural phenomena. Science education would not be about science if it did not include opportunities for students to learn about both the process and content of science. Within the notion of the scientific processes come the following goals of laboratory and inquiry experiences:

- Enhancing mastery of subject matter
- Developing scientific reasoning
- Understanding the complexity and ambiguity of empirical work
- Developing practical skills
- Understanding of the nature of science
- Cultivating interest in science and interest in learning science
- Developing teamwork abilities (p. 3)

Unfortunately, crafting inquiry-based laboratory experiences, rather than linear procedural-based labs with only one right answer, can be difficult. The best laboratory experiences include more opportunities for students to think, adjust, and make and support decisions, while also putting the science content in an authentic context for students to experience and master. Fortunately, there are many sources to draw on to develop inquiry-based experiences. An Internet search lists many sites with information and examples of inquiry strategies. One of the better sites is "Case Studies in Science" at the State University of Buffalo. These cases are located at http://library.buffalo.edu/libraries/projects/cases/case.html and meet many of the goals listed above.

Precautions and Potential Pitfalls

Most state science standards recommend that students understand and develop appropriate skills related to scientific inquiry, yet, as we have discussed, many state science assessment systems do not adequately target these skills. Under these circumstances, the requirements for alignment between standards and assessments cannot be met. Also, state and local school departments have long left decisions about hands-on curriculum and pedagogy to teachers.

America's Lab Report (NRC, 2005) documented a disconnect between procedure-based laboratory experiences and integrated, inquiry-based laboratory experiences. Students engaged in inquiry-based labs receive problems and questions to solve and answer their own way. However, inquiry-based investigations typically require more teacher time and more knowledge and safety are required.

Another factor is that high-stakes tests tend to reshape the curriculum, and there is a prevalent belief that hands-on experiences deprive students of traditional test-prep time regardless of what much of the current literature reveals. This is more prevalent in low-level classes. In February of 2007, the National Science Teachers Association issued a position paper promoting integrated, inquiry-based labs for students in all classes.

It is very difficult to measure the effectiveness of hands-on science, and the authors of *America's Lab Report* (NRC, 2005) found that evidence is currently lacking to definitely determine the efficacy of both typical laboratory experiences and integrated instructional units in enabling students to achieve a number of the higher-order learning goals set by instructors. There's no doubt that many lab-deprived students score as well on standardized tests as their lab-rich peers. However, we worry that students may be missing out on the spark that ignites a passion for science. They miss the opportunity to discover if they might enjoy working and thinking like scientists.

We believe in the value of well-designed, inquiry-based, hands-on curriculum. Don't let the pitfalls discourage you. There are enough reasons to support the notion that hands-on, inquiry-based instruction works, regardless of the educational inertia to the contrary.

Sources

National Research Council. (2005). *America's lab report: Investigations in high school science.* Washington, DC: National Academies Press. Retrieved January 18, 2006, from http://books.nap.edu/catalog/11311.html

NSTA. (2007). *Position Statement. The integral role of laboratory investigations in science instruction.* Retrieved March 3, 2010, from http://www.nsta.org/about/positions/laboratory.aspx

Strategy 19: Convert traditional labs to inquiry-based activities.

What the Research Says

The NRC (2000) has identified the essential features of classroom inquiry. Students and teachers are engaged in inquiry when they do the following:

1. Grapple with scientifically oriented questions

2. Give priority to evidence

3. Formulate evidence-based explanations

4. Evaluate the strength of explanations based on the evidence

5. Communicate and justify explanations (p. 25)

The NRC (2000) asserts that these features should be applied across science content areas and grade levels. To see how these might apply to your classes, reference the NSES standards for the appropriate grade levels (NRC, 1996).

The idea of inquiry assumes a shift in who does what kind of work in the classroom. The teacher's role shifts from that of information dispenser to task developer, and students take on more responsibility for their own learning. The taxonomy developed by Schwab (1962) and modified by Herron (1971) provides a lens for categorizing laboratory activities based on who provides the problem and method of solution and whether the answer is already known to the students (as in confirmatory labs). Laboratory activities in which the problem and methodology are provided to the students and the answer is already known are classified as level 0. As teachers and students move toward level 3, which is the highest, students assume more responsibility for the actual cognitive work. Level 3 activities constitute those in which the answer is unknown and both the problem and method of solution are left open to the student.

Volkmann and Abell (2003) discuss a process for adapting traditional laboratory activities into those that are much more representative of inquiry. One of the tools they introduce is something they call the "Inquiry Analysis Tool" (p. 39). This tool is based on the NRC's five features of inquiry and takes the teacher through a series of questions that asks the teacher to focus on various aspects of the tasks and required actions by the students. The questions focus broadly on the nature of what is under investigation; how the students collect and represent data; who is responsible for explanations, when this occurs (prior to a laboratory activity or after), and how this occurs; and what kind of opportunities students have to communicate their explanations and critique others' explanations. The questions help teachers identify aspects of the laboratory activity to change so that it becomes more inquiry like.

Volkmann and Abell (2003) then identify 10 potential actions that teachers can take to increase the amount of inquiry in any particular laboratory activity. In revising their currently used laboratory activities, teachers can use this tool to change portions of these labs to move some, or all, sections toward more inquiry-like laboratories.

Classroom Applications

 Start small. It is usually best to first introduce a change like this with just one part of a lab and then expand it. Think about where you might get the most out of a lab, especially if time is a big consideration. It may be less important to have the students generate the questions but much more important for students to wallow around in the data, figuring out which data are important, how to represent them, and just how to present them in a convincing way. If this is the case, you choose the question the students are to investigate, saving the time for the students to spend working with the data.

The same is true for the data collection. If there really is only one best way to get the data, don't spend valuable class time having students try to determine a procedure. In some cases, you might want the students to learn about the ups and downs of data collection, and then *that* would be the goal of the lab. However, if the goal is something that the students will learn from the pattern in the data, then provide the opportunity for the students to really work with the data in a meaningful way.

In a more inquiry-like activity, students need to share their data so that their data set is large enough that they are able to determine if any patterns emerge. Making these data (or their "answers") public and discussing what the pattern(s) might mean is very different from the enactment of a traditional lab in which the students carry out the lab, complete the post-lab, and turn it in, with little discussion.

Converting traditional labs that you are already using into more inquiry-like labs that ask more of the students needn't be as intimidating and time-consuming a process as might first be anticipated. It can be possible to change pieces of an already existing lab in relatively small ways and in the process engage your students in a much greater degree of inquiry. Just asking students to do something different with their data from what is normally expected of them can be a big start. The Volkmann and Abell (2003) framework provides a nice tool for thinking about this process of transformation.

Precautions and Potential Pitfalls

Asking students to do more of the work and more of the thinking is definitely more time-consuming, so plan ahead for this. Discussion of how to represent data and why that representation might be important can take 30 minutes. Think about how to use charts and graphs and be sure that the students know *why* scientists do this. Ask students if they understand the real difference between bar graphs and line graphs and why and when they might use one and not the other. You might be surprised at the responses that you get.

Discussions with students about their data, the patterns that emerge, and the explanations that they are developing can take time. The inclination on the part of the teacher might be to hurry things along and just tell the students what they should be seeing. However, it is important to continue to help the students to develop their own understandings by probing and questioning, rephrasing, and adding information as appropriate. The teacher should always go back to the students' own data and ask the students to do the same, using evidence to support all statements.

Students might also gripe and even ask why you don't just tell them the answer. It helps if you explain the process to them and that they may be frustrated in the beginning. For many students, especially those who are uncomfortable with not knowing a definitive answer, this can be challenging. Often, it is the honors students who struggle most with the transition into more inquiry-based lessons. They are accustomed to being successful and learning in ways that have most likely been easy for them. Persevere.

Sources

Herron, M. D. (1971). The nature of scientific inquiry. *School Review, 79*(2), 171–212.

McComas, W. (2005). Laboratory instruction in the service of science teaching and learning. *The Science Teacher, 72*(7), 24–29.

National Research Council. (2000). *Inquiry and the national science education standards: A guide for teaching and learning.* Washington, DC: National Academy Press.

National Research Council. (1996). *National science education standards.* Washington, DC: National Academy Press.

Schwab, J. J. (1962). The teaching of science as inquiry. In J. Schwab & P. Brandwein (Eds.), *The Teaching of Science.* Cambridge, MA: Harvard University Press.

Volkmann, M. J., & Abell, S. K. (2003). Rethinking laboratories: Tools for converting cookbook labs into inquiry. *The Science Teacher, 70*(6), 38–41.

✓ Strategy 20: Align the goals of dissection to the curriculum.

What the Research Says

The current role of dissection in high school has sometimes become the focus of intense debate or at the very least careful scrutiny in the last several years. It may be time to redefine the goals and objectives of this activity and involve students in determining when and how dissection should be used. Furthermore, the definition and scope of dissection needs to be broadened to include high-level problem solving, and the experience needs to be structured in an inquiry-based or problem-based pedagogy. Ultimately, the goal here is not to take sides but to generate thought and reflection on what role dissection should play in the science classroom.

Hug (2008) undertook a reexamination of this subject. She first examined the historical notion of dissection via academic literature. She searched the literature for references defining dissection as an instructional strategy and also the examination of the practice from an ethical perspective. Hug then visited classrooms to analyze more carefully the levels of engagement and learning and at what cognitive levels the students interacted with the activity. She did an analysis of a number of classes experiencing the dissection of a yellow perch and sea lamprey. As a framework for observation, she used the following guidelines (Doyle, 1983) to define dissection as an academic task:

1. The products students create as a result of engaging in the assigned activity

2. The manner by which the students complete the task

3. Any resources, examples, and/or models that students have access to in order to complete the activity and create the product

Hug (2008) stated that, in the classrooms she observed, there were opportunities for inquiry, as illustrated by the engagement and questioning, but she felt in most cases teachers were unable to capture the teachable moments or expand them into periods of extended investigation and reasoning. She added that for the most part, the activity remained focused on procedures involved in the dissection activity itself.

Hug's (2008) observations within her investigation led her to comment, "The students rarely succeeded in going beyond the basic factual information about reproductive strategies or digestive systems. It was not clear that the dissection added depth to the students' understanding or provided sustained opportunities to learn structures and functions of these systems" (p. 93). Hug felt that if the instructional goals were the observation of anatomical structures or comparisons of structure and/or function, the students could have observed images via simulation or demonstration without sacrificing or using large numbers of animals.

Hug's basic argument is that teachers need to examine whether the pedagogical value in dissection is worth the ethical compromises that surround it. She points out that the tradition of dissection in secondary school science classes is increasingly being questioned for its ethical dimensions.

Classroom Applications

 Are dissections as curriculum outdated in the contemporary science classroom? It seems that dissections are not so much outdated as much as they are in need of modification and enhancement away from linear procedures to more of a comparative high-level thinking experience.

Dissections are driven by historic inertia within the very traditional educational model for what parents and students expect biology to be. Anecdotally, it also seems that more and more students would prefer to opt out of the traditional dissection experience and accomplish the tasks of learning structures and framing contrast and comparison questions in virtual labs or experience them as a demonstration and class discussion.

Beyond the basic factual anatomical information that dissection provides, teachers can and should strive to raise the cognitive levels in which students engage in typical dissections. Multiple intelligence theory and differentiated curriculum proponents might argue that a tactile interaction within the curriculum is a good way to develop multiple learning pathways. There are several authors that have spoken of the benefits of the multisensory learning environment provided by the dissection laboratory experience with certain groups, specifically English language learners. Self-directed learning, peer teaching, communicative skills, and in some cases team building can come from dissection experiences. Also, there is no doubt that some students' interest in biology can be piqued during dissections.

It's very common for teachers to develop their own laboratory procedures. For example, Meuler (2008) presents a vertebrate anatomy lab that involves a guided-inquiry approach. While students perform a dissection in this lab, they ask scientifically oriented questions, think critically, and problem solve.

For those interested in laboratory models of inquiry, the supplier Carolina Biological has attempted to create, develop, and structure an inquiry approach to some of their laboratory experiences. Examples in different science disciplines are located at http://www.carolina.com/category/teacher+resources/dissection+activities+and+resources.do. There may be other suppliers that offer similar curricula. Finally, the National Science Teachers Association position statement on dissection and the use of live organisms can be accessed at http://www.nsta.org/about/positions/animals.aspx.

Precautions and Potential Pitfalls

Dissections continue to be a morally and ethically sensitive subject for many students. Many college or university-bound students take classes where dissections are mandated by the nature of college preparatory class experience. Some schools transfer students out of college-prep science classes when they refuse to do dissections. Rather than confront students with the dissection requirements, use the requirements as an opportunity to develop alternative inquiry-based curriculum and instructional practices that meet your original goals.

Sources

Doyle, W. (1983). Academic work. *Review of Educational Research, 53*(2), 159–199.

Hug, B. (2008). Re-examining the practice of dissection: What does it teach? *Journal of Curriculum Studies, 40*(1), 91–105.

Meuler, D. (2008). Using a guided inquiry approach in the traditional vertebrate anatomy laboratory. *The American Biology Teacher.* Retrieved March 24, 2009, from http://findarticles.com/p/articles/mi_6958/is_1_70/ai_n28524382?tag=content;col1

3

Collaborative Teaching and Learning

Strategy 21: Fine-tune collaborative student relationships with the Socratic Seminar.

What the Research Says

 Sampson and Clark's (2008) curiosity motivated them to explore three questions:

1. Do groups craft better arguments than individuals?

2. To what degree do individuals adopt and internalize the arguments crafted by their groups?

3. Do individuals who work in groups learn more from their experiences than individuals working on their own?

To answer these questions, the researchers studied 168 high school chemistry students, who were randomly assigned, using matched pair design to collaborative or individual argumentation conditions. Students in both instructional conditions first completed a task that required them to produce an argument articulating and justifying an explanation for a discrepant event. The students then worked on their own to complete mastery and transfer problems.

The results of the study indicated the following:

- Groups of students did not produce any better arguments than students who worked alone.
- A substantial proportion of the students adopted at least some elements of their group's argument.
- Students from the collaborative condition demonstrated superior performance on the mastery and transfer problems.
- Collaboration was beneficial for individual learning but not for initial performance on task.

Classroom Applications

Argumentation, in the real world outside the classroom, is described as a process of debate or discussion between people with different viewpoints. As parents and teachers know, students are often skillful at supporting their ideas, challenging, and counter challenging ideas and points during conversations that usually focus on everyday issues. The qualities of these discussions can be compared and contrasted with those of scientists. Students are often skeptical of new ideas; they use analogies, support their claims with evidence or data, and prefer causal explanations. You can say that students enter your classroom with useful and productive cognitive resources and abilities to engage, generate, and assess explanations, arguments, and phenomena in the context of science.

In the science classroom, students need the opportunity to propose, support, participate in critique, and revise or alter their ideas and those of their peers. They need to examine the validity or acceptability of alternative explanations based on available data and new information, and also be able to clearly articulate and participate in scientific argumentation.

Collaborative learning in the science classroom would seem to be a natural outgrowth of the way science is practiced in the world outside the classroom. Peer review, collaborative effort, and argumentation are the gold currency of scientific discourse and process. Why haven't these types of interactions made it into the K–12 classroom, and where do future scientists and science workers learn these processes? There are some obvious problems in accomplishing this task in a school setting:

- Teachers themselves need to understand the nature of scientific collaboration and argumentation. Many teachers who have been involved in science education or classroom science haven't experienced scientific argumentation themselves within authentic inquiry.

- The nature of the school social structure makes it difficult for students to drop their student identities and relate to others in new ways more appropriate for a science workplace.
- An additional obstacle for students, especially gifted students, is a transition to a science classroom emphasizing cooperative learning strategies. In prior academic experiences, gifted students' self-concepts were formed largely on their ability to find the right answers. They may have limited experience in truly participating as a member of a learning community and sharing ideas for the purpose of mutual understanding.

How should or could a science teacher overcome these problems and orchestrate collaborative learning in the science classroom? The current academic literature, including research-based and anecdotal, presents a range of ways to structure cooperative or collaborative learning in class-rooms. Sampson and Clark's (2008) work included a literature search. These researchers felt that rather than yield definitive answers regarding effective strategies, the findings tend to be mixed based on the class demographics and the specific tasks at hand. In tasks such as making products, model building, or mathematical problem solving, they found that groups tend to perform better. In contrast, regarding tasks such as story writing or rote memorization, Sampson and Clark found studies that concluded that groups do not perform any better than individuals. The mixed results support the conclusion that the benefits of collaboration for academic performance are very dependant on student demographics, the specific tasks, and the overall context for the activity. When Sampson and Clark looked for science-specific research, they found few studies that have examined the benefits of group work in evaluating alternative explanations and generating an argument, both of which are key in scientific discourse. They found evidence in the literature that some groups tend to spend a great deal of time discussing procedural aspects and little time discussing the underlying concepts or using higher-level thinking skills. Individual group members can also have a detrimental effect on how others participate, and assertive individuals can drive and shape the whole group as they try to accomplish a task.

So where does all of this lead us? The benefits of collaboration for individual learning do not simply emerge from teachers haphazardly distributing students within group work. To be certain that individuals within groups are engaged in certain types of learning processes, teachers must provide opportunities for individuals in groups to encounter new ideas, opinions, and perspectives within discussions. Teachers also need to facilitate opportunities for students to defend and explain their own thinking and listen to the ideas and explanations of others. In the limited framework of this text, it is difficult to explore and offer all of the potential models of collaborative learning. The best strategies will come close to engaging students in the types of discourse and thinking usually found in scientific laboratories. However, whatever model you decide to adopt needs to be well thought out ahead of time. Let's consider, for example, the Socratic Seminar, which has been used in humanity classes for some time, is highly structured, and has a record of effectiveness.

The Socratic Seminar teaches research and speaking skills and higher-level thinking skills by having students relate and respond to other students' thinking and draw parallels to similar topics. Socratic Seminars work well in literature classes, science classes, and social studies classes, and with a bit of simplification these seminars can also work in lower grade levels.

The key is the Socratic Seminar's tight structure, clear expectations, and easily understood assessment goals. It also is conducted in a visible style rather than in isolation. Student participation is highly observable. Using the Socratic method in the classroom takes some practice, and the topic needs to be carefully selected for the seminar to work well. For those new to the strategy, there are Internet sites that specialize in helping teachers structure the technique. Each site presents a version of the Socratic Seminar that may be a little different or is presented for a specific discipline. If you choose to use the Socratic Seminar, you will, as with other instructional activities, need to adjust, modify, and learn by experience. Be sure to design a rubric explaining instructional goals, assessment, and grading so that they are clear for individual students and student groups. Rubrics are very personal instruments that teachers use to help students and themselves focus on what is important. They define the "destination" for instruction and demonstration of mastery. Given out beforehand, a rubric provides students with an outline of exactly what they will be graded on and what they have to demonstrate to receive a certain grade. It also provides teachers with a fair grading standard that is applied to all students. Below is an example best suited for a high school class. The following grading rubric outlines two levels of performance as a participant in group discussions.

Meets Standards

- Communicates cooperatively and effectively with the collaborative team. The quality of contribution meets standards in tone, articulation, appropriate science vocabulary, and eye contact
- Participates effectively within the group, actively participating, respecting others, carefully listening, encouraging silent members, and using techniques like paraphrasing and summarizing the comments of others to use in rebuttal
- Contributes thoughtful responses to the topic and the overall discussion, supporting with evidence from the textbook and other resources
- Demonstrates knowledge of the material and preparation through quality of language, vocabulary, responses, and discussion
- Is able to adopt science language or academic language in their contribution to classroom discourse

Exceeds Standards

- Demonstrates the ability to examine and then respectfully accept or reject the procedures, relationships, or connections in an explanation or argument and can connect and present their ideas based on the evidence presented and the ideas invoked
- Shows informed leadership and helps keep the group on task by asking questions of the large group, refocusing the group's attention, and directing questions or statements to members of the group who need a chance to speak
- Supports statements with specific and appropriate references that include mastery of textbook information and scientific inquiry process

A checkmark or X can be put next to each item the student successfully demonstrates.

Once finished with the discussion phase, students who have met or exceeded standards will find it easy to write an analytical essay on any of the topics.

Precautions and Potential Pitfalls

First, the greatest pitfall in all of this is expecting mastery of scientific discourse and reasoning after a short period of time. It helps to make it a departmental rather than an individual goal. Teaching students to think like scientists is always work in progress, and sadly, some will never get it. The world of academic science can be intimidating for many, and adopting a new way of reasoning, thinking, and speaking is difficult. Don't let early frustration or one tough class detour your efforts!

Second, keep in mind that students often rely on their personal views, rather than support their arguments with data generated by their book or laboratory research or inquiry. They are so accustomed to regurgitating "right" answers and are biased to ignore, discount, or distort information or data that threaten strongly held beliefs. Students often have a great deal of difficulty generating arguments or explanations that articulate their understanding in the style of scientists. They have a tough time identifying "what counts" from a scientific perspective rather than a personal one. Because they rarely use scientific knowledge to support their decisions in everyday life, they find it difficult in the science classroom. Teachers should realize that their students' success in completing inquiry practices, such as using appropriate evidence and scientific reasoning to support or refute an idea, is dependent on their ability to understand the argumentative nature of science in its complete context. Without the basic knowledge of what counts as evidence in science, it is unlikely that students can apply data or scientific information when asked to construct an argument or to justify an idea. Teaching students to think like scientists will take time and practice.

Source

Sampson, V., & Clark, D. (2008). The impact of collaboration on the outcomes of scientific argumentation. *Science Education, 93*(3), 448–484.

Strategy 22: Teach your students collaborative strategies and skills.

What the Research Says

Anderson, Thomas, and Nashon (2009) explored the underlying metasocial and metacognitive factors that can adversely affect, influence, and shape academic relationships and collaborative learning efforts. They found that even when group work was optimized with highly collegial and collaborative student groups, consistent with the recommendations found in the literature for collaborative group work, there were factors that teachers have a difficult time controlling. Their study revealed that in addition to the more obvious traditional individual-centered perspective, there exist other social agendas that can alter the collective and individual actions of group members on both learning tasks and social relationship levels. They propose that students are highly aware of their social positioning and status within a group and the group's overall social condition, and students spend a considerable amount of monitoring these conditions and carefully use strategies that facilitate success in both the academic tasks and also social relationships. They also were not surprised to find that students make decisions to maintain friendships and their associated social agenda and capital rather than engaging in argumentative discussions more related to the science teacher's instructional agenda. In this way, group structures might be counterproductive to effective learning in science.

While not obvious, Anderson et al. (2009) saw barriers to discourse that might lead to more meaningful learning arrangements and emphasized that these barriers could limit higher-order thinking. They concluded that certain types of assumptions that parents, teachers, and educators in general make regarding collaborative work foster a false sense of security about the power of group work to promote and facilitate meaningful learning group environments.

Classroom Applications

Here are the main instructional points that teachers need to consider to help science students in collaborative settings:

- Respectful peer argumentation and discourse is an important part of science.

- Differences of opinion are important points for discussion and a normal occurrence in science and science learning environments, especially within inquiry-based instruction.
- Students need to be taught to appreciate that debate on certain points can benefit the learning of all group members without compromising collegial social harmony and relationships.
- The way science is practiced in the world outside the classroom proceeds on the basis of conjecture and debate among close science colleagues and peers.
- Teachers must model scientific discourse as part of scaffolding the development of this type of interaction within instruction.

Collaborative group work in science can best be taught within a whole department as a universal departmental goal. Teachers who really know their students well and can "read" the social arrangements and agendas within classes are most successful at developing collaborative learning strategies. A sense of trust between the teacher and the students is fundamental.

Precautions and Potential Pitfalls

 It is widely acknowledged both in adolescent psychological research and in anecdotal evidence that friendships are important in developing young minds. Adolescents without friendships may suffer a range of problems, most notably stress and low self-esteem. Teaching the main points of scientific discourse and actually engaging students in them takes time. Students must be willing to take risks and learn that they can engage in debate without a social penalty. Still, there will be students who will not engage in discussions that might result in conflict between group members. They simply will not compromise their social relationships.

Source

Anderson, D., Thomas, G. P., & Nashon, S. M. (2009). Social barriers to meaningful engagement in biology field trip group work. *Science Education, 93*(3), 511–534.

 Strategy 23: Utilize formal cooperative learning methods in the classroom.

What the Research Says

The research in cooperative learning is quite substantial and clearly identifies what cooperative learning is and what it is not. Cooperative learning is often mistaken with group work or collaborative learning. Children in elementary schools often work in groups; this starts early as young children are placed in reading and math groups. However, just because students work *near* other students does not mean that they are working cooperatively. As children age and progress through the grades, teachers recognize that some students are more capable and often assume an unbalanced load of the work assigned to the group. This may be because some students are incapable of doing the assigned work, are uninterested in doing the work, or are not allowed to do the work by other students in the group. As a result, the experience for students in groups is not equal, and all students do not benefit equitably. Johnson and Johnson (1999) refer to these as pseudo groups or traditional classroom learning groups.

In recognition of this, Johnson, Johnson, and Holubec (Johnson & Johnson, 1989, 1999; Johnson, Johnson, & Holubec, 1998) embarked on their seminal work on cooperative learning. These researchers recognize different types of cooperative learning but identify common features to cooperative groups that result in high-level learning outcomes for students. The basic features, or elements, that Johnson, Johnson, and Holubec identify as essential for an activity to be considered cooperative include the following:

• *Positive interdependence.* The success of each individual is tied to the success of the group and vice versa. Positive interdependence can be encouraged by rewarding each member of the group for meeting a certain individual performance level, thereby creating an incentive for each member of the group to work to ensure that all members of the group are learning. Teachers can also use jigsaw strategies so that individual group members have only part of the necessary information or materials to complete the task.

• *Individual accountability.* Individual students are assessed, and feedback is provided both to the individual student and to the group. Strategies that Johnson, Johnson, and Holubec suggest for holding students individually accountable include giving students tests and/or quizzes, randomly selecting students to explain their group's work, or reciprocal teaching.

• *Interpersonal interaction.* Johnson, Johnson, and Holubec state that the face-to-face interaction that occurs in the cooperative learning process is essential. They recommend forming groups of two to four students. Groups that are too large provide opportunities for some students not to participate.

• *Social skills.* Students learn to encourage and support each other as they learn together in a social setting. Initially, teachers need to teach the social skills necessary to be successful in these activities and reinforce them as the students develop facility in their use.

- *Group processing*. This element includes a metacognitive component that requires students to reflect on the extent to which they have met the goals of both the task and of working together.

Research abounds on the relative effectiveness of cooperative learning versus competitive and individual modes of learning. Johnson and Johnson (1989) identify and review over 550 experimental and 100 correlational studies. These studies and others have revealed that students engaged in cooperative groups demonstrated greater academic achievement and greater productivity than those students who worked alone. Studies also showed that students showed greater time on task, greater high-level reasoning and problem solving, and improved ability to transfer learning. These studies also indicated that students demonstrated improved interpersonal relationships, including an improvement in attendance, and cooperative learning helped to create an environment in which students viewed themselves as capable.

While it is important to keep in mind the five elements identified by Johnson and Johnson (1989) when structuring tasks for cooperative learning groups, group composition is also important. Webb (1997) found that group composition is important in the overall performance of the groups. Below-average student performance was significantly improved when these students were placed in heterogeneous groups as compared to placement in homogeneous groups or working alone. Above-average students showed no such effect. Their performance on academic measures was largely flat, indicating no real academic benefit for high-performing students but no detriment either.

Classroom Applications

As with trying anything new in the classroom, you might want to start with a task that is fairly small and of relatively low risk. For example, the first task might involve a reading from a chapter in the textbook that you have structured as a jigsaw activity in which the students will each read different parts, and then teach their piece to the other group members. They might then take a short quiz on the whole chapter that is worth a relatively small number of points. You probably would *not* want their first experience with formal cooperative learning to be a large project worth a substantial percentage of their grade. Students may need to be convinced that they, too, will learn just as well, if not better, this way.

Using a jigsaw of a section of reading is actually a nice way for students to engage in text and content as opposed to the rapid dissemination of that same content via teacher lecture. This is particularly true if the content is relatively unfamiliar to the students and fairly complex. The less experience students have with content and the more complex the ideas, the more time students will need to come to understand them. Providing a structure that will encourage discussion is just one way that students can come to understand some of the more challenging ideas in science. As is true with all activities that occur in the classroom, the teacher should closely monitor what is occurring and can intercede in any group, or with the class as a whole, if the students become stuck on a particular point or idea. This is not a situation where students are simply observed and allowed to work unassisted.

Make sure to structure the experience in a way that encourages positive interdependence so that one or two students do not co-opt a group and do all of the work or so that some students do not become what Webb (1997) terms "social loafers" (p. 208). Assigning roles and using a jigsaw structure can work nicely. An article by Emily Lin (2006) provides some practical advice for integrating cooperative learning into middle and high school classrooms. She includes suggestions for shifting through a jigsaw structure that can be used as a framework for a variety of tasks.

Precautions and Potential Pitfalls

Group work or loosely structured collaborative work has not been shown to produce the positive outcomes identified in the research. These participation structures have their place in classrooms. Perhaps what should determine the participation structure is the intended learning outcome—if the outcome is something integral to understanding the *big idea* being studied, then perhaps the participation structure might be more tightly constrained and formal cooperative groups used.

As with all new strategies, students will need to learn the component pieces that will allow them to be successful. Care should be taken to provide the necessary instruction of the group and social skills that will enable the students to work together in productive ways.

Sources

Johnson, D. W., & Johnson, R. T. (1999). Making cooperative learning work. *Theory Into Practice, 38*(2), 67–73.

Johnson, D. W., & Johnson, R. T. (1989). *Cooperation and competition: Theory and research.* Edina, MN: Interaction Book Co.

Johnson, D. W., Johnson, R., & Holubec, E. (1998). *Cooperation in the classroom* (7th ed.). Edina, MN: Interaction Book Co.

Lin, E. (2006). Cooperative learning in the science classroom: A new learning model for a new year. *The Science Teacher, 73*(5), 34–39.

Webb, N. M. (1997). Assessing students in small collaborative groups. *Theory Into Practice, 36*(4), 205–213.

Strategy 24: Introduce students to constructive, cooperative, and academic controversy.

What the Research Says

Constructive, Cooperative, and Academic Controversy is a strategy in which students are responsible for developing and then arguing both sides of an issue. This differs from a more traditional debate in that students do not argue just one side of the issue, but must develop arguments for both sides of the issue and then seek to reach a consensus agreement (Johnson & Johnson, 2007). This process requires students to organize information as they create their arguments that they will then present to their peers. Students must advocate for multiple positions, defending and elaborating on those positions using evidence along with prior scientific knowledge. These processes necessitate that students synthesize and integrate the best evidence and arguments as they move into the consensus segment.

In a scientific sense, issues are considered controversial if there is disagreement around evidence, explanations, or theories. An example of this might be the case of cold fusion in which experimental results were not reproducible, or in the case of observable increases in levels of atmospheric CO_2 and the implications for global warming in which the data are not disputed, but their interpretation are not agreed upon.

Controversy may also arise when the technological applications of science create debate, such as in the increasingly common use of antibacterial soaps and sprays by the public and the potential link to "superbugs" or in the growing market of genetically modified foods.

Note that what is controversial to the lay public is not necessarily controversial to scientists for scientific reasons. It can be problematic for science teachers to venture into areas of teaching values or representing and/or advocating their own perspective. In some cases, it will be important for a teacher to present a balanced view of a topic. In others, law prevents teachers from doing so, as in the case of giving equal time for creationism (*Edwards v. Aguillard*, 482 U.S. 578, 1987). See the National Science Teachers Association Position Statement on the Teaching of Evolution (http://www.nsta.org/about/positions.aspx) for more information on the implications of this court case and the "equal time" issue.

What is probably best to remember is that the issue must be controversial for scientific reasons, not for moral, ethical, or religious reasons. The discussions in science class should focus on the reasons why *science* considers the issue to be controversial (reduced reproductive success, lack of genetic variability, increased likelihood for mutations, inadequate testing, lack of safe storage, inadequate modeling, lack of agreement on modeling parameters, etc.).

The teaching strategy of constructive controversy was developed in the mid-1960s in the field of conflict resolution (Johnson & Johnson, 2007) and is used in teaching across content areas and grade levels. Research on constructive controversy has been conducted over the past 35 years, investigating various dependent variables, including student achievement, cognitive reasoning, motivation, and attitude toward task. The research subjects have included students across grade levels from elementary school through college. In the meta-analysis conducted by Johnson & Johnson (2007), they conclude that students involved in controversy demonstrate greater content mastery, greater recall of information and reasoning, more skillful transference of learning, and greater generalization to new situations. In addition, students exhibited greater motivation for continued learning of the content being considered in the issue. Students involved in a controversy tended to search for more information regarding the controversy (Johnson & Johnson, 2007). All of these are the types of outcomes we would like to see for our students and are representative of those lifelong learning skills we often talk about.

Classroom Applications

The steps to a Constructive, Cooperative, and Academic Controversy are quite prescribed. They are described in a number of places, including in the publications by Johnson and Johnson and their colleagues (1985, 1998, 2007) and at the Wide Angle website of the Public Broadcasting Service (Educational Broadcasting Company, 2002–2007). The steps essentially break down into the following:

1. Students are either provided with information about a topic or research the topic. Initially, a pair of students is responsible for only one side of the issue, and the pair prepares an argument for their position. The issue should have two sides—pro or con, for or against, and so on.

2. Student pairs present their position to a pair of students who has the opposing position.

3. Students have their position challenged by engaging in an open discussion. They must defend their position, rebut attacks, and pose questions to challenge the opposing viewpoint.

4. What makes this process very different from a debate is this next step. The groups now switch positions and reverse perspectives. Each group must now present the opposing position as persuasively as possible using all information available.

5. In the last step, the students must reach some agreement on the issue. This requires the students to integrate and synthesize the information that has been presented on both sides and to reach a consensus.

A variation on this for older students is available in Johnson, Johnson, and Smith (1998).

The initial preparation for this activity can be a bit time-consuming. You'll need to prepare at least three hand-outs: (1) a general overview introducing the issue, (2) a pro position, and (3) a con position. It's important to keep both the pro and con positions parallel in construction—similar in length, appearance, amount of content, and so on. The amount of information you provide will depend on who your students are—grade level, prior knowledge, and so on. It will also determine how much time you provide for them to work through each step of the controversy. If they get less information to work with, they will need less time to develop their argument. Giving them a time limit for each step and moving them through each step as a whole class works best. You might find that you need two class periods to complete this activity, or a double period. The nice thing about the structure of Constructive, Cooperative, and Academic Controversy is that it is easy to break up into two periods. You might get through the development of the argument one day and then start up with the argument presentation on Day 2 and then go to completion.

Students may not know what it means to develop a scientific argument the first time you do this, so you may need to have an up-front discussion about what this means if you want your students to develop a quality product. Providing tools for students to organize their thinking and their arguments is helpful and will not only keep them accountable, it will also allow you to assess their work.

Students often find topics that are "closer to home" more interesting, and information can often be drawn from local newspapers. For example, a controversy about what to do with an expanding deer population in a local suburban community might be of interest to students in that community.

Precautions and Potential Pitfalls

When engaging in this activity for the first time, it might be best to provide students with "fact sheets" that they can use to create their arguments. This will steer them in the direction of using scientific, rather than nonscientific, information in their arguments. A discussion with your students about what is science and what is not considered science will be helpful. Students can get confused when trying to distinguish between the kinds of questions that science can and cannot answer. Handouts to help students organize the development of their argument aid in keeping them on task. They also provide something tangible for the teacher to collect and assess. The Wide Angle website has some useful examples.

It is also important to check the reading level of the material that you provide to students. Microsoft Word has a function that will allow you to do this, and you can also use one of the other readability formulas (Flesch-Kincaid, Fry, etc.).

This strategy is a great way to get students reading and writing in science. Supports in both reading and writing can be tailored to meet the needs of your students.

Sources

Educational Broadcasting Company. (2002–2007). *Wide Angle: The Global Classroom*. Academic Primer. Available at http://www.pbs.org/wnet/wideangle/classroom/controversy.html

Edwards v. Aguillard, 482 U.S. 578. (1987). Retrieved March 1, 2010, from http://www.law.cornell.edu/supct/html/historics/USSC_CR_0482_0578_ZS.html

Johnson, D. W., & Johnson, R. T. (2007). *Creative controversy: Intellectual challenge in the classroom* (4th ed.). Edina, MN: Interaction Book Company.

Johnson, D. W., Johnson, R., & Smith, K. (1998). *Active learning: Cooperation in the college classroom*. Edina, MN: Interaction Book Company.

Johnson, R., Brooker, C., Stutzman, Hultman, D., & Johnson, D. W. (1985). The effects of controversy, concurrence seeking, and individualistic learning on achievement and attitude change. *Journal of Research in Science Teaching, 22*(3), 197–205.

Strategy 25: Communicate beyond the classroom by using electronic pen pals.

What the Research Says

According to Louanne Smolin and Kimberly Lawless (2003), a technologically literate person is someone who understands what technology is and how to use it with relative ease. As the U.S. Department of Education (1997) suggests, students must move beyond just knowing how to use technology, such as computers and the Internet, to being able to manipulate these technologies to increase academic performance. Reading teachers must thus be able to help their students become technologically literate by showing them how to use these technologies and how to express their ideas and communicate with diverse groups.

Classroom Applications

Smolin and Lawless (2003) suggest that by working in small-group activities, students can learn to interact independently while at the same time learn from each other. The authors propose the use of

ePals.com (http://www.epals.com) to foster such independence. One of the largest online classroom communities in the world, ePals allows teachers and students alike to locate electronic pen pals in all regions of the world. Science teachers can have students perform basic communication skills such as developing e-mail communications, but they can also get students to work in groups or perform collaborative science projects. Students can join weblogs and e-mentoring groups. This website translates from one language to another so that students can communicate with others anywhere in the world, even though their e-pals may speak a different language. Teachers can set up common science projects with other teachers and students from around the world, and they can all share and compare data on the same project from different contexts. According to Smolin and Lawless (2003), teachers can find collaborative projects across curriculum areas by using the Internet Projects Registry (http://gsh .lightspan.com/pr/index.html), which lists curriculum-based projects from a variety of organizations. Teachers can search for projects by subject area, age level, or project starting dates.

Precautions and Potential Pitfalls

Like all Internet-related projects, both teachers and students must be proficient not only in manipulating technology, such as computers and the Internet, but also in knowing how to critically interpret what is presented on the web. Students must be monitored at all times while involved with Internet use. Most schools have some type of blocking software installed to restrict student access to certain Internet sites. You can set up some type of fair use technology policy to be shared with parents and students to alert them to the expectations teachers have for the students' Internet use. Finally, unfortunately only those countries and schools that are linked to the web can participate in creating such e-pals projects.

Sources

Smolin, L., & Lawless, K. (2003). Becoming literate in the technological age: New responsibilities and tools for teachers. *Reading Teacher, 56*, 22–29.

U.S. Department of Education. (1997). President Clinton's call to action for American education in the 21st century. *Technological Literacy*. Retrieved June 10, 2006, from http://www.ed.gov

4

Utilizing Technology for the Classroom and Professional Development

> **Strategy 26: Add technological tools to your students' learning.**

What the Research Says

As reported in Runge et al. (1999), a traditional undergraduate physics course on math methods was redesigned to incorporate the use of a computerized algebra program during all aspects of the course. The goal of this redesign was to expose beginning students to professional tools currently used by mathematicians and physicists. At the same time, a new "multimedia" physics class sought to integrate math and physics content with other multimedia forms. These two classes served as research laboratories to begin a qualitative case study to describe the courses and develop an understanding of the effect technology had on instruction and learning in the courses. It was found that the instructors made rather substantial changes in both of their courses the second time through, based on their early experience.

The research provided an overview of the issues as follows:

1. Students resisted the additional process orientation of adding technology as another layer of course requirements. Computers add another layer of process skills to learn.

2. Teachers needed to be better prepared and have their own technological act together.

3. The advanced workload preparing for such courses is enormous and goes unnoticed by the students. To the students, book content represents the curriculum: reduced use of books equates to little student-perceived structure.

4. There needs to be a means used for demonstrating the technology and teachers should have a backup plan in case of problems.

5. Clear procedures needed to be developed for students to follow when they encounter problems.

6. Whenever students seemed to have strong learning preferences and styles, their expectations about how they "ought to be taught" conflicted with the design of the courses. Expectations need to be described explicitly and explained for possible conflicts. Problematic conflicts in how and why instruction is implemented need to be resolved.

7. Instructors somewhat underestimated the basic instruction needed. Teachers were challenged to provide guidance and examples without providing "simple" templates that structure the students' homework with little imagination or editing. Technology used as professional tools required in-class instruction that modeled real problem-solving modes.

Overall, the research suggested that the necessary transition from traditional instruction to tool-based instruction is dramatic and fraught with difficulty for teachers and students. The researchers found their data far less positive or encouraging than they would have liked. As experienced teachers, as technology users, and as scientists foreseeing drastic changes in the kinds of intellectual skills students are likely to bring to the professional world, they saw a long developmental role ahead.

Classroom Application

The "technology" of the book is standardized today, and both teachers and students are familiar with these book standards. When you teach a course from a book, most of the time, all involved know what to expect. Calculators, seen as routine today, required a good deal of time to filter through instructional practices and find a niche. Most teachers today have no problem finding a context in their courses for calculators. There are no such "standards" yet on Internet use.

As new technology continues to filter into the secondary science classroom, we must await more technologically savvy students from the lower grades. Second, teachers need to address the concerns listed in the research reviewed above and accept a rather steep learning curve for implementing technology for themselves and their students. The researchers found a remarkable similarity in problems and pitfalls between these two independent classes using very different technologies. "Real-world" professional tools impose a rather drastic transition for all stakeholders. Become as informed as you can about the technology but also be aware of the potential transitional pitfalls you will need to address as a professional educator. Course content always seems to grow, and much of today's testing requires coverage of a wider range of material than ever before. Adding technology to the mix may be necessary for students to keep up with the tools of the field, but teachers need to balance its implementation with important content.

Precautions and Possible Pitfalls

Do not underestimate the huge amount of work, for both you and your students, involved in making technological transitions. Frustrated students can sabotage your best efforts by not authentically engaging in the "new" type of instruction. Students that would do well in traditional classes need nurturing and assurance when the rules change.

In some cases there are problems with intellectual property rights. Teachers should be aware of fair use policies and laws before putting resources online for their students. Many resources are already available online for students, so linking parents to those resources instead of republishing them avoids the risk and liability associated with copyright laws.

Source

Runge, A., Spiegel, A., Pytlik, L., Dunbar, S., Fuller, R., Sowell, G., & Brooks, D. (1999). Hands-on computer use in science classrooms: The skeptics are still waiting. *Journal of Science Education and Technology, 8*(1).

Strategy 27: Put your students' Internet skills to use in the classroom.

What the Research Says

Burnett and Wilkinson (2005) enthusiastically comment on all the new possibilities for engaging students with information associated with a wide variety of literacy practices. Their study explores the purposes for which young children, with routine availability, access the Internet, the attitudes and orientations they demonstrate in their approach to web-based texts, and what has enabled them to develop as Internet users. The focus of the study was out-of-school uses. Their findings are used to make suggestions for supporting and framing the literacy uses of the Internet. They define "reading" Internet and digital texts as functionally distinct from print-based text and describe decoding text, moving images, still images, sounds, and words where meaning is created in different ways.

Their study focused on six-year-olds, three boys and three girls from a small rural primary school. Individual and whole-group interviews were conducted over a six-week period, focusing on key questions regarding Internet use. The researchers gathered the following information:

1. Reasons why children used the Internet

2. Descriptions of the sites they liked and visited

3. Advice for other students on how to access these sites

4. General reflections on skills needed to be effective Internet users

5. Experiences that had been significant in enabling them to become users

The researchers found the students' reasons for using the Internet were diverse. Most frequently, they accessed free stuff such as games, music, images, and so on. They also entered into special Internet communities for shared interests and enthusiasms and communicated with the world around them.

Classroom Applications

Students rarely see the use of the Internet as "literacy" or as a learning activity. Their agendas are usually very "un-school"-oriented; although, as students get older, e-mail and research for school activities become areas of focus. Veteran teachers of students in the upper grades know the educational pitfalls of easy access to questionable information. Because of such pitfalls, younger students should have help using web information appropriately. This is where the Internet can become the focus of science-based literacy activities in the middle grades.

The Internet is an ideal mechanism for encouraging students to assume responsibility for their own learning and build on and improve skills some have already developed. As students find different learning resources on the Internet, they become active participants in their quest for knowledge and information. Incorporating the Internet into your classroom provides students with more opportunities to structure their own explorations and, hopefully, learning. Once trained, students are able to define their learning needs, find information, assess its value, build their own knowledge base, and engage in discourse about their discoveries. Before you and your students can begin to use the Internet in your classroom, students need the foundation of two main sets of skills to (1) navigate the Internet and (2) manage the large amounts of information they find.

People rarely read webpages word by word; instead, they scan the page, picking out individual words and sentences. In a recent study, Morkes and Nielsen (1998) found that 79% of their test users always scanned any new page they came across; only 16% read word by word.

It's likely that you are already familiar with two very important strategies for reading on the web—skimming and scanning. Skimming is glancing quickly over a text to get a general idea of the topic. When skimming, do the following:

- Quickly look over the entire page, focusing on any titles and headings.
- Look at the illustrations, diagrams, and captions. What do they describe?

Scanning is looking for key words and phrases that will give you the specific information you need. When scanning, do the following:

- Look for key words, headings, and terms in bold or italics that refer to information you need.
- Read the first and last sentences of the paragraphs on the page to see if they connect to information you need.

The amount of information available over the Internet, on the news, in newspapers, and in magazines and books is overwhelming for most adults, let alone children. Beyond just gaining webpage fluency, it is critical that students learn to find, analyze, use appropriately, and credit the information at their fingertips. These are information literacy skills, and the sooner we begin teaching them, the better students' chances are of succeeding in the Information Age.

Information literacy skills entail complex thinking and reasoning. These types of skills take time and practice to learn, and many students passing through your classes do not have strong information literacy skills, so be patient and encourage students to practice, practice, practice.

Many of the following information literacy skills and techniques can be taught by first discussing the concept, followed by modeling and conducting guided practice. As students observe you and other students manage information, think aloud about what is being analyzed, and reach conclusions, they will begin to use similar strategies for themselves. Keep in mind that many of these skills are defined as advanced thinking skills by Higher-Order Thinking Skills (HOTS) or Bloom's (1956) taxonomy criteria. The Bloom's taxonomy skill(s) used in each skill set are included in parentheses.

1. Identify if there is a need for information within a task (Comprehension).
- Recognize when information is needed to solve a problem or develop an idea, concept, or theme.
- Brainstorm multiple pathways for approaching a problem or issue.
- Identify, organize, and sequence tasks and specific activities to complete an information-based project.

2. Locate, identify, categorize, and analyze information needed (Comprehension and Analysis).
- Formulate questions based on information needs.
- Use effective search techniques; use key words to search for information.
- Analyze various sources for validity and overall relevance.
- Read competently to understand what is presented.

3. Assess the information found (Analysis and Evaluation).
- Evaluate the quality of information by establishing authority.
- Determine age, accuracy, and authenticity.
- Distinguish among opinion, reasoned arguments, and fact.

4. Organize the information (Application).
- Learn how knowledge is organized.
- Organize and store data in searchable formats.
- Organize information for practical application.

5. Use information effectively to address the problem or task (Synthesis).
- Create new information by synthesizing data from primary and secondary sources.
- Integrate new information with existing knowledge.
- Summarize information found in sources.

6. Communicate information and evaluate results (Application and Evaluation).

- Present information in a product form.
- Revise and update the product in ongoing evaluation.

7. Respect intellectual property rights.

- Develop knowledge for how information and knowledge is produced.
- Document sources using appropriate formats.

As you work through the information science-based literacy skills with your students, remember that these are not the types of skills you can model and teach once and assume students will learn and utilize. You are building on skills they have already developed on their own. They require very advanced thinking and organizing skills, and therefore need multiple visits and hands-on and minds-on practice. Keep in mind that every classroom has students with a range of information literacy, and it is important for a teacher to assess prior knowledge before starting this unit.

Once your students have basic skills on searching and navigating the Internet and strategies to manage and make sense of the information they find, you can begin using the Internet in your lessons, learning centers, and individual assignments and projects.

Here are a number of websites, some of which are interactive, that offer collections of science-based content. Many are suitable for inclusion in your instructional strategies.

1. SciLinks—http://www.scilinks.org

2. Science.gov—http://www.science.gov

3. Lunar and Planetary Institute—http://www.lpi.usra.edu

4. Best Science and Technology Sites—http://www.worldbest.com/science.htm

5. Interactive Science Web Sites—http://jc-schools.net/tutorials/interact-science.htm

6. Spartacus Educational—http://www.spartacus.schoolnet.co.uk/REVscience.htm

7. Insanely Great Science Websites—http://www.eskimo.com/~billb/amateur/coolsci.html

8. KidSites.com—http://www.kidsites.com/sites-edu/science.htm

9. Earth Science—http://www.ncsu.edu/imse/1/earth.htm

Finally, it is important for teachers to completely and smoothly integrate traditional instructional strategies with Internet sites and Internet assignments. The connections or "fit" should be tight and relevant and in complete context with curricular standards. Teachers should also be completely knowledgeable about each site they want to use to help students stay focused on the major learning outcomes.

Precautions and Potential Pitfalls

The Internet is a "time bandit." Without structure, it is easy for kids to lose their direction and purpose. Here are a few hints:

1. Give them a list of a few selected websites related to their unit that relate directly to the lesson. Never start lessons by having students use search engines without guidance.

2. Require students to find very specific information, not just surf. A rubric might be appropriate here.

3. Always require students to write down the URLs of the sites they use for reports in a bibliographic format. You might teach them a cut-and-paste technique to help develop their bibliography or references.

4. Don't send the entire class to the same site at the same time. Once you get them started, encourage the development of search engine techniques.

5. Always preview sites or do the easy key word searches before students visit them.

Finally, access can be a problem for some students. Not all students come from homes with Internet access. You will need to accommodate and support these students also.

Sources

Bloom B. S. (1956). *Taxonomy of educational objectives, handbook I: The cognitive domain*. New York: David McKay.

Burnett, C., & Wilkinson, J. (2005). Holy lemons! Learning from children's uses of the Internet in out-of-school contexts. *Literacy, 39*(3), 158–177.

Morkes, J., & Nielsen, J. (1998). Applying writing guidelines to web pages. Retrieved April 26, 2006, from http://www.useit.com

Strategy 28: Use technology to accommodate students' different learning styles.

What the Research Says

Differences exist within and among student groups, and not all curricula or technological innovations developed by teachers or science experts should be expected to achieve similar ends for all students. Technological implementations for students should consider ways that tools can expand opportunities to all students by offering different kinds of access to knowledge. One way to honor students' diverse skill sets is to incorporate opportunities into lessons by offering students choices for demonstrating science competency through musical, dramatic, artistic, or other representations. Orchestrating collaboration of diverse student knowledge and skill sets around a central problem or concept can also offer greater opportunity to various students to be successful in classrooms.

Becoming familiar with differences in learners' specific styles of preferred knowledge acquisition allows in-depth understanding and interaction with the interests and needs of a greater diversity of students. Research studies confirm the need for identifying students' preferred learning style and for teaching in ways that complement that style. Confirmation from research findings report that academic achievement is elevated when teachers use instructional strategies consistent with students' preferred learning styles (Ballone & Czerniak, 2001). In addition, the converse of student learning has also been demonstrated—that students tend to achieve lower when their learning style and environment are mismatched (MacMurren, 1985; Pizzo, 1981). In fact, some have even argued as strongly for a direct correlation between the match of learning styles and environment and student grade point average (Cafferty, 1981).

Classroom Applications

To achieve the goal of having all students succeed in science requires that teachers' practices and curriculum content be designed to meet their various interests, abilities, experiences, understandings, and knowledge. Accepting diversity in learning styles means also accepting that all students can learn, and effective teachers consider not only the content to be learned but also the learning context, including the background of the students. Teachers must identify instructional materials that are not only flexible but also supportive of diversity and capable of accommodating a wide range of learning styles. Technology integration has been argued to initiate the desired curricular and pedagogical change given the opportunity, equipment, and support.

Lessons should incorporate as many different representations of content as reasonably possible and offer multiple access points for students to use the information presented in ways that they feel confident applying. The following is an example extracted from a 50-minute lesson with elementary students about heat transfer:

- The lesson began with a question and a demonstration activity where students were asked, "Which will heat up more: a cup of water with boiled pennies placed in it or a cup of water with boiled rocks?" Children were allowed to discuss their prediction in small groups, which assisted the social-oriented learners.
- Students then produced graphs of their predictions for what they believed would happen as the demonstration continued with two temperature probes in the two different cups projected in front of the class. This live graphing activity allowed the logical-oriented students to access their knowledge about the event.
- Predictions, as well as the reasoning, were varied so the teacher brought the students over to the side of the room and engaged them in a simulation of metal particles moving back and forth inside the penny and inside the rocks to discuss the notion of specific heat. Students moved faster and slower, bumping into one another, as the teacher discussed heat transfer and conduction—making connections with the kinesthetic-oriented learners. This was also supplemented by a software simulation that showed what particles were likely doing on a microscopic level. Students were given the opportunity to either draw a picture (visual and spatial-oriented) to explain what was happening in the two glasses or to write explanations on their own using vocabulary words emphasized during the lesson (intrapersonal-oriented). These pictures and descriptions were then posted on the class website for students to share with others and discuss on their blogs. Each of these different strategies was used in the same lesson and reached a wider audience than a lecture or even simply a hands-on application. Two other examples of how learners can be brought into the mainstream with assigned tasks to make the content their own are as follows:
  o Have students in heterogeneous groups take the roles of photographer, leader or director, editor, and actor for a video production demonstrating their acquired knowledge.
  o Allow students to create visual concept maps with software that demonstrates connections between important ideas.

Integrating a variety of subject matter areas through the production of podcasts builds upon children's natural curiosity and skills and makes learning more meaningful. Literacy instruction in particular can be enhanced by expanding experiences and vocabulary, stimulating creative writing and graphical representations, expanding knowledge of literary genres, and fostering student voices and knowledge of audiences through writing about relevant issues. Through each of these strategies, shared experiences and technology tools encourage students to compare their own personal knowledge and skills with that of others, thus building a greater sense of purpose for school.

Precautions and Possible Pitfalls

Some educators and administrators have wrongly used the theories of multiple intelligences and learning styles for defining prescriptive measures for teaching children. There are *not* simply eight kinds of students in the world (or any other discrete number). Over-generalizations are easy to make as teachers are required to make dozens of important decisions every day, and there is little time to probe deeply into all children's backgrounds and learning preferences. Just because a student is fidgety or talkative, sings a lot, or is simply of a specific ethnic background does not mean that one can apply the same strategies for that student that have worked for similar students. Students usually have a collection of attributes that all work together to make each of them unique. It is also impossible to expect that any teacher would offer lessons that reach all defined learning styles every day.

It is also important to consider that the same teaching strategies may not work to engage this kind of learner in all situations. Students change, and the moods that drive their engagement may have ebbs and flows. Siblings are often different from one another as well, and making comparisons can also be counterproductive. Offering the widest and most reasonable options of access to a planned lesson is the best approach.

Sources

Ballone, L. M., & Czerniak, C. M. (2001). Teachers' beliefs about accommodating students' learning styles in science classes. *Electronic Journal of Science Education, 6*, 1–43.

Cafferty, E. (1981). An analysis of student performance based upon the degree of match between the educational cognitive style of the teacher and the educational cognitive style of the students (Doctoral dissertation, The University of Nebraska-Lincoln, 1980). *Dissertation Abstracts International, 41–07,* 2908.

MacMurren, H. (1985). A comparative study of the effects of matching and mis-matching sixth-grade students with their learning style preferences for the physical element of intake and their subsequent reading speed and accuracy scores and attitudes (Doctoral dissertation, St. John's University, 1985). *Dissertation Abstracts International, 46–11,* 3257.

Pizzo, J. (1981). An investigation of the relationship between selected acoustic environments and sound, an element of learning style, as they affect sixth-grade students' reading achievement and attitudes (Doctoral dissertation, St. John's University, 1981). *Dissertation Abstracts International, 42–06,* 2475.

Strategy 29: Give students opportunities to use media production for classwork.

What the Research Says

With the influx of technology into classrooms and the afford-ability and ease of digital media editing, increasing numbers of teachers are using video and podcasts for instruction. Since assessment ought to be matched with pedagogical practices, evaluating students' learning should also incorporate digital media editing as a form of assessment. In a study of student achievement and evaluation of teaching strategies, students were given laptop access and a set of digital tools (e.g., blogging, podcasting, mobile devices), that were compatible with what they had available outside of school (Yerrick & Johnson, 2009). Students were given the opportunity to create podcasts; create, narrate, and edit iPhoto books; and edit iMovies to supplement their teachers' assessment of their new learning environment.

Teachers reported over five weeks less instructional time spent on "covering material" as they substituted digital media editing as a strategy for students to co-construct knowledge. The result of less time spent teaching by traditional means was an increase in scores on the New York State Regents exam, one of the oldest and most consistent measures of student content achievement.

At the end of the first year of implementing technology in their classrooms, the number of students achieving at the highest level grew from 41% of the total population to 54%. Students reported that the technology infusion and adapted teachers' strategies were better fits for their needs as learners. In addition, nearly 75% of the more than 400 students surveyed at the school reported that the teachers using technology were preparing them for the future, while only 38% of students at the same school whose teachers were not using computers felt this way.

Classroom Applications

Teachers can identify areas in which content and literacy can be woven together without losing a conceptual, investigative approach to teaching. The potential for integration and commonality when using digital media editing is endless. Teachers can use digital media editing to have students write stories, make predictions, design projects, report events, and create entertaining and informational artifacts that are good assessments of children's learning as well. Teachers can deepen content understanding by increasing the variety of students' experiences with the content beyond traditional text-based instruction. Some goals that teachers might share when infusing media editing into content instruction may include the following:

- Expanding students' experiences and the vocabulary available to them for their writing through the introduction of external artifacts and events
- Stimulating creative writing, photo, and graphical representations through inquiry lessons
- Expanding students' knowledge of literary genres through the writing, editing, and production of public service announcements
- Fostering development of students' voices and their understanding of audience through writing about problems with societal impact

Digital video enhances certain central communication and problem-solving processes, and this relatively new technology of digital video editing addresses specific, perplexing issues of authentically engaging children through their roles as writers, directors, and editors of their own productions. It can shine new light on difficult concepts while also engaging all students in the process of learning.

In addition to providing alternative ways to engage students, digital video editing also invites different modes of engagement and appeals to a wider variety of learning styles and experiences, which in turn opens the door for a wider variety of children to succeed. For example, research in science classes has found that girls receive less positive reinforcement and less of the teachers' attention, are asked fewer complex questions, get less remedial help, and volunteer less in class than boys. Many of these same findings are true for children of color, both boys and girls, when compared to white, middle- or upper-class students. Because developing and editing digital videos is highly motivational and allows students to share scientific understandings and explanations in a small group prior to presenting to the larger class (Ross, Yerrick, & Molebash, 2003), this strategy promotes student success.

A well-planned teaching event combines heterogeneous grouping with project-based learning. To complete a digital video science project, students must plan and execute together several strategies of production, including composing, shooting, and editing. The students must plan using storyboards as they role-play and tell the story they have planned. Students must think carefully about how to integrate spoken scripts, digital images, data, and conclusions into a completed storyboard. Expert teachers only provide students the desired equipment after students complete and successfully pitch their stories to their peers and teacher.

It is during the facilitation of filming, acting, and editing that the specific skills and characteristics of diverse students can be highlighted and best used through a collaborative process. Some students love to be funny, and others attend carefully to details. Some students are very creative, and others like to operate technology. Thoughtful selection of groups and task design can assist all the students in having an important and vital role in the learning process—thereby including a diverse set of learners in an authentically engaging project of reaching far beyond the capabilities of any traditional assignment or written report. In this way, digital video projects can traverse learning style and gender gaps in science through collaboration in heterogeneous groups.

In addition, the National Education Technology Standards for students, promoted by the International Society for Technology Education, is now calling for the increased sophistication of students' use of technology for communication—extending the expectation of students' composition beyond presentations and webpages. Creating digital media artifacts aligns directly with the recommendations for improving communication as well as other kinds of national and state standards.

Precautions and Possible Pitfalls

When using digital media editing as an assessment tool, it is essential to lay out specific expectations for students before the process begins. Teachers who do not use rubrics and examples are likely to have a wide variety of kinds of productions that are dependent upon the kinds of media students regularly interact with. Some students may spend time watching music videos, while others play video games. Since neither of these are appropriate genres for learning proposed science content, expectations must be made clear.

Included in these rubrics, teachers should make content connections explicit. "You must use this vocabulary list and must have a central question that deals with the topic of_____" would be an appropriate way to explain expectations at the beginning of the assignment. Students are more likely to achieve goals that are made explicit in advance. One of the best ways to do this is to keep an archive of successful students' artifacts and play them when introducing a project, along with holding a discussion of strengths and weaknesses in the final products.

Finally, planning cannot be over emphasized as a part of students' preparation to shoot video. Detailed storyboards should be expected from students before they are issued any equipment. One of the biggest consumers of instructional time is the editing of video that students took at random, hoping to capture something important, rather than deliberate clips and rehearsed lines. If students are poor planners or slow planners, they will be encouraged to hurry and improve their planning when they see all of their peers receiving cameras as they refine their storyboards to pass the pitch to their teacher or peers.

Sources

Ross, D., Yerrick, R., & Molebash, P. (2003) Lights! Camera! Science? Using digital video in elementary science classrooms. *Leading and Learning With Technology, 34*(3), 18–24.

Yerrick, R., & Johnson, J. (2009). The impact of digital tools on middle school science literacy technological implementation and instructional improvement. *Contemporary Issues in Technology Education, 9*(3), 280–315.

Strategy 30: Incorporate mobile technology into student assignments.

What the Research Says

 Authors have pointed out that fundamental differences in our American culture are changing who students are and the way they learn best (Friedman, 2005; Pink, 2005). For example, according to the Pew Internet and American Life Project (Pew Research Center, 2005), 87% of children ages 12 to 17 use the Internet regularly. This number has increased more than one-fourth since the year 2000. Of today's teens, 75% use at least two digital devices daily and spend an average of nearly 6.5 hours a day with media. Such observed changes in student behavior represent a challenge for teachers to incorporate technology familiar to students. Since the popularization of Gardner's (1983) work with multiple intelligences, much attention has been given to different kinds of students' intelligences mediating the engagement with different academic subjects. His theory of multiple intelligences has been applied to a variety of learning environments and can be defined as the manner in which students of all ages are affected by sociological needs, immediate environment, physical characteristics, and emotional and psychological inclinations (Carbo, Dunn, & Dunn, 1986). Differences exist within and among student groups, and not all curricula or technological innovations developed by teachers or experts should be expected to achieve similar ends for all students. For all students to succeed at learning, teacher practices and curricula must be designed to meet students' various interests, abilities, experiences, understanding, and knowledge. Technological implementations for students should consider ways in which tools can expand opportunities to all students by offering different kinds of access to knowledge.

Classroom Applications

Since it is clear that students today use technology tools more often than adults, adults should try to adapt their teaching strategies to incorporate the culture and tools of students to connect skills and knowledge teachers want to impart. Students want their learning environments to match the strengths, knowledge, and experiences that they bring with them to school. Yet there is often a great disparity between the kinds of tools and resources students use outside of school compared to in the classroom. If teachers change their routines, adapt their strategies, and embrace the kinds of tools students use regularly, students will take note. The following text describes some examples of teachers incorporating students' everyday technology that is widely used outside of school into their intended learning outcomes.

Teachers who typically assign written reports on famous contributors to philosophy, art, science, mathematics, or politics can assign students to create a Facebook page for that person where students are supposed to vicariously live out and view the world from a different perspective. Teachers can learn much from the ways students portray the thoughts, quotes, and perspectives of Locke, Gauss, da Vinci, or Copernicus.

Teachers are often looking for additional resources to teach contemporary content developments or historically complicated ideas. Assigning students to go on an Internet scavenger hunt and post their best finds on a social bookmarking site like Delicious.com can save teachers hours of searching and preparation. Students are also more likely to find less-obvious but high-quality resources due to their savvy in using the tools of the day. These bookmarks also are available to all in the class, establishing a more equitable access to knowledge and a resource that lasts for years and can be updated and refined.

Making connections by immersing content in the events and lives of actual data in nonoffensive and anonymous ways is easy with social networking sites and polling tools. Teachers can assign students to find the prevalence of certain trends among their peer groups and family members without revealing sources and digging deeply into actual data. Students can use the devices to gather data from their friends about trends including the following:

- *Student Work Ethics.* How many hours of homework do 16- to 17-year-olds do per night?
- *Human Population, Birth Rates, and Overcrowding.* What is the average size of families in your neighborhood?
- *Genetics.* Which diseases are common in your family?

Teachers can also post data, readings, media, and other resources on their class website, which requires students to use their devices outside of class and post their data online. For example, a teacher who has taught a science lab in as a single demonstration station at the front of the class can require students to analyze the data at home using their technology outside of class. In addition, if the data are posted online and accessible, students who were absent from the demonstration still have access to the collective knowledge of the class and have greater choice over which tools they might use to complete the task.

As demonstrated in learning-style research, children are most likely to learn with methods matching their learning style. An attempt to use methods that match students' learning style with a good balance of teaching strategies during instruction makes good sense, and shifting teaching to incorporate more technology that is properly aligned with the needs of today's teens is a promising practice.

Precautions and Possible Pitfalls

It is important to note that there are increased instances of students treating other students poorly through technology. Cyber-bullying and other forms of misuse require the teacher to closely monitor how students are using the devices. Teachers should intervene immediately on behalf of students who are subjected to inappropriate treatment and enforce ethical violations strictly with the code of school policies. To avoid many abuses, teachers should teach self-monitoring techniques to students and clearly demarcate appropriate versus inappropriate responses to assignments. Finally, teachers should not assume that all students have access to the same devices in the home. The greater the options that students have to complete the tasks, the more likely the activities will connect with the lives and learning styles of children.

Sources

Carbo, M., Dunn, K., & Dunn R. (1986). *Teaching students to read through their individual learning styles.* Englewood Cliffs, NJ: Prentice Hall.

Friedman, T. L. (2005). *The world is flat: A brief history of the twenty-first century.* New York: MacMillan Publishers.

Gardner, H. (1983). *Frames of mind: The theory of multiple intelligences.* New York: Basic Books.

Pew Research Center. (2005). *Trends 2005: Information for the public interest.* Washington, DC: Pew Research Center. Available at http://pewresearch.org

Pink, D. (2005). *A whole new mind.* New York: Penguin.

Strategy 31: Model inquiry with students using limited resources.

What the Research Says

Whether social studies educators are arguing about students learning the modes of inquiry for historians or science educators are debating the benefits of process skills over achievement scores, inquiry has been the subject of much conversation of school reform of late. Inquiry has been argued to be beneficial to students as it represents more of the kinds of thinking, speaking, and acting that experts do when practicing their discipline. Scholars argue that teaching about facts and theories that have been "proven" by experts in the past denies students the opportunity to construct knowledge for themselves and hence the students do not really understand the essence of the body of knowledge.

Reforms in a variety of disciplines are calling for inquiry-learning opportunities to be made available to students, but the majority of research demonstrates that inquiry is not a regular part of teachers' routine practices (Cazden, 1988; Fine, 1991; Lemke, 1990; Oakes, 1990; Tobin & Gallagher, 1987). Rather than promoting inquiry and opening up classroom talk, teachers call upon a variety of strategies to limit student input, direct and constrain contributions, and control the learning experiences toward predictable outcomes.

In national studies, less than one-fourth of students see school as offering them learning environments that are engaging and make relevant content connections outside the classroom (National Center for Education Statistics, 2002). These findings have been well documented by many researchers who also argue that when it comes to infusing learning technologies in their classrooms, teachers have even more difficulty making changes toward a constructivist orientation (Becker & Reil, 2000; Rakes, Flowers, Casey, & Santana, 2001; Windschitl, 1999). For example, in a recent survey of 655 teachers (Grades 4 to 12), Becker and Riel (2000) found that less than 4% of the teachers surveyed used computers during instruction to assist students in constructing their own understanding of content knowledge in accordance with constructivist learning frameworks. In addition, Rakes et al. (2001) also found that in a survey of 435 teachers, who use technology in K–12 contexts, less than half of the teachers who professed to be constructivist even acknowledged implementing six out of 14 commonly identified constructivist strategies. Furthermore, only 40% of the participating teachers used even three of these strategies, and less than 20% of those who claimed to use constructivist strategies in their classrooms implemented them "fairly often" (monthly).

At the same time, the literature is replete with studies demonstrating the value of inquiry teaching in improving student learning (Follansbee, Hughes, Pisha, & Stahl, 1997; Middleton & Murray, 1999; Wenglinsky, 1998). There are many obstacles good teachers face when trying to implement inquiry teaching. One commonly reported obstacle is the limited amount of resources available to teachers. Because limited resources are a legitimate concern, it is the goal in this chapter to outline ways teachers can think about promoting inquiry with limited resources. Students today need engaging teachers who are willing to employ appropriate strategies and resources that further content learning in authentic ways (Mann, Shakeshaft, Becker, & Kottkamp, 1999; Newmann, Bryk, & Nagaoka, 2001; Sivin-Kachala, 1998).

Classroom Applications

Science teachers sometimes skip over labs they intended to do simply because they ran out of time or didn't trust that students could complete the lab, analysis, and clean up in the allotted class time. These decisions to offer students inquiry opportunities or omit them because of resources could be false dichotomies. In fact, there can be ways to engage students in inquiry through alternative pedagogies and accomplish the same goals. Take, for example, a teacher's desire to have each student gather his or her own heart rate response to chocolate or cola. There are a variety of limitations good teachers automatically consider to decide the feasibility of this lab (e.g., Do I have enough sensors? How do I have students look across all the data for trends? What do I do with students who are now bouncing off the walls because of other effects besides increased heart rate?). These are all legitimate concerns. Let's consider the options that contrast with giving each student a monitor and chocolate. A teacher could do the following:

- Make a station in the back of the room where each student (or pair) is required to rotate through and collect the data. These data can be written down or stored on a single computer out of the way in the corner of the room. As each student comes to the station, the instructions are available at the station.
- Use a single probe demonstration to make the point. This technique works best when the adequate discussion precedes the demonstration. Teachers can pose an important question to the whole class but use a single student's data to answer the question live. Discussion should include documented (written down) student predictions of outcomes and questions like, "Will body type affect the kind of results we get? (Thin, tall, gender?)" "Whom shall we pick to test our hypothesis?" "How many people wrote down their predictions?"
- Acquire "canned" data from other classes who may be ahead of schedule. Some classes work faster than others, and their data can

be collected and used for the rest of the teacher's day instead of omitting the activity from the day altogether.

- Offer a demonstration *during* instruction as a way to accomplish more than one thing at a time. For example, a teacher may want to conduct a 20-minute lecture on information that she or he *must* cover by Friday's test. During the lecture regarding the connections between the nervous and circulatory system and involuntary functions, a student could be wired to the heart rate monitor and the data projected live in front of the class. This student would be taking notes like every other student, but another advantage of this method is the observed difference in note-taking ability or ease of distraction in comparison to other students. The student can report how difficult it seemed to take notes with a racing heart as he or she was eating chocolate.
- Collect data in a brief demonstration in class and post the data on the school website for students to download and analyze in a formal lab write up. These data could be connected to a blog of a student who was in the demonstration. Other students could ask direct questions about the experience.
- Give credit for peer instruction to other classes as sometimes teachers see the great success of another teacher's idea but don't have time to learn it themselves. Students from the class who have gone through the inquiry experience can give talks or even facilitate the inquiry experiences in other classrooms as a way to share teachers' best practices. This technique is often used for high school students to teach younger students in elementary grades difficult concepts, but there is little reason not to share inquiry experiences in this same way.

We must admit that we work in schools with real limitations of resources and time. We do not have the luxury of taking as long as we want to explore ideas from an infinite variety of perspectives. However, no limitation is good reason to dismiss inquiry experiences out of hand. In fact, several studies have shown that taking more time and exploring ideas from a more constructivist perspective has *increased* student learning. Covering less and exploring more deeply with particular attention to inquiry processes is a dilemma that won't go away soon, and it is a balance that must be sought according to today's vision for American schools (see also Strategy 4).

Precautions and Possible Pitfalls

It is easy to fall into the mental trap of considering equity from a disabling perspective. Giving equitable computer access to students doesn't necessarily mean all children have their own machine. There are a variety of ways to reconsider the learning environment to make the lesson equitable, even with limited resources. Teachers should be aware that offering the same mediocre experiences to all can limit many. Just because one class can't get it done shouldn't deprive others.

It is also important to keep in mind that learning goals should be kept in the forefront of lessons that have a variety of activities happening simultaneously. Elementary teachers may have more experience with this kind of multitasking than high school teachers. When learning goals are kept in sight for each station and students are clear about what they are accomplishing, student products will be of high quality. Students need to know exactly what is expected of them if they are going to complete a station on their own. Instructions at that station should also be written in a way that covers the variety of learning styles represented in the class. Pictures, words, and example artifacts can be helpful in making independent instructions more clear. Language diversity should also be a consideration for these environments, as it is easy for English language learners to get lost in the apparent flurry of activities.

Sources

Becker, H. J., & Riel, M. M. (2000). *Teacher professional engagement and constructive-compatible computer usage* (Report No. 7). Irvine, CA: Teaching, Learning, and Computing.

Cazden, C. (1988). *Classroom discourse: The language of teaching and learning.* Portsmouth, NH: Heinemann.

Fine, M. (1991) *Framing dropouts: Notes on the politics of an urban high school.* Albany, NY: SUNY Press.

Follansbee, S., Hughes, R., Pisha, B., & Stahl, S. (1997). Can online communications improve student performance? Results of a controlled study. *ERS Spectrum, 15*(1), 15–26.

Lemke, J. (1990). *Talking science: Language, learning and values.* New York: Ablex.

Mann, D., Shakeshaft, C., Becker, J., & Kottkamp, R. (1999). *West Virginia's basic skills/computer education program: An analysis of student achievement.* Santa Monica, CA: Milken Family Foundation.

Murray, J. (1999). *An inclusive school library for the 21st century: Fostering independence.* IFLA Council and General Conference, August 20–28, 1998.

National Center for Education Statistics. (2002). *The condition of education 2002.* U.S. Department of Education, Washington, D.C.

Newmann, F., Bryk,, A. & Nagaoka, J. (2001). *Authentic intellectual work and standardized tests: Conflict or coexistence?* Chicago: Consortium on Chicago School Research.

Oakes, J. (1990). *Multiplying inequalities: The effects of race, social class, and tracking on opportunities to learn mathematics and science.* Santa Monica, CA: Rand Corporation.

Rakes, G. C., Flowers, B. F., Casey, H. B., & Santana, R. (1999). An analysis of instructional technology use and constructivist behaviors in K–12 teachers. *International Journal of Educational Technology, 1*(2), 1–18.

Sivin-Kachala, J. (1998). *Report on the effectiveness of technology in schools, 1990–1997.* Washington, DC: Software Publisher's Association.

Tobin, K., & Gallagher, J. J. (1987). What happens in high school science classrooms? *Journal of Curriculum Studies, 19*, 549–560.

Wenglinsky, H. (1998). *Does it compute? The relationship between educational technology and student achievement in mathematics.* Princeton, NJ: ETS Policy Information Center-Research Division.

Windschitl, M. (1999). The challenges of sustaining a constructivist classroom culture. *Phi Delta Kappan, 80*(10), 751-755.

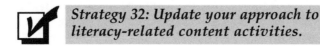

Strategy 32: Update your approach to literacy-related content activities.

What the Research Says

Behrman (2003) examined content-area literacy by observing a summer six-week high school biology class. The class featured a problem-based instructional approach by examining and working with biology-related realistic scenarios that include a community component.

The community component required students to spend a considerable amount of time outside of school interacting with community mentors and biology-related workplaces. The students analyzed and acted on each scenario in a somewhat workplace-like procedure. Students were free to select any sources of information that would help them learn and respond successfully to the problems as problem solving was stressed over information retrieval. This can best be described as "field-based learning."

Behrman (2003) found that students placed high reliance on human resources (mentors) and the Internet and limited their use of print media and sources. Behrman explains that the use of multiple literacies and varied print material call for reexamining the definitions of content literacy and adolescent literacy in general. The limited instructional focus on traditional print-based literacy needs to be expanded to include multiple texts, including electronic, spoken, nonlinguistic, and other representations of meaning and knowledge.

Behrman's (2003) data sets included notes of classroom observation and events, instructional experiences with mentors at field sites, and interviews with students and the teacher. In addition, students provided end-of-the-course surveys and reviews of student project reports. Data were analyzed qualitatively.

Behrman (2003) discovered that, without a textbook, the class supported students in a rich assortment of literacy activities. Students sorted out digital and oral forms of content information to construct responses to project prompts and the authentic problems posed within the scenarios. The Internet was used far more than the class library of traditional print texts and other reference material. The author concludes by asking readers to rethink the primacy of print text in acquiring content knowledge.

Classroom Applications

 It is common for teachers to help students learn to use and read traditional textbooks. However, more and more textbooks are taking a
back seat to the oral transfer of information, the multimedia Internet,
and other sources of information (television, radio, magazines). Most
teachers are now aware of the problems and benefits the Internet provides.
Textbooks in many classes have been reduced to use only for reference or
as a source of answers if a lecture is not totally understood. The biggest
problem, when the textbook is no longer the primary source of information, is determining the validity and relevance of information from other
sources. A second problem is outright plagiarism as many students copy
and paste Internet information into their papers and don't understand
exactly what's wrong with that strategy (the principles of the ownership of
intellectual property).

As students begin to use these new resources, teachers need to extend
the potentially limited scope of how content literacy is defined beyond the
textbook. Many times, when students are asked for their sources, they just
say, "I mostly used the Internet." This indicates that the students do not
acknowledge the human intellect behind the sources. They place a higher
value on web-based sources than text-based sources without carefully
assessing the validity, relevance, and value of the content.

Ongoing curriculum development is needed in all classes to reflect the
potential of content-area learning in nonschool sources (nontextbook or
other school material) and contexts. To further this idea, teachers need to
consider how information is obtained in most workplace settings and use
that information in curricular design, stressing how to move content learning beyond the traditional textbook.

Search engines and directories specifically organized for teachers and
children can be used to quickly find sites on the Internet containing useful
information related to your classroom unit and at an appropriate grade
level. It is important that these tools also screen out sites inappropriate for
children. You might begin with one of these locations:

- *Yahooligans* is a directory and a web guide appropriate for ages seven
  to 12.
- *Ask Jeeves for Kids* is a directory and a search engine based on natural
  language. You simply type in a question, and it finds the best site
  with the answer.
- *Searchopolis* is a directory and search engine organized for K–12
  students.
- *KidsClick!* is a directory and search engine developed for students in
  Grades 5 through 12 by the Ramapo Catskill Library System.

A second strategy is to select one of several central content sites for
each subject area and explore the resources for use during an Internet

workshop. A central site is one that contains an extensive and well-organized set of links to resources in a content area. In a sense, it is like a directory for a content area: science, math, social studies, reading, or another subject. Most are located at stable sites that will not quickly change. As you explore the Internet, you will discover these well-organized treasure troves of information. They will become homes to which you will often return, and you will develop your own favorites. Here are a few examples of central content sites:

Science

Eisenhower National Clearinghouse—http://www.goenc.com

Science Learning Network—http://www.sln.org

Yahoo—http://dir.yahoo.com/science/education

NASA—http://teachspacescience.org/cgi-bin/ssrtop.plex

ACADEMICINFO—http://www.academicinfo.net/edteachsci.html

Math

Eisenhower National Clearinghouse—http://www.goenc.com

The Math Forum—http://mathforum.com

Social Studies

Virtual Middle School Library—http://www.sldirectory.com/teachf/socsci.html

Reading/Literature

SCORE Cyberguides to Literature—http://www.sdcoe.k12.ca.us

The Children's Literature Web Guide—http://www.ucalgary.ca

The Literacy Web—http://www.literacy.uconn.edu

Designing a specific activity could be the third step related to the learning goals of your unit, using a site you have bookmarked. The activity may be designed for several purposes:

- To introduce students to a site that you will use in your instructional unit
- To develop important background knowledge for an upcoming unit
- To develop navigation strategies
- To develop the critical literacies so important to effective Internet use

It is important during this step to provide an open-ended activity for students in which they have some choice about the information they will bring to the project. If everyone brings back identical information, there will be little to share and discuss during the activity session. You may wish to prepare an activity page for students to complete and bring to the Internet activity discussion, or you may simply write the assignment in a visible location in your classroom.

The potential for innovative approaches to Internet literacy are endless. Be prepared to teach your students to retrieve information in ways that will serve them well both inside and outside of your classroom while respecting intellectual property rights.

Precautions and Potential Pitfalls

 Many teachers who have not yet integrated the Internet into their curriculum feel as if the effort will be too time-consuming. Some say they don't have time to learn new instructional strategies for using a complex tool like the Internet.

More sources of information are available to students than ever before. The textbook and the school library were once the extent of 95% of class research. Now, information can come from anywhere. It would be a mistake to not help students learn to sort and deal with the vast range and quality of content available. You can avoid many problems with plagiarism and related issues by embedding respect for intellectual property rights into your assignment and curriculum in general. By doing this, you will also help them become better writers and turn in more interesting papers for you to evaluate. Preparing children for their future is not an extra; it is central to our role as science educators.

Source

Behrman, E. (2003). Reconciling content literacy with adolescent literacy: Expanding literacy opportunities in a community-focused biology class. *Reading Research and Instruction, 43*(1), 1–30.

 Strategy 33: Foster literacy development through visual texts and media.

What the Research Says

Walsh's (2003) small study examined the oral responses of young children to the texts of two narrative picture books, *I Went Walking* by Sue Machin and *Felix and Alexander* by Terry Denton.

Walsh cited a single question that guided her research, "What does the 'reading' of pictures reveal compared with the reading of print?" The data for this study were taken from a larger study Walsh conducted in 1997 in several primary schools in Sydney, Australia. The 2003 study featured the responses of children from kindergarten and first grade, while the larger study investigated the beginning reading behavior of young second-language learners compared to native English speakers. A theoretical framework of reader-related variables was compared to reading behavior, both qualitatively and quantitatively. A framework of text-related variables for narrative picture books was proposed and compared with oral responses to these books, and some of these students' oral responses were examined.

Walsh's (2003) findings emphasize how images can evoke a variety of levels of response. According to Walsh, the study confirms that teachers need to reconsider the nature of reading and reading education in an environment where words and print are no longer the dominant medium of knowledge transfer. Images now take on a much bigger role in the transfer of information.

It should also be noted that the English language learners (ELLs) responded with the same range of comments and understanding as the native speakers. Although the ELLs did not have the same mastery of language structures, they were able to infer, evaluate, and develop the conceptual process of reading. Therefore, the research found that picture books offered a rich resource to assist ELLs in their understanding of "content" knowledge, cultural practices, and linguistic structures of English.

Classroom Applications

 While this study deals with very young readers and a small educational scope, it is interesting to consider a wider and important context for this small study. When you look at science instruction, the ability to decode pictures, illustrations, and images is very important as these often communicate just as much information as text-based knowledge. In these days of fast-paced changes in visual stimuli, people have less patience for digesting visual details, especially young people. It is not unreasonable to try to build observation and analysis skills into your curriculum in decoding and critically thinking about images.

Based on the idea that visual images and multimedia are a language, visual literacy can be defined as the ability to understand, process, and produce visual messages. These skills are becoming increasingly important with the ever-proliferating mass media in society. As increasing amounts of information and entertainment are acquired through nonprint media (such as television, movies, and the Internet), the ability to think critically and visually about the images presented becomes a crucial skill. Based on Walsh's small study, visual literacy is something that can be taught and learned, just as reading and writing are learned. Although it is not yet taught in schools, the ability to process visual images efficiently and understand the impact they have on viewers is nevertheless very important.

From the beginnings of human culture, visual awareness has been a key element in communication. Just as information conveyed by the written word held significance for humanity in the 20th century, the symbols of early cave paintings held a deep significance for the artists and cultures that produced them. Over time, these symbols and meanings evolved into the alphabets of today, which are the basis for verbal literacy.

To be verbally literate, one must be able to manipulate the basic components of written language: the letters, words, spelling, grammar, and syntax. With mastery of these elements of written communication, the possibilities of verbal expression are endless. Visual literacy in the 21st century operates within the same boundaries. Just as verbal literacy depends on basic components and common meanings, visual literacy involves basic elements and common meaning.

Twenty-first century literacies refer to the skills needed to flourish in today's society and in the future. Discrete yet integrated literacy disciplines have emerged around information, media, multicultural paradigms, and specific professional workplaces, all of which require a specialized and often unique visual literacy. This range requires the combination of these literacies to help K–12 students and adult learners address the issues and solve the problems that confront them. Rather than simply transcribing print from page to screen, students need to work with still and moving images, graphics, and text. Organizing and arranging these elements on the screen requires expertise in visual language and human perception. It requires individuals who are skilled in the design and display of electronically produced, stored, and accessed information.

Today's technologies represent a startling fusion of sight and sound that frequently makes it difficult for us to discern illusion from reality and fact from fiction. Given these trends, responsible citizens need to possess the ability to question the accuracy and authenticity of information in all of its forms, not just print. They need the ability to make reflective critical responses to this information. It is essential that students be guided to develop the critical thinking skills necessary to understand the complex issues facing modern society as presented in the media. As you begin to consider how your curriculum might reflect a shift toward integrating elements of visual literacy education, the following websites offer additional discourse and links about the topic:

Center for Media Literacy—http://www.medialit.org

21st Century Schools—http://www.21stcenturyschools.com (a list of visual literacy links)

Tasmania Department of Education—http://www.education.tas.gov.au (ideas for seven- and eight-year-olds in English)

Precautions and Potential Pitfalls

Literacy is seen by most as the ability to read and write. The definition is changing to include the new ways film, television, and the Internet communicate ideas and information. Literacy is painted with a wider brush in the 21st century. Parents may need to be enlightened to this newer and wider literacy paradigm. Take the time to educate them along with your students.

Source

Walsh, M. (2003). "Reading" pictures: What do they reveal? Young children's reading of visual texts. *Literacy, 37*(1), 123–134.

 Strategy 34: Utilize portable media players to bring exemplary resources into teaching.

What the Research Says

Study after study demonstrates that student achievement increases and student engagement improves when teachers engage students through methods that students recognize as authentic; when teachers connect lessons to students' thinking, prior knowledge, and experiences; and when teachers use a variety of strategies to match instructional practices to the cultural and contextual artifacts of their students while maintaining high expectations (Hodgkinson, 2000; Lemke & Martin, 2006; Newmann, 1992; Newmann & Byrk, 2001; Trimmel & Bachmann, 2004; Wenglinsky, 1998).

Critics have historically argued that technology has been "oversold and underused" (Cuban, 2001). Because technology is so closely connected with the attributes of students in this generation of learners, it is often considered a tool for exchanging culture with the youth of today. Digital media players can play a strong role during instruction by bringing exemplary media into the classroom and in communicating work from the classroom to parents. If all parents have at their disposal are paper and pencil tests to assess their children's progress, chances are they will not be able to assist their children in other national standards like process skills, communication skills, and higher-level analysis of data and information. In contrast, providing multiple opportunities for students to revoice acquired content knowledge and share it with teachers and parents creates a common and shared understanding of the students' needs, thus creating a community of educators interested in the success of each and every child.

Classroom Applications

Through digital media, exemplary resources can be brought into the classroom. Many informal education institutions like museums, research organizations, and archives are investing in preparation time to magnify the learning outcomes of visitors to their collections. Consider Robert Ballenger's live explorations with the Jason Submersible vehicle, the Grand Canyon online exhibit, NASA's International Space Station webcasts, and the Lewis and Clark reenactment. Each of these web events were accompanied by collections of audio and video assets to prepare students for the events and to offer the opportunity to others subsequent to the event. These assets provide a major inroad for establishing equitable learning opportunities. Though students may not be able to go to the Grand Canyon for a geology lesson or visit a space station, these resources are just one click away. All students can take advantage of podcasting from experts and other extraordinary resources.

Podcasts also enhance the learning experience for those classes actually attending museums, aquariums, and exhibits. Prior to their coordinated visits, teachers and students can access assets that familiarize them with the facility and provide important instruction and background on vital concepts they will be exposed to during the trip. For teachers, previewing exhibits, classroom simulations, hands-on and minds-on activities, and other preparatory resources can help them organize tasks, group work, and even assignments of parent volunteers who will assist on the trip. While at the facility, tours for students can be guided by video and audio assets that give them specific purpose and engagement as well as be stored for review at a later date.

With the iPod, educators have an instruction tool that offers portable professional development for teachers, as well as a way to extend classroom resources. Some of the ways in which educators have used iPods include the following:

- Bringing experts and other resources into teachers' and students' pockets
- Providing the power to play back significant historic and instructional events
- Sharing data and data analysis anywhere and at any time
- Giving access to pristine research facilities and state-of-the-art demonstrations and simulations
- Facilitating supplemental instruction through multiple languages
- Extending the everyday classroom lab experience beyond the classroom walls, and promoting equity by giving this access to every student

Even major tourism projects are being produced that can be of use to teachers and the students. Entire city tours are available for download to iPods, as well as tours of aircraft carriers, historical monuments, and other significant social, civic, and scientific artifacts. Teachers can take advantage of the endless supply of free assets available to the general public.

The use of digital media should be thought of as a two-way street, as exemplary classroom practices can be brought to the attention of the community. Teachers are working harder than ever to provide equitable and excellent instruction for all learners on limited time and budgets. However, nearly every time achievement scores from local schools are announced, there are often scathing criticisms of teacher performance—usually without any evidence from the actual classroom practices or even a loose causal connection between teaching efforts and learning outcomes. Teachers take it on the chin repeatedly, not necessarily because they deserve it but because they are so busy with the onerous task of teaching that they do not have time to build a case for themselves of the great practices that happen weekly in their classrooms. Teachers can use podcasting to provide regular communication to parents about what is actually happening in classrooms. Here are but a few ways in which teachers can use podcasting to improve their relationships with the larger community:

- Put teaching and learning artifacts of teachers and students online to promote a greater sense of community and connection to the lives of students in and out of school.
- Make certain assignments or instructions available in multiple languages. Parents can support language and vocabulary at home by seeing content in a variety of ways.
- Solicit specific help for teaching by showing some examples from prior years' work. Parents can better plan for their volunteer work in the classroom by reviewing what concepts and activities teachers are promoting in school.
- Publish and share students' work as formative assessments to better connect parents to students' progress.

Mobile devices like iPods provide ways to cheaply disseminate exemplary resources and to share more widely the work of teachers who are making profound impacts on the lives of students with innovative practices.

Precautions and Possible Pitfalls

 Most teachers avoid using digital media editing tools and mobile devices in their teaching because the devices seem too hard to learn or because they take too much time away from teaching to learn. It is important to remember that students can be a great asset not only for finding good resources but also editing and managing them. Many students in your class have already created a movie, song, or podcast, and they welcome the trust and responsibility of the task to manage a set of assets for the class. Bilingual Spanish-speaking students, for example, can re-record instructions for major assignments and have them available for download in minutes. This does not need to be an additional responsibility of the teacher.

Editing and podcasting artifacts from classrooms also require permissions. Teachers should be aware of the preferences of parents and have on file written permissions for which students can and can't be seen online. Permissions also apply to educational resources seen in class. Teachers should be aware of fair use policies and laws before putting resources online for their students. Many resources are already available online for students, so linking parents to those resources instead of republishing them gets around the risk and liability associated with copyright laws.

Finally, podcasting and the production of web and media artifacts should not be an all-or-nothing ordeal. Teachers should start small and incrementally without pressuring themselves to do it all at once. Research shows it takes three to six years for teachers to become an expert at any particular technology, so teachers should be content with baby steps and celebrate their first podcast with enthusiasm, even if it is the only one that is up for many months to come.

Sources

Cuban, L. (2001). *Oversold and underused: Computers in the classroom.* Cambridge, England: Harvard University Press.

Hodgkinson, H. (2000). Educational demographics: What teachers should know. *Educational Leadership, 58*(4), 6–12.

Lemke, C., & Martin, C. (2006). *One to one learning: A review and analysis by the Metiri Group.* Culver City, CA: Metiri Group.

Newmann, F. (1992). *Student engagement and achievement in American secondary schools.* New York: Teachers College Press.

Newmann, F. & Bryk, A. (2001). *Authentic intellectual work and standardized tests: Conflict or coexistence?* Chicago: Consortium on Chicago School Research.

Trimmel, M., & Bachmann, J. (2004). Cognitive, social, motivational and health aspects of students in laptop classrooms. *Journal of Computer Assisted Learning, 20*(2), 151–158.

Wenglinsky, H. (1998). *Does it compute? The relationship between educational technology and student achievement in mathematics.* Princeton, NJ: ETS Policy Information Center-Research Division.

Strategy 35: Find opportunities to record yourself teaching to share with peers.

What the Research Says

The emphasis on critical reflection in and on practice has taken an increasingly prominent role in the discussion of teachers' knowledge. Reflection has been recognized as a main vehicle for teacher education (Grimmett & Erickson, 1988), and many argue that understanding the subtleties of personal experiences and interpretations that teachers bring to teaching can help develop a critical consciousness for the visions that teachers and teacher educators strive for amidst the tumultuous sea of reform. Unfortunately, research has shown that simply modeling best practices or challenging prospective teachers' beliefs is insufficient for making dramatic change (Abell & Bryan, 1997; Abell, Bryan, & Anderson, 1998; Yerrick & Hoving, 2003).

When teachers reflect in ways that are aimed at explaining their reasoning and defending practices with current learning theory, it also "enhances understanding or readiness for acting in the moment," and as such, "their future praxis will likely change" (Roth, 2003, p. 15). However, researchers warn that reflection on teaching cannot bring about instant change in teaching and argue that the reflection process is less engaging if it is vicarious rather than focused on one's own personal and recent events (Abell et al., 1998).

Classroom Applications

There are many reasons and many ways to share one's teaching through video. Teachers could explore generally their use of strategies over a particular time period, or they could focus upon a particular issue like engaging children in group work where the camera is simply focused on a small group of children. What teachers should carefully consider before turning on the camera is, "What exactly am I looking for?" It is a very common mistake to put the camera in the back of the room, pan out to collect the whole class, and turn it on with the hope of capturing something interesting. The result, however, is usually a distant general shot of the teacher and the back of children's heads with the audio only heard from students in the back row. While lavaliere microphones and wireless transmitters can help, nothing can replace a well-planned placement of a camera and microphones for examining practice. Here are some scenarios and suggestions for teachers trying video reflections for the first time:

- *Recording successful strategies to share with less-experienced teachers.* There are many times when successful teachers want to share their practices, and yet because there is no mutually available time to observe one another, the teachers' lounge is the only venue to discuss briefly one's efforts. For example, one teacher may be the rare expert using inquiry methods with second language learners. Recording the example strategies in action can be a great resource for other teachers. A general rule is two minutes maximum for sharing lessons as few people choose to spend time to watch much more. Some free places to host example teaching with lots of hits and collaboration from teachers include TeacherTube (http://www.teachertube.com), iTunes (itunes.apple.com), LearnersTV (http://www.learnerstv.com/), VideoLectures (http://videolectures.net/), and Free Science Videos and Lectures (http://www.freesciencelectures.com/).

- *Recording new strategies for exploring shifts in practice.* Sometimes, teachers want to try something new. These are not likely videos that will be shared, so quality will be less of an issue. Because students are often more technologically savvy that adults, inviting students to help film can be helpful in many ways. It can bring more buy-in for students trying to help the teacher's innovative teaching work better. It can also be helpful in getting more honest feedback from students as they are likely to ask good questions of their peers about what students liked or disliked. Pre-planning and storyboards help students to shoot what the teacher is interested in, and if a teacher has more than one class period for his or her particular innovation, a dry run is helpful to make the second taping more fruitful.

- *Recording children's pre– and post–problem-solving skills in an interview.* Sometimes teaching aims for shifts that are more esoteric in students' performance than a written exam can account for. Having a few students involved in pre- and post-interviews with a particular unit can demonstrate shifts in the way students think, speak, and act differently with the content in more conversational contexts. Be sure these interviews take place in sequestered environments where sound and distractions will not affect the recording.

- *Recording class discussions.* Sometimes students need to also step back from their perspective and see the impact of their actions on the whole group. Modeling students' behaviors and discussions can be used for teachers to debrief where complex social interactions may break down. Debates are examples of one teaching strategy where a teacher might record discussions to help students to look back and refine their own speaking in a social context. Wide camera angles are not always good for this setting, and camera angles can make audiences dizzy from the camera moving back and forth from point to point. Multiple cameras set up for closer angles without motion are good for this format.

- *Recording students in small-group work.* Students often talk differently in small groups than whole-class discussion. If teachers want to know how students are interpreting a particular collaborative task with students in multiple roles, recording small segments can help. Positioning the camera to face all three group members around a semicircle is better than shooting a square venue since half the students' facial expressions would be absent in the square configuration. Camera microphones are sufficiently powerful for up-close shots like this, and a tripod is helpful as well.

- *Recording students problem solving at a learning center.* Learning stations or centers that students rotate through is a popular elementary strategy. With the camera poised, queued, and ready, children can be responsible for turning on and off the camera if teachers want to record students for such things as performance assessments or process skills. Most cameras also allow the viewfinder to be rotated fully around so the students can see themselves as they perform.

- *Recording student presentations.* Capturing students' work for future students is always a good practice as the recordings can be shown as examples for assessment purposes. Students are always better at meeting goals when teachers are explicit about them in advance. Recorded presentations can accompany rubrics to capture certain nuances like intonation or eye contact that are hard to describe but easy to demonstrate. A single camera close with a chest-up shot is often best. Have them work with an appropriate backdrop to make their "talking head" video more engaging.

- *Recording class for parent night or open house.* Teachers sometimes have only limited opportunities to showcase their best to parents because of everyone's busy schedules. Recording different aspects of the classroom is helpful to open up conversations with parents about class expectations, format, student contributions, and even opportunities for parent volunteering. Teachers should make the most of video for these events.

There are significant lessons to be learned from engaging teachers in adventurous teaching and digital video reflection. As digital video editing becomes increasingly affordable and accessible, teachers engaging in reflections on their own practice may save time and resources spent on other endeavors. In addition, thoughtful practices like reflecting on children's thinking, planning, and teaching for specific interventions or outcomes, or even reexamining requisite knowledge for given topics may be informed by teachers' video reflections.

Precautions and Possible Pitfalls

 Teaching is a deeply personal practice and requires real risk to share one's events that are usually practiced behind closed doors. Because teachers' work environments are not highly collaborative and visitors from outside the classroom often function in an evaluative capacity, teachers do not trust how these accounts may be used by others. In order to use video as a tool for professional development, trusted learning communities of teachers must be developed with those who have expertise in examining practice while honoring the participants' perspective and efforts (Yerrick, Thompson, McLaughlin, & McDonald, in press). Typically it requires the involvement of teacher educators who are familiar with the teachers' settings in order to support them in designing, developing, implementing, taping, and reviewing the lesson. However, outsiders need not be involved if only a few local teachers want to share their practice. If a teacher purchases or borrows camera equipment, most laptops and media labs have equipment to edit quickly.

It is not an easy path teachers choose to engage in a deeper reflection to examine classroom dilemmas. Each issue we explore about our teaching has the inherent potential to confront our own discrepancies between teaching beliefs and actual practices. In addition, since school environments are generally not supportive or helpful to teachers to provide time, equipment, and teacher space for reflection, some of the issues teachers find may have no simple solution.

Another issue about using cameras in the classroom that teachers will need to overcome is getting permissions from students' parents. Students cannot be filmed without parents' permission if the video will be seen by anyone outside the classroom, and specific permission must be gained by teachers to show video on venues like the Internet where they can be identified by viewers outside of school. Signed permissions should be multi-tiered with possible responses ranging from (1) "No, I do not want my student recorded, " to (2) "Yes, my student and her work can be recorded but any identification must be removed before it is posted on the Internet," to (3) "Yes, my student and his work can be shared outside the classroom, including use by the media." For their own protection, teachers should keep these forms on file in case of dispute. Teachers also must be certain that the camera does not impose an inequitable context for students who do not choose to be filmed. This is easily resolved by pointing the camera away from the group of students who are sitting together who do not give their permission, and by using wireless microphones to selectively collect audio.

Sources

Abell, S. K., & Bryan, L. A. (1997). Reconceptualizing the elementary science methods course using a reflection orientation. *Journal of Science Teacher Education, 8*, 153–166.

Abell, S. K., Bryan, L. A., & Anderson, M. A. (1998). Investigating preservice elementary science teacher reflective thinking using integrated media case-based instruction in elementary science teacher preparation. *Science Education, 82,* 491–510.

Grimmett, P. P., & Erickson, G. L. (1988). *Reflection in teacher education.* Vancouver, British Columbia, Canada: Pacific Educational.

Roth, W.-M. (2003, April). Video as tool for reacting on practice: Theoretical perspectives. Research paper presented at the annual meeting of the National Association for Research in Science Teaching, Philadelphia.

Yerrick, R. K., & Hoving, T. J. (2003). One foot on the dock and one foot on the boat: Differences among preservice science teachers' interpretations of field-based science methods in culturally diverse contexts. *Science Education, 87,* 390–418.

Yerrick, R., Thompson, M., McLaughlin, S., and McDonald, S. (in press). Collected from the cutting room floor: An examination of teacher education approaches to digital video editing as a tool for shifting classroom practices. *Current Issues in Technology Education.*

5

Science
Assessment

> ☑ *Strategy 36: Look at formative assessment in a coherent and cohesive way.*

What the Research Says

Assessment is an integral component of the National Science Education Standards (NRC, 1996). A follow-up document issued by the NRC (2001) focuses on classroom assessments, both formative and summative, and the relationship that this type of ongoing assessment has for student learning. This document particularly looks at the ongoing assessment that occurs on a daily basis and how these assessments can link to a more comprehensive system of assessment. In short, we should all be looking at assessment in a much more coherent and cohesive way; looking for specific data and evidence for student understanding, using that data to make decisions in the classroom to improve instruction, while understanding the different roles that assessment plays. The following is explained by NRC:

> Assessments that resonate with a standards-based reform agenda reflect the complexity of science as a discipline of interconnected ideas and as a way of thinking about the world. Assessments must not be only summative in nature, that is, offering a cumulative

summary of achievement level, usually at the end of a unit or after a topic has been covered. These summative assessments can serve multiple purposes: they help to inform placement decisions and to communicate a judgment about performance to interested parties, including parents and students. Assessment also must become an integral and essential part of daily classroom activity. (p. 12)

Highlights of the findings in this report include the following that are relevant to this discussion:

- Research shows that regular and high-quality assessment in the classroom can have a positive effect on student achievement.
- The information generated must be used to inform the teacher and/or the students in deciding the next step. The results provide effective assessment to improve learning and teaching.
- Student participation is a key component of successful assessment strategies at every step. If students are to participate effectively in the process, they need to be clear about the target and the criteria for good work, to assess their own efforts in light of the criteria and to share responsibility in taking action in light of the feedback. (NRC, 1996, pp. 1–2)

The research is clear that formative assessment, or assessment that is embedded in instruction, has been shown to have a positive effect on student learning (Black, 1998; Black & William, 1998a, 1998b). However, teachers often exhibit several weaknesses in their formative assessment practice, including emphasizing questions that focus on superficial rather than higher-level learning, focusing more on assessment for grading purposes than for learning purposes, approaching assessment from a criterion-referenced stance rather than from a norm-referenced stance, and seldom discussing their assessment practices with their peers (Crooks, 1988; Black & William, 1998b).

In their study, Furtak and Ruiz-Primo (2008) looked at four kinds of curriculum embedded formative assessment prompts. Each type of prompt consisted of two phases. The students first worked independently to respond to the prompt. This was followed by a whole-class discussion where the students shared their ideas. The authors refer to these types of prompts generally as formal formative assessment prompts and distinguish these from informal formative assessment prompts that they describe as on-the-fly questioning. These formal prompts are those that are planned as part of instruction and include a "question or task that is aligned with learning goals and serves the purpose of eliciting students' conceptions as a basis for teachers to make instructional decisions to reduce the gap between learning goals and students' present state of understanding" (pp. 800–801).

The four types of formative assessment prompts were as follows:

- *Graph.* Students had to complete a graph similar to one they had constructed in a previous investigation. They were then presented with a correctly completed version of the graph and asked to compare their graph to the correct one, identifying any errors they might have made. Students were then asked to interpret the graph.

- *Predict-observe-explain.* Students were presented with an experimental situation and asked to predict what they thought might occur. They then observed the experiment and discussed whether they had correctly predicted the outcome, to explain their reasoning and if they might have changed their ideas after observing the experiment.

- *Constructed response.* Students responded to an open-ended question.

- *Predict-observe.* This is a variation on the predict-observe-explain situation, but the students were not asked to explain their thinking or if and why they might have changed their minds.

Results of the study indicated that all types of prompts successfully elicited the students' conceptions in writing. Students' misconceptions were more likely to be uncovered in the constructed response and predict-observe conditions; however, the predict-observe condition also elicited a high number of "no conception" responses. Discussions following the students' writing to the prompt tended to be more conceptually oriented in the predict-observe-explain and predict-observe conditions. These discussions were also of longer duration than those of the other two conditions. Furtak and Ruiz-Primo (2008) concluded that while all prompt conditions elicited high percentages of student ideas, below-level ideas were more likely to emerge in writing than in discussion. Written responses were also more likely to contain multiple ideas than those shared by students in class. Those ideas appeared to be filtered by students as they shared them. Therefore, as a means of gathering important information about what students are thinking and what they know, written formal formative prompts are critical tools for teachers.

Classroom Applications

One of the things that is clear from the research is that assessment alone does not lead to improved student learning. Both the teacher and the students need to *do* something with the information that they get from the assessments. Teachers need to evaluate the information that they get from both formative and summative assessments to determine the next best course of instructional action on their part. Students also need to evaluate not only the work they have produced but also the feedback on their work as well. If we expect students to assume more responsibility for their own learning, we need to equip them with the tools to do so. Students will need to become accustomed to revising their work but will also need to receive substantive feedback to guide them in the process.

It can be helpful to think about assessment—formative and summative— more systematically. Prior to the start of a chapter or unit, identify the major ideas or conceptual understandings that your students are to master. Identify the questions and/or products that will allow you to identify whether they have developed the necessary understandings. Decide where and how these pieces will be integrated into instruction. Take a more planful, rather than spontaneous, approach to assessment.

Precautions and Potential Pitfalls

Shifting responsibility for learning from teacher to student can be difficult. In many classrooms, students are accustomed to teachers "giving" them grades and feel little sense of control over the process. In one scenario, a student was asked how he was doing in his 12th-grade English class. He responded that he had no idea, although he had turned in all his work. But none of it had been returned (verified by other students who had the same teacher) and that he really had *no* idea what his grade was. Students were quick to state that they had experienced this over the years with many other teachers across schools, grade levels, and content areas. No wonder students feel that they have little control over grades, which seem to be assigned based on teachers' personal preferences.

The message here is that assessing students is an active ongoing process that requires teachers to provide meaningful feedback to students in a timely manner that will allow students to improve their performance. This means finding time in an already-packed day to read what students have written and provide some type of response. Some teachers are finding that using technology has reduced some of the time involved. There may be times when a group response might be an appropriate form of feedback. This might take the form of an e-mailed response that is a synthesis of the various pieces of individual feedback. This is a bit less personal and may not work all of the time, but might be effective in some situations, especially if students have submitted work electronically or if much of the individual feedback is repetitive.

Sources

Black, P. (1998). Formative assessment: Raising standards inside the classroom. *School Science Review, 90*(291), 39–46.

Black, P., & William, D. (1998a). Assessment and classroom learning. *Assessment in education: Principles, Policy, & Practice, 5*(1), 7–74.

Black, P., & William, D. (1998b). Inside the black box: Raising standards through classroom assessment. *Phi Delta Kappan, 80*(2), 139–148.

Crooks, T. J. (1988). The impact of classroom evaluation practices on students, *Review of Educational Research, 58*(4), 438–481.

Furtak, E. M., & Ruiz-Primo, M. A. (2008). Making students' thinking explicit in writing and discussion: An analysis of formative assessment prompts. *Science Education, 92*(5), 799–824.

National Research Council. (2001). *Classroom assessment and the national education standards.* Washington, DC: National Academy Press.

National Research Council. (1996). *National science education standards.* Washington, DC: National Academy Press.

Strategy 37: Use standards-based inquiry to prepare students for standards-based tests.

What the Research Says

In the era of high-stakes assessment, it can seem at cross purposes to spend valuable instructional time on what might not be easily recognized as scientific content in the traditional sense. However, since the publication of the National Science Education Standards (NSES) (NRC, 1996), many states have based their standards on both this document and the *Benchmarks for Science Literacy: Project 2061* (AAAS, 1993). Central to the NSES is the idea of inquiry both in terms of students learning *about* inquiry and in terms of students learning *through* inquiry. This idea also appears in many of the state standards—with inquiry in not only content the students need to learn but also process. For example, North Carolina, California, New York, and Pennsylvania (all four of which were chosen as representative) have science standards that include language around students coming to understand and engage in the process of inquiry—that of recognizing and/or developing testable questions, gathering and analyzing data, developing explanations from that data, and justifying explanations from evidence. Scientific inquiry *has* become content and is therefore eligible for testing on state assessments. Clearly, it is important to find ways to meaningfully engage students in learning both through and about inquiry.

Geier and colleagues (2008) examined the concept of combining standards-based science instruction with project-based and inquiry-based science units. The work was one component of a systemic reform effort in the Detroit Public Schools. Two cohorts of seventh- and eighth-grade science students participating in the project units were compared to the rest of the district population, using the results of high-stakes state standardized tests in science. During the three-year implementation, 37 teachers in 18 schools and roughly 5,000 students participated. The results demonstrated that the participants had increases in science content and process skill over their peers, with gains occurring up to a year and a half after engagement in the curriculum. There were also significantly higher pass rates on the statewide test.

The findings support the conclusion that standards-based, inquiry science curriculum can lead to standardized achievement test gains with populations of historically underserved urban students when the instruction is highly specific, developed, and aligned with administrative and professional development support.

In addition to these findings, Geier et al. (2008) found in their literature search that there has been an identified pattern of measured lower achievement in urban minority boys in comparison to their female peers. They found a similar gap in achievement within their comparison pool; however, the effect was essentially eliminated in their experimental population. The at-risk boys had caught up with their female peers. The researchers felt that the phenomenon was due to the more robust instruction, including technology, inquiry, and peer collaboration and interaction, therefore increasing positive attitudes and greater participation.

Classroom Applications

All of the major science national standards and most state standards now stress mastery of science inquiry as a major pedagogical and content goal for science teachers, curriculum developers, and students. While teaching using an inquiry-based approach can be a daunting process for many teachers, and teachers may feel conflicted when faced with the pressures of content coverage for standardized assessments, it is important to remember that some of the standards on which students are being assessed are those that incorporate an understanding of the modes of scientific reasoning and the demonstration of their use. Thinking broadly about ways to incorporate multiple standards into activities and investigations will be a more efficient way to ensure that students have access to the maximum amount of required content.

The concepts of "hands-on" or "problem-based" teaching and learning are one way to start to provide ways for students to engage in more of the work of inquiry—that of recognizing and/or developing testable questions, gathering and analyzing data, developing explanations from that data, and justifying explanations from evidence.

The inquiry-science curriculum developed and implemented in Detroit was centered on outcomes from state and national standards that were aligned with the Detroit Public School's curriculum framework. Details of the program are described in the following.

The curriculum was developed and designed as a series of somewhat integrated eight- to 10-week science units centered around science inquiry-based investigations focused on selected basic questions. These types of units can be constructed by teachers or, better yet, by groups of teachers to embed standards into inquiry and a more authentic context. They are summarized here (Geier et al., 2008):

1. *What is the quality of the air in my community?* Students examined sources of air pollution in their communities and used archived data to compare Detroit air quality with air quality in other cities. The unit focused on the factors that influence air quality, along with the basic science content such as the particulate nature of matter and its chemical and physical properties.

2. *What is the water like in my river?* Students acquired an integrated understanding of science concepts such as watersheds, soil movement (erosion and deposition), and the chemistry concepts of pH and dissolved oxygen.

3. *Why do I need to wear a helmet when I ride my bike?* A physical-science-based unit was designed to develop the students' understanding of force, velocity, acceleration, and Newton's laws. This is all within the context of examining the nature of collisions in the real world and developing strategies for interpreting and visualizing physical phenomena graphically.

Precautions and Potential Pitfalls

The really positive message here is that standardized tests and engaging students in inquiry have been shown to coexist per the research by Geier et al. (2008). This research also concluded that the teaching style within the study exhibited the potential to close a male-female achievement gap. Many in science and science education have emphasized the importance of involving students in the processes of scientific knowledge making or inquiry. The goal is to have students learn the processes and content of science by actually engaging in guided inquiry.

While the Geier et al. (2008) study looks promising, many teachers will still be concerned that standardized test preparation and positive performance don't mix well in classroom instruction with an inquiry emphasis. If teachers are not experienced or knowledgeable about inquiry, experimental design, or the related scientific reasoning, it is difficult for them to develop these units on their own without help or significant motivation and resources.

Teaching within an inquiry-based pedagogy can be rewarding and yet frustrating at times when developed from scratch. Teachers in Detroit benefited from significant professional development before implementing the curriculum. If inquiry or problem-based learning works, as shown in this study (not conflicting but enhancing test preparation), science teachers will have wider choices to make in their professional development and choice of teaching resources. It is clear that inquiry more clearly represents how science is practiced outside the classroom. Inquiry learning enhances the metacognitive skills and motivates students in ways that chapter marches and lecture cannot.

The researchers also examined the factor of teacher bias. Researchers discussed the potential nature of the type of teachers that choose to participate and felt that the reform efforts might favor teachers who show a greater level of commitment to self-improvement and bring a greater range of techniques to the classroom.

Also, sadly, the research did not provide the details of class management or organizations within the units or any other instructional or content details. It is assumed the experimental design was very structured and developed by adults, not students. This raises the question on how much "inquiry" was truly experienced by the students versus an activity with a procedural emphasis only.

Sources

American Association for the Advancement of Science. (1993). *Benchmarks for science literacy: Project 2061*. New York: Oxford University Press.

Geier, R., Blumenfeld, P. C., Marx, R. W., Krajcik, J. S., Fishman, B., Soloway, E., & Clay-Chambers, J. (2008). Standardized test outcomes for students engaged in inquiry-based science curricula in the context of urban reform. *Journal of Research in Science Teaching, 45*(8), 922–939.

National Research Council. (1996). *National science education standards*. Washington, DC: National Academy Press.

> **Strategy 38: Align instruction and assessment tools to state curriculum standards.**

What the Research Says

 Liu and Fulmer (2008) report on an analysis of alignment between the New York State core curriculum and the New York Regents tests in physics and chemistry. The investigation found that overall there was a high alignment between New York core curriculum and cognitive levels and the New York Regents test, and the alignment was said to remain fairly stable from test to test. However, there were considerable discrepancies in emphasis on different cognitive levels and topics between core curriculum and the test. Questions were raised about the nature of the alignment and the nature and validity of the content standards. The implications for science curriculum and instruction were also examined.

Evaluating the content and cognitive alignment are very important factors in monitoring and evaluating of the state standardized assessment system. This is because the No Child Left Behind (NCLB) Act requires that the state standardized test be aligned with the state standards. (Soon, of course, the tests will need to be aligned instead with the new national or "common" core standards, at least in those states that adopt them. For more information about the national science standards, to be released in 2011, see http://www7 .nationalacademies.org/bose/Standards_Framework_Homepage.html.)

Classroom Applications

In science department meetings across the nation, you often hear conversations about content coverage, simply "covering" what's on a standardized test. Rarely do you hear about how teachers or departments adjust their content based on rigor or cognitive levels or how their instructional rigor and complexity align with the state curriculum standards or state test. It is assumed that time equals rigor or emphasis on a given topic, which simply is not a good way to gauge how students interact or engage in the selected content, concept, or topic. For example, just think about how the topic of energy can engage students. The cognitive level and the rigor of the instruction will vary between age groups and science disciplines. Curriculum coverage discussions alone don't tell you how the students should experience the instruction. You have to dig deeper.

The implications from the Liu and Fulmer (2008) study are simply stated. The authors suggest that teachers focus more on identifying ways of increasing alignment between their instruction and the state curriculum standards, rather than on student feedback from standardized test content alone. Liu and Fulmer suggest that teachers trust their state's alignment between the state curriculum and the standardized tests.

Research has shown that just covering topics is not a good predictor for how well students will perform on tests. Coverage and teaching science disciplines at an appropriate cognitive and language level serve as better predictors of student performance on standardized tests (D'Agostino, Welsh, & Corson, 2007). Most state curriculum standards cover both content and the cognitive level that is appropriate for the various age groups to understand a topic. When you read the standards, you can see how the topics are visited and revisited at various cognitive levels as you move through the grade levels. The complexity of the concepts, the language complexity, and the overall rigor of understanding increase as you go.

When you are discussing standardized test results and using those results to make decisions about your instruction and coverage, remember that your state's curriculum guidelines and frameworks may be more reliable and wide-ranging sources of information on curriculum issues. It is very important that teachers balance content, cognitive, and language levels and the overall rigor associated with understanding a topic. Only when there is a good match between a teacher's instruction and the state standardized test's operationalization of the state's science framework or curricular guidelines that instruction can really be fine-tuned.

Precautions and Possible Pitfalls

It is likely that the new core content standards, like the existing state standards, will not specify how content should be taught, what resources should be provided, and/or the depth of knowledge and skills associated with any topic. Content standards are not neutral, and they carry values and power. Teachers need to maximize the input they need to make informed instructional decisions and not just rely on looking at test results.

Sources

D'Agostino, J. V., Welsh, M. E., & Corson, M. M. (2007). Instructional sensitivity of a state's standards-based assessment. *Educational Assessment, 12*(1), 1–22.

Liu, X., & Fulme, G. (2008). Alignment between the science curriculum and assessment in selected N.Y. State Regents exams. *Journal of Science Education and Technology, 17,* 373–383.

Strategy 39: *Utilize formative assessment to better engage students in content and instruction.*

What the Research Says

The theory and application of formative assessment in academic literature has a relatively long history, over 40 years and counting. Formative assessment ideas and concepts have evolved and been adapted over time as a means to adapt to student and teacher needs. Historically, formative assessments were used with instructional units as diagnostic assessments for placement purposes. Today, formative assessments are part of instruction designed to provide crucial feedback for teachers and students. A typical claim today is that formative assessment is about discovering what the learner knows, understands, or can do. Summative assessment, in contrast, is about whether the learner knows and understands a predetermined fact or concept, or can do a task or other cognitive function. As opposed to a summative assessment designed to judge student performance and produce grades, the role of a formative assessment is to improve teaching and learning for a diverse range of students. As opposed to benchmark tests that are used to predict student performance on other tests (most often state assessments), formative assessments are designed to be more intimately connected with smaller units of instruction.

Although much recent attention has focused on gaps in the achievement of different groups of students, the problem has been with us for decades. Benjamin Bloom (1968, 1976) argued that to reduce variation in students' achievement and to have all students learn well, we must increase variation in instructional approaches and learning time. The key element for teachers in this effort was well-constructed, formative classroom assessments. Bloom outlined a specific strategy for using formative classroom assessments to guide teachers in differentiating their instruction and labeled it "mastery learning." With this strategy, teachers first organize the concepts and skills they want students to learn into instructional units that typically involve about a week or two of instructional time. Following initial instruction on the unit, teachers administer a brief assessment based on the unit's learning goals. Bloom recommended calling this a formative assessment, borrowing a term that Scriven (1967) had coined a year earlier to describe the informative, rather than judgmental, aspects of program evaluations. Instead of signifying the end of the unit, this formative assessment's purpose is to give both students and teachers information, or feedback, on students' learning progress within a unit. It helps students and teachers identify specifically what has been learned well to that point and what has not (Bloom, Madaus, & Hastings, 1981).

Classroom Applications

The everyday, more informal assessment that occurs in the classroom is often overlooked as an informed source of data in assessing students for instructional purposes. Teachers commonly view assessment as something different and separate from their regular teaching—more for assigning grades than examining instruction. However, for instruction to be effective, teachers must also assess their students while learning is in progress to obtain information about their developing comprehension and understanding so that instruction can be adapted to the classroom and individual situation. Teachers can also use this information to inform and involve students since they need to observe and recognize, evaluate, and react to their own learning, misunderstandings, and misconceptions. The major goal of formative assessment is to *make the students' thinking visible* so that their level of cognitive understanding can be compared to the goals of where we want them to go.

Formative assessment can inform instruction not only for a class but also for individuals and groups within the same class. As differentiated instruction and multiple intelligence theory have become the models for learning, formative assessment has become the model for informed classroom instructional assessment. While formative assessment is a general concept that can be applied to a wide range of classes, it finds a good fit in the science classroom. The National Research Council (2001) described their general version of formative assessment and then applied their interpretation specifically to the sciences. They suggest a simple template for designing and using formative assessment in regular classroom practice. Three essential questions are used to guide teachers:

- Where are you trying to go?
- Where are you now?
- How can you get there?

1. *Where are you trying to go?* Think beyond the retention of facts. Keep in mind that the goals talked about and emphasized in the National Science Education Standards build around the active nature of science. A range of activities are recommended that involve what it means to do science and understand how specific topics and concepts fit into science as a whole. Facilitating a student's understanding of science must go beyond the coverage of basic facts to the basic steps in the actual processes of science. Consequently, any formative assessments must attend to gaining student feedback on the entire range of learning in science—content understanding, application, processes, reasoning, teamwork, and the literacy skills to make sense of it all. The question, "Where are you trying to go?" requires a complex and thoughtful answer.

To add to the complexity, teachers also need to emphasize the importance of student understanding of what constitutes quality work (Sadler, 1989). Sadler states, "The indispensable condition for improvement is that the student comes to hold a concept of quality roughly equivalent to that held by the teacher" (p. 121). It is critical that teachers convey to their students the guidelines and criteria for how they define "good" work for their own self-assessment. Rubrics work here, but they also can hinder students' ability to develop their own internal standards. At some point, students may need to be weaned from rubrics.

2. *Where are you now?* After developing a clear picture of where teachers want students to go and what they want students to know and to do, they must define a starting point for instruction. All the elements and techniques of determining prior knowledge come into play here. Each concept, topic, or process can be known and experienced at different levels of complexity and rigor. For example, although a simple understanding of energy is developed at the elementary school level, in a high school physics class, energy becomes complex with a mathematical structure. The cognitive level in which a topic is understood needs to be assessed, and once established, needs to become a starting point to be built upon. Each student in the class has his or her own starting point, and each class will have a range of starting points.

Simple questioning is an informal way to gather information. There are powerful questioning strategies that can be developed with carefully crafted leading questions and appropriate wait times (see Strategy 6). This also requires teachers to have a solid mastery of the subject matter to really understand the knowledge and also the misconceptions. Teachers can work with students individually, in small groups, and in whole-class discussions.

The examination of student work can also help to establish prior learning; however, past work is not always available. A nonthreatening pre-test is also a possibility for formative assessment and can serve to help familiarize students with specific testing formats they could face. A less threatening strategy is to give students a list of vocabulary words as concepts and ask them to create graphic organizers using the words while adding their own prior knowledge to the concepts. The results of this exercise can yield insight into the cognitive levels in which students are interacting with the concepts and vocabulary.

3. *How can you get there?* This is where teachers make, adjust, and refine decisions about both teaching and learning. They decide on the experiences they think can help their students better understand and use instruction and meet standards. They begin by deciding how to introduce and approach a concept, while determining an appropriate pace and rigor for the curriculum and required processes. In addition to the more obvious components of curriculum and pedagogy, teachers also monitor the students' level of interest and engagement in any curricular activity. They want their students to be challenged and motivated without reaching frustration points. Skilled teachers use the knowledge gained from sound assessment to help struggling students, whether they need to revisit specific points, practice more, or be reminded of a quality standard.

Furthermore, recognizing multiple intelligences as a classroom theme, teachers practice the concept of differentiated curriculum with multiple learning pathways within the same unit. Formative assessment techniques can help clarify standards for quality work, clear up misconceptions about the nature of a task or language used, provide a scaffold for self-assessment, and help facilitate cooperative learning activities.

Precautions and Potential Pitfalls

It should be noted that the value of testing is continually being examined and critiqued. For example, Crooks (1988) and Black and William (1998) have demonstrated that there is little evidence that classroom assessment has assisted in the learning process. Black and William, for example, reviewed 578 publications related to the role of assessment in learning and concluded that classroom assessment "typically encourages superficial and rote learning, concentrating on recall of isolated details, usually items of knowledge, which pupils soon forget . . . teachers do not generally review the assessment questions that they use and do not discuss them critically with peers, so there is little reflection on what is being assessed" (p. 17).

It is also important to note that the National Research Council (2001) posed their model as only one example of formative assessment. They state, "It is important that no one blueprint or single best model existed for using assessment as a tool that, first and foremost, supports and facilitates student learning" (p. 26). Teachers, within their own community and student demographics, need to develop a system that works for their unique situation. Those three critical questions, either formally or informally, are considered most days by reflective teachers and hopefully, by their students also. The key is to begin ongoing professional dialogue with colleagues and other professionals to help make the features of formative assessment more explicit and connect it more intimately to teaching and learning.

From a teaching and teacher perspective, changing assessment practices and philosophies within a classroom is not as easy or straight forward as it is often portrayed. Changes require a re-examination of entrenched routines and teaching styles. Negotiating change can be difficult even for seemingly worthwhile and promising goals, and there is no uniform approach to modifying assessment practices for teachers or their students as every teacher's style is different (Sato & Atkin, 2007). However, despite the challenges to successful implementation, the studies reviewed in this strategy illuminate promising techniques for improving learning outcomes.

Sources

Black, P., & William, D. (1998). Assessment and classroom learning. *Assessment in Education: Principles, Policy & Practice, 5*(1), 7–74.

Bloom, B. S. (1976). *Human characteristics and school learning.* New York: McGraw-Hill.

Bloom, B. S. (1968). Learning for mastery. *Evaluation Comment* (UCLA-CSIEP), *1*(2), 1–12.

Bloom, B. S., Madaus, G. F., & Hastings, J. T. (1981). *Evaluation to improve learning.* New York: McGraw-Hill.

Crooks, T. J. (1988). The impact of classroom evaluation practices on students. *Review of Educational Research, 58*(4), 438–481.

National Research Council. (2001). *Classroom assessment and the national science education standards.* Washington, DC: National Academy Press.

Sadler, D. R. (1989). Formative assessment and the design of instructional systems. *Instructional Science, 18*, 119–144.

Sato, S., & Atkin, J. M. (2007). Supporting change in classroom assessment. *Educational Leadership, 64*(4), 76–79.

Scriven, M. (1967). The methodology of evaluation. In R. E. Stake (Ed.), *Perspectives of curriculum evaluation* (Vol. 1, pp. 39–55). Chicago: Rand McNally.

Strategy 40: Add a classroom response system for instant formative assessment.

What the Research Says

One piece of technology making inroads in classrooms in the aide of assessment is the classroom response system (CRS), often called "clickers." Initially introduced in college classrooms as a way to make large lecture classes seem smaller, these systems are routinely showing up in high school and middle school classrooms around the county. College students now are routinely required to purchase "clickers" in the college bookstore when they purchase their textbooks. A 2006 web search found over 3,000 K–12 schools that were using CRSs (Abrahamson, 2006).

These systems allow teachers to pose questions and elicit responses from students. The system consists of a set of input devices that connect to the teacher's computer. Students can enter their responses to the teacher's question. The students' responses are aggregated and typically displayed as a bar graph, allowing the teacher to easily see the array of responses.

An article by Beatty and Gerace (2009) describes how they introduce the idea of technology-enhanced formative assessment (TEFA). They distinguish this from CRS by separating the discussion of the technology (hardware and software) from the pedagogy. The authors identify four principles for the implementation of TEFA:

1. Motivate and focus student learning with question-driven instruction.

2. Develop students' understanding and scientific fluency with dialogic discourse.

3. Inform and adjust teaching and learning decisions with formative assessment.

4. Help students develop metacognitive skills and cooperate in the learning process with meta-level communication. (p. 153)

These principles are general and are to be used flexibly within a broader framework called the *question cycle*. The question cycle presumes that a question is posed to the students prior to the instructional sequence. The question serves as the basis for discussion and provides the opportunity for the students to articulate what they already know about the concept. The CRS is used to collect data on the students' early understandings— even if the students are unsure of their responses. These data are displayed for the students to see. The teacher then asks the students to provide explanations for their various responses—regardless of the correctness of those responses. The correct response is not shared with the students at this time. The teacher uses this opportunity to develop scientific language based on the students' language, to elicit any misconceptions and/or preconceptions, and to develop the beginning understanding of the concept and idea. This extends into a more focused discussion of the topic in which students are encouraged to engage in the majority of the discussion. The teacher's role is that of facilitator. In the last piece, the teacher summarizes the concept that was developed during the discussion. This may close out the lesson or may be used to move on to the next question.

The article by Beatty and Gerace (2009) is not an empirical study but rather describes a cycle of instruction using technology based on theories of learning (NRC, 1999). Among the outcomes of this cycle of instruction are the following: assessment of prior knowledge, identification of misconceptions and preconceptions, promotion of higher-order thinking and problem-solving skills, and stimulation of discussion.

Classroom Applications

Implementing a participation structure such as TEFA represents a significant departure from that of most classrooms. The roles of the teacher and the students look much different. The teacher acts as a facilitator rather than directing all discussion. The typical initiation-response-evaluation pattern of discussion in the classroom to which both teacher and students are accustomed does not exist when using TEFA. Getting used to not doing all the talking can be difficult for teachers, and getting used to doing more of the purposeful talking can be difficult for the students.

Ask a question in class, and generally six students raise their hands. While some of the rest of the students may know the answer or may be thinking, others just don't bother. CRSs make it difficult for students to hide. Once the teacher asks the question, the number of students who respond is recorded along with their response. Because many systems automatically graph the responses, the teacher can clearly see where the preponderance of responses lie and what the most common incorrect response is. The graph can be projected for the class to see and to discuss. The right response can be discussed along with the features of incorrect responses that made those responses seem attractive. While it isn't immediately possible to identify who hasn't responded, the likelihood that students will respond increases just because at least at the time of response, it's anonymous. Teachers can track down the nonresponders later.

You can still use these same principles even if you don't have the technology. You can do a low-tech version with small dry-erase boards or even index cards, although a CRS provides both anonymity and accountability. The immediate display of a bar graph that depicts students' thinking is a useful representation around which to center an initial discussion. You could quickly tally the data from boards or index cards, but it's less flashy.

In this case, it's more about the pedagogy or what you do with the CRS than the technology itself.

Precautions and Potential Pitfalls

Students will likely look at the clickers as toys. Various response systems will allow teachers different levels of control, and most will provide ways to track back individual student responses. Expect some abuses from students who will likely misbehave regardless of the circumstances. Limiting exposure initially may be the way to go.

It is likely that this technology may come under the blanket "acceptable use" technology policy that is in place in your school. You might want to explore this option. You may also want to consider adding something in your safety contract about these potential "missiles." Attaching the "clickers" to larger boards (e.g., a one-square-foot marine board) can reduce the likelihood for loss or misplacement, although it does dramatically increase the need for storage space.

Sources

Abrahamson, L. A. (2006). A brief history of networked classrooms: Effects, cases, pedagogy, and implications. In D. A. Banks (Ed.). *Audience response systems in higher education: Applications and cases* (pp. 1–25). Hershey, PA: Idea Group. Available at www.igi-global.com/downloads/excerpts/ITB12186.pdf

Beatty, I. D., & Gerace, W. J. (2009). Technology-enhanced formative assessment: A research-based pedagogy for teaching science with classroom response technology. *Journal of Science Education Technology, 18,* 146–162.

National Research Council. (1999). *How people learn: Brain, mind, experience, and school.* J. D. Bransford, A. L. Brown, & R. R. Cocking (Eds.). Washington, DC: National Academy Press.

Strategy 41: Design formative assessment for data to inform instruction.

What the Research Says

In many classrooms, instruction occurs on a daily basis and assessment occurs perhaps weekly with a quiz or a test as the teacher determines what the students have *not* learned. In recent years, the emphasis on teacher dissemination of content has shifted to teaching for understanding and making assessment part of the instructional process (Wiske, 1998). This shift requires teachers to think in fundamentally different ways about what they do in their classrooms. In addition to planning *what* their students will do, teachers must also plan for ways to *know* what their students have learned. Teachers need to reconsider how often and in what ways they will assess students' understanding and then what to do with the information gleaned from those assessments. It is no longer enough to decide where you want your students to go; you also need to know that they get there.

In the report *Knowing What Students Know: The Science and Design of Educational Assessment*, the National Research Council (2001) contends that assessment cannot be designed or implemented without consideration of the three elements in what they call the assessment triangle. The three elements are cognition, observation, and interpretation. The cognition domain includes a teacher's theory of how learning occurs as well as the identification of the knowledge and skills to be learned. It is arguably most effective if a teacher is grounded in the most current research in how students learn. The observation element of the assessment triangle is based on a teacher's observations about the kinds of tasks that will elicit the necessary demonstrations of the students' understandings. The teacher needs to clearly understand the specific features of tasks and the understandings those features will elicit. The interpretation piece of the assessment triangle refers to how the teacher will utilize the information that is obtained from the assessment.

The assessment triangle can be seen as a tool to help teachers better understand the process of reasoning about formative assessments. Formative assessments are any and all activities (written or otherwise) designed to provide feedback to both teachers and students to modify teaching and learning. Think back to the old maxim of "monitor and adjust" that was common in education lingo many years ago. Elementary school teachers seem to be very comfortable with this concept, secondary teachers far less so. It implies making changes to instruction as warranted by the data that are collected from assessment (NRC, 2001).

Teachers are not shy about assessing students, although assessment typically occurs for grading and evaluation purposes (Brookhart, 2004). This type of assessment has changed little over the years—consisting of the typical quizzes and tests. Research in mathematics (Saxe, Gearhart, Franke, Howard, & Crockett, 1999) indicates that teachers who implement new forms of assessment (aligned with mathematics reform) do so not because of the potential that these assessments provide for illuminating the mathematical thinking of the students, but because of previous beliefs about the functions of assessments for evaluation and grading purposes. Other teachers have made minor modifications to existing assessments to meet some minimal requirements of the reform movement. This is a case of where old forms of assessment may serve new purposes. Both students and teachers can be asked to put more into and take more away from specific assessment tasks. Open-ended tasks that were subsequently evaluated as either "right" or "wrong" can be assessed to expose students' patterns of thinking. Tomanek, Talanquer, and Novodvorsky (2008) suggest that the situation in science regarding assessment is likely similar to that in mathematics.

Classroom Applications

The report from the NRC (2001) is available online at no charge. While it is a bit lengthy, it does contain useful examples of how to use the assessment triangle (found in Chapter 2 of the report) and is certainly worth a look.

As you design formative assessments to collect data to inform instruction, consider the following:

- *The cognitive level of the students.* What level of thinking is required by the students to complete the task? Is it comparable to that required by the students in the initial learning situation? If you would like to accurately assess what the students have learned, the assessment task should be at the same approximate cognitive level at which the knowledge and/or skill was learned.

- *The skill level of students.* Asking the students to perform a novel task as an assessment may prove to be frustrating for all and may not provide the type of feedback regarding what the students have learned that you had hoped for.

- *The targeted knowledge or skill.* The task should provide an opportunity for their students to demonstrate their level of understanding, but they should not be required to do what does not relate directly to the targeted knowledge and/or skill. A focused task reduces the amount of "noise" you get in the data.

- *What is being assessed.* If you want to know what the students understand about a concept, don't give points for creativity if that's not what you intend to assess.

Precautions and Potential Pitfalls

Adding in additional quality assessments can be time-consuming to create, assess, and interpret the information. You then also need to decide what to do with that information. The purpose of this type of assessment is the improvement of both your instruction and therefore student learning. This is an active, iterative process and requires effort.

Incorporating this type of assessment also takes class time, which means that you'll need to find time to implement these types of assessments by condensing, eliminating, compacting, or somehow dealing with the constraints of your curriculum. One of the helpful things about these types of assessments is that you can choose a format that complements the format of the standardized assessments that your students may need to take. In many states, the state tests now include a constructed response portion to the assessment. Your formative assessments may be just the practice your students need to help prepare them for these high-stakes tests.

Sources

Brookhart, S. M. (2004). Classroom assessment: Tension and intersection in theory and practice. *Teachers College Record, 106*(3), 429–458.

National Research Council. (2001). *Knowing what students know: The science and design of educational assessment.* James W. Pellegrino, Naomi Chudowsky, and Robert Glaser (Eds.). Retrieved June 1, 2009, from http://www.nap.edu/open book.php?isbn=0309072727

Saxe, G. B., Gearhart, M., Franke, M. L., Howard, S., & Crockett, M. (1999). Teachers' shifting assessment practices in the context of educational reform in mathematics. *Teaching and Teacher Education, 15*(1), 85–105.

Tomanek, D., Talanquer, V., & Novodvorsky, I. (2008). What do science teachers consider when selecting formative assessment tasks? *Journal of Research in Science Teaching, 45*(10), 1113–1130.

Wiske, M. S. (1998). What is teaching for understanding? In M. S. Stone (Ed.), *Teaching for understanding: Linking research to practice* (pp. 61–86). San Francisco, CA: Jossey-Bass.

Strategy 42: Encourage assigned textbook reading by giving open-book tests.

What the Research Says

Phillips (2006) was interested in finding out if three open-book tests in community-college biology classes could be used to improve students' study skills. He also wanted to find out if the students with weaker study skills benefited more than students with moderate or strong study skills. This study involved 1,080 students over a 10-year period. The mean improvement for the entire sample was 4.47 points. The students with weak study skills improved an average of 23.79 points, the students with moderate study skills improved 4.88 points, and the students designated as strong decreased 4.88 points. The most obvious reason for the improvement in the weak group and moderate group stems from their being provided with study strategies and an opportunity to turn those strategies into skills. The most dramatic improvement was seen between the first and second open-book tests of the year. Phillips assumed that students with strong study skills were not assimilating any new strategies, or they were not incorporating any new skills. However, after a drop in scores in the second test, they rebounded for the third test. Although they did not show an improvement in their overall study skills, their drop was minimal.

Classroom Applications

 Phillips (2006) used his open-book tests as a vehicle for teaching study skills within only the three tests that made up a portion of overall class assessment. These open-book tests targeted information that was related to lectures but not directly covered during class. Also, he prepared students by going over examples of open-book questions and discussing strategies for effectively and efficiently using the class text. Finally, Phillips made the importance of completing the assigned readings clear early in the class.

He also taught instruction strategies for comprehending the layout of the targeted chapters and highlighting, tabbing, and using the index, as well as understanding the significance of bolded pages and bolded key-words within the text. The open-book test questions contained contextual clues that directed the students to the correct chapters and subheadings. Students who used the study skills and read the material prior to the test could more quickly narrow their search.

You can see that Phillips's efforts were not typical of college and university classrooms. In this class instruction, goals included not only teaching the subject matter but also providing students with the study skills necessary to help them learn. To do this, teachers need to see testing, assessment, and evaluation as an opportunity to embed teaching and learning devices within the targeted assessment goals. This may require a change in perspective regarding using tests for evaluation purposes only. The rewards students take with them can be seen as greater than just subject matter knowledge.

In a variation of this technique, try giving students the test essay questions a few days before the test. Use those questions as an opportunity to teach study strategies. In this example, consider giving them 10 essay questions, only two or three of which will be used on the actual test. They won't know which ones they will see come test day.

It is also useful to design a rubric for grading each answer to the questions you use. In the test review, explain to your students how you saw the question and analyzed it and also the response you expected. In this way, you model the techniques they need to assimilate to better structure their answers to essay questions. These types of test-taking strategies can also be taught for other assessment styles.

There are many other ways to incorporate a literacy-specific, study-skill agenda into testing. Again, you just need to see tests as opportunities to teach within an assessment component.

Precautions and Potential Pitfalls

More successful students, especially in secondary schools, some-times feel that their study skills and test-taking strategies work just fine and are not open to new or different ideas. If you try to push your test-taking strategies or literacy agenda too hard, you will lose them, and they will lose respect for the rigor of the class. You'll have to decide on the needs of the class and do your best to help those in need. Better test scores should reinforce and reward those who assimilate more effective study skills.

Source

Phillips, G. (2006). Using open-book tests to strengthen the study skills of community college biology students. *Journal of Adolescent & Adult Literacy, 49*(7), 574–582.

Strategy 43: Focus on students' writing strengths.

What the Research Says

 In a review of current research, Gregg and Mather (2002) note that many factors influence the perception that a student is not a proficient writer. They propose that by considering writing skills (spelling, syntax, vocabulary) and the task format (dictating, copying, timed writing), teachers will discover a student's writing strengths and also notice areas that require support. They point out that it is vital to remember that writing is integrally related to social interactions and dialogue. In other words, writing is not simply the attempt to represent linguistic structures such as sentences, words, or phonemes; written expression requires a social process achieved through dialogue and interaction.

Classroom Applications

Early on in a science class with students new to you, it is important that you establish a base or starting point for all students, especially students challenged by literacy skills. You may go into a class with some unrealistic expectations. You may also go into the class focusing on science content and forget that teaching overall literacy might be as important or more important than the content. Students with special needs often view writing as a hated task, and as standards move toward embedding writing in more curricular areas, poor writing skills can lead to a broader dislike of classwork and school in general. Writing itself is a very personal enterprise, and for a student who struggles with it, writing can be a very personal failure. They may like thinking about science, but the literacy expectation could damage their class experience.

When teaching writing, teachers should pay close attention to how students view themselves as writers and encourage them to focus on finding and writing in their own unique voice. By modeling the writing process for them—showing how ideas come first, then a rough draft to give the ideas shape, followed by an editing process that addresses the mechanical aspects of the writing—teachers can begin to facilitate student success.

When assessing written assignments, teachers should consider grading the first draft for content only, engaging the student in a written dialogue about what the student is saying in his or her writing. Teachers must quell their urges to point out paragraphing, capitalization, and spelling errors as they read. They should demonstrate the difference between content and mechanics by isolating them in the teaching and assessment-evaluation process.

Experienced teachers recognize that, like science content mastery, writing skill develops on a continuum, and they help their students to see individual growth along that continuum. Students who understand that what they have to say is unique and valuable are much more likely to risk committing their thoughts and ideas to paper. They know that the mechanical components of writing can be addressed concretely further along in their writing process.

Precautions and Potential Pitfalls

In recent years, many teachers and parents have lamented the lack of spelling and grammar instruction in schools. Students need to learn the principles behind spelling patterns, as well as the basic grammatical components of standard written English. Most students learn these basic rules more effectively in context, so teachers should consider embedding a lesson on a specific rule of grammar by asking the students to correct it or apply it in their own writing.

Source

Gregg, N., & Mather, N. (2002). School is fun at recess. *Journal of Learning Disabilities, 35*(1), 7–23.

6

Culturally Responsive Teaching and Learning

 Strategy 44: Avoid culturally stereotyping science students.

What the Research Says

Prime and Miranda (2006) investigated the connection between urban high school teachers' beliefs about student preparedness to achieve academic success and the curricular responses to those beliefs reported by the teachers. Eight high school science teachers were selected and interviewed from a range of schools with different achievement levels.

The findings and results suggest that teachers view science as a special subject that requires special qualities and see the students in their own schools as mostly lacking the qualities necessary for success in science. The teachers expressed what is commonly known as a deficit view of many urban students. They were seen as deficient in many of the skills, experiences, prior achievement and/or knowledge, attitude, and motivation and/or interest needed to grasp science concepts and develop patterns of high achievement. Because of their views, teachers reported a number of modifications they made to the curriculum and pedagogy such as "slowing down," deemphasizing some topics, and reducing the depth of coverage.

Furthermore, Prime and Miranda (2006) discussed how this deficit model was also reflected in negative teacher beliefs about their students' parents' lack of interest in their children's education. The impact of teacher beliefs can have a profound effect on teachers' instructional decisions.

Classroom Applications

Even though the sample size in this study was extremely small, it is not unreasonable to feel that the problems described in the research are widespread. Collectively, the teachers believed that their students did not measure up to the high intellectual and personal attitudinal demands of the science classroom. Many times, teachers are unaware of other, more culturally sensitive ways of viewing and reacting to students, parents, and the community. Culturally responsible teaching requires a change of mindset. Fortunately, teachers can find help in adopting new perspectives and ways to develop and construct more appropriate curriculum.

Reviewing the following description of culturally responsive science teaching is a place to start thinking about the topic and potential instruction changes. It comes from the Alaska Science Consortium and the Alaska Rural Systemic Initiative (Stephens, 2000). Culturally responsive teaching begins with personal reflection on a teacher's current practices and beliefs.

What are the characteristics of culturally responsive science curricula?

- It begins with topics of cultural significance and involves local experts.
- It links science instruction to locally identified topics and to science standards.
- It devotes substantial blocks of time and provides ample opportunity for students to develop a deeper understanding of culturally significant knowledge linked to science.
- It incorporates teaching practices that are both compatible with the cultural context and focus on student understanding and use of knowledge and skills.
- It engages in ongoing authentic assessment that subtly guides instruction and taps deeper cultural and scientific understanding, reasoning, and skill development tied to standards.

What are some strengths of culturally responsive curriculum?

- It recognizes and validates what children currently know and builds upon that knowledge toward more disciplined and sophisticated understanding from both indigenous and Western perspectives.

- It taps the often unrecognized expertise of local people and links their contemporary observations to a vast historical database gained from living on the land.
- It provides for rich inquiry into different knowledge systems and fosters collaboration, mutual understanding, and respect.
- It creates a strong connection between what students experience in school and their lives out of school.
- It can address content standards from multiple disciplines.

What are some difficulties associated with culturally responsive curriculum?

- Cultural knowledge may not be readily available to or understood by teachers.
- Cultural experts may be unfamiliar, uncomfortable, or hesitant to work within the school setting.
- Standard science texts may be of little assistance in generating locally relevant activities.
- Administrative or community support for design and implementation may be lacking.
- It takes time and commitment.

If you feel you could use some help in any or all of these areas of culturally responsive teaching, a quick look on Amazon.com will yield a range of books on the topic of culturally relevant teaching. A few of the books target the science classroom. Taking up this professional development challenge could enlighten you, improve your work environment, and give you the tools to move past frustrating obstacles to more effective teaching strategies.

Precautions and Potential Pitfalls

Although most teachers do show great concern for the academic progress of their students, many may have little understanding of how to teach science in a culturally relevant style. This is especially true for teachers coming from programs that do not sensitize teachers to the principles and practices of culturally relevant teaching. Before teachers can make the necessary changes, they have to become aware of how their teaching is affected by their own personal cultural background. Teachers need effective professional development to begin the journey toward a more culturally sensitive teaching style.

If urban students, or those in any other demographic setting, are perceived by their teachers as lacking the necessary qualities for high achievement in science, these perceptions are going to influence a teacher's instructional decisions and choices. In this way, teachers are going to possibly limit their students' opportunities to learn science, as there is a link between teachers' beliefs and classroom practice.

Sources

Prime, G. M., & Miranda, R. J. (2006). Urban public high school teachers' beliefs about science learner characteristics. *Urban Education, 41*(5), 506–532.

Stephens, S. (2000). *Cultural responsive science curriculum.* Alaska Science Consortium and the Alaska Rural Systemic Initiative. Retrieved May 6, 2009, from http://www.ankn.uaf.edu/Publications/Handbook/front.html

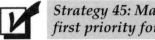

Strategy 45: Make academic success your first priority for all students.

What the Research Says

In a research study examining the link between school culture and effective schools, Gaziel (1997) surveyed 20 schools in Israel. Ten of the schools were rated as average and 10 were rated as highly effective, both based on student performance. Gaziel determined that the differences between the two groups could be accounted for largely as a result of school culture factors. Interestingly, the research determined that the highest priority at the highly effective schools was academic achievement. The highest priority at the average schools was orderliness. The researcher noted that teachers in the average schools working with disadvantaged students believed that academic success of the students could not be achieved before order was established.

Gaziel (1997) goes on to conclude, " . . . to be effective in a disadvantaged environment, where education is less highly valued, a school must have a school culture that, first, values academic achievement; second, values continuous school improvement and teamwork; and, only then, values the creation of an orderly environment" (p. 319). Although orderliness is important in schools, when it becomes the sole important norm, it prevents other norms from being expressed within the school.

Classroom Applications

School culture can be a difficult thing to define, and needed changes in school culture most effectively begin at the ground level. While administrators may be concerned about test scores and minimizing conflict on school campuses, teachers have the opportunity to set the tone, expectations, and high standards for student performance in their classrooms with the way they approach instruction. Science can be rigorous for all academic levels of students without the teacher being considered "hard." Positive academic achievement is a better indicator and defines success more precisely than class management or orderliness.

There is no question that some orderliness is essential to be able to effectively deliver instruction, but teachers need to place the greatest emphasis on academic growth and increasing achievement in their classrooms. This is particularly important for students who are economically disadvantaged and may not have school success and higher education on their own priority list.

Teachers can demonstrate their own commitment to academic growth and success through simple techniques, such as the following:

- Weight grading for content with less weight on structure and format.
- Be willing to find things that are right with student work rather than wrong. Value content over writing skills.
- Allow students to correct their work and resubmit it for partial or extra credit.
- Focus on application of higher-level thinking skills.
- Encourage students to take pride in their own and each other's academic successes.
- Share personal experiences regarding higher-level education and the positive difference it can make in one's life.
- Encourage students to articulate and track their personal academic goals. Simple surveys can provide helpful information on goals and how they view the role of science in their lives.

Although science may not be practiced by all students once leaving school, teachers should foster students' respect for science and make sure that the limited time the students are interacting with science, as an academic subject, is a positive one. By doing this, a teacher may be breaking a student's history of lack of success in a rigorous academic class.

Precautions and Possible Pitfalls

Changing school culture takes time and effort, but choosing to emphasize academic success over an orderly environment does not mean that the quest for order is abandoned. Teachers who create sound processes for classroom procedures and who take the time to teach those procedures concretely often find they have more time and focus to devote to instruction.

Source

Gaziel, H. H. (1997). Impact of school culture on effectiveness of secondary schools with disadvantaged students. *Journal of Educational Research, 90*(5), 310–319.

Strategy 46: Reach out to students from unfamiliar cultural and linguistic backgrounds.

What the Research Says

The majority of future teachers in the United States are white, monolingual, and female (Cushner, McClelland, & Safford, 1996). In contrast, the demographics for their students will increasingly be of a diverse culture and feature children of second-language learners (Hodgkinson, 1985; Pallas, Natriello, & McDill, 1989). Because of this potential mismatch, future teachers will be called upon to teach in classrooms to a student clientele that is very different from their own cultural background. As a group, these new teachers will generally come from rural colleges and universities and will find their first assignments teaching in urban classrooms populated with second-language learners. They will bring a certain cultural, racial, linguistic, and economic background and expectations for urban life. These expectations will not likely be based on firsthand experiences.

Various studies (Terrill & Mark, 2000) point to future teachers' exhibiting negative attitudes and perceptions toward urban schools and minority learners. They point out that most people tend to be culture-bound, and teachers with no experience in the backgrounds of their students are limited in their ability to interact effectively and professionally. They are not ready to shape cultural partnerships and teach in culturally diverse classrooms. These studies also found that teachers' personal experiences during childhood and adolescence were the major determinants of their cultural perspectives and most had little experience in diverse cultural settings.

Classroom Applications

Science teachers can look upon the potential problems presented by the research as their own or pass them off as a problem for the teacher education institutions. Future teachers may think they will get that job in their first school of choice, but are they prepared to move on if they don't? What if a preservice teacher's institution of higher education doesn't include a heavy dose of multicultural education throughout the curriculum? Will the student be prepared? The reality is that education graduates will be competing for jobs in very diverse settings. The demographics point out that it is very likely a teacher will be working in a cultural demographic very different from his or her own. It is up to the individual preservice teacher to squeeze every bit of help he or she can find within a program to become prepared. Students should seek out the professors who seem to be more in tune to multicultural themes and training. In this way, there is a greater chance for the new teacher to be better prepared for a greater range of placements to bridge potential cultural and linguistic gaps.

Next, consider service-learning opportunities in science classes with diverse settings. These experiences will increase levels of comfort and reduce anxiety. Teachers should be prepared to confront their cultural and linguistic assumptions, perceptions, and expectations. With an expanded awareness and a more inclusive, tolerant, and larger knowledge base, they will be able to help students.

Finally, science teachers should consider developing strategies to explore their own cultural, linguistic, and racial identities and biases. Teachers will find it is difficult to explore and appreciate the world views of others without a grasp of their own. As a teacher, it is important to develop a knowledge base of the major paradigms and concepts of multicultural education, diverse cultures, and ethnic and social groups and how the sciences relate to these groups today and in the past. Educators can't be effective if they are afraid of their communities, expect the worst in the classroom, and rarely see their students as gifted and talented and being motivated.

Precautions and Possible Pitfalls

Teachers shouldn't assume that their science subject matter or content mastery is the most important factor in preparation for the classroom. Depending on the settings in which teachers find themselves, management and people skills will make the job much easier. Multicultural educational settings require diverse teaching tools. One size doesn't fit all, and teachers will need to provide multiple learning pathways in the same class. Many students and classroom demographics will exhibit needs well beyond the curriculum content.

Sources

Cushner, K., McClelland, A., & Safford, P. (1996). *Human diversity in education: An integrative approach.* New York: McGraw-Hill.

Hodgkinson, H. (1985). *All one system: Demographics of education, kindergarden through graduate school (ED 261 101).* Washington, DC: Institute for Educational Leadership.

Pallas, A. M., Natriello, G., & McDill, E. L. (1989). The changing nature of the disadvantaged population: Current dimensions and future trends. *Educational Research, 18*(5), 16–22.

Terrill, M. M., & Mark, D. (March 2000). Preservice teachers' expectations for schools with children of color and second-language learners. *Journal of Teacher Education, 51*(2), 149.

	Strategy 47: Structure homework for success for students from nondominant backgrounds.

What the Research Says

Brock, Lapp, Flood, Fisher, and Han (2007) state that in the past decade, the number of English language learners (ELLs) in the United States has more than doubled. Also, students from nondominant backgrounds comprise the majority of the students in the nation's largest school systems. Finally, Brock et al. estimate that ELLs will make up 40% of the school-age population by the 2030s.

Their research was prompted by the resurgence of public opinion about the value and importance of homework coupled with the rising numbers of children from nondominant backgrounds. This phenomenon has raised questions about how students from nondominant backgrounds in American schools, especially in the urban areas, are impacted by teachers' homework practices. Brock et al. (2007) designed a study to explore:

- Why teachers in one large urban community assigned homework and what their homework practices were
- What kinds of homework they assigned and how they described their students' homework practices
- What the teachers' beliefs were about the impact of this homework on their students' success at school

They collected surveys from 133 elementary school teachers that were all working on master's degrees in literacy and interviewed 27 of those teachers about their homework practices. The researchers found the results encouraging:

- Although teachers engaged in "typical "homework practices (i.e., the kinds of homework they assigned and their reasons for assigning it), they did make provisions to help their students to be successful with homework.
- Almost all of the teachers they interviewed made provisions to ensure that their students had the support they needed to successfully complete their homework.
- Knowing that the parents of ELLs may not be able to support their students' homework in English, teachers made provisions for other ways for students to receive help (e.g., before and afterschool homework clubs, being available for them).

Interestingly, this study found the following about teachers:

- They did not question the broader issues relating to the nature and usefulness of homework in general.
- They assigned homework to meet parent expectations and to meet the district's requirements that are different from purely instructional purposes.

Classroom Applications

Unfortunately, no precise guidelines emerged from this research, and teachers and schools will need to ask themselves the hard homework questions and develop local policy that suits their individual settings, students, and parents.

Science teachers assign homework for many reasons. Most teachers see homework as a paradigm for students to practice skills, especially the science-related skills of math, reading, vocabulary, and spelling. Science teachers routinely include these skills in their homework agenda. Most of the time, this can be seen as a review and reinforcement of what the students are doing in school.

Teachers assign homework to help students develop self-discipline and responsibility. Some teachers also assign homework because parents and the school or district want and expect homework and worry if it's not assigned, and in some districts, there is a mandate or a set of guidelines for homework. While there are no precise and perfect guidelines for the role and structure of homework for every situation, there are topics for discussion that need to take place.

Many students from nondominant cultures and their families may not have the materials and linguistic resources to successfully engage in the historic canons of homework practices, especially in the sciences. Therefore, what questions should science teachers ask themselves while structuring homework activities, and what assumptions should they make? First, do all of the students have the resources to complete their assignments?

In the study by Brock et al. (2007), two-thirds of the teachers wouldn't assign homework requiring the Internet. The respondents in the study stated that they or their schools provided all of the materials necessary for the students to complete their homework. Pencils, paper, crayons, worksheets, and/or books for reading were considered the basics. Only two out of 27 stated they also needed to provide glue, scissors, or other craft items.

Second, should all students receive the same assignments? In the study by Brock et al. (2007) 22 out of 27 used scaffolding techniques like assigning a reduced work load for struggling students or varying the nature and reading level of books assigned. Differentiating the homework for a class is more work for a teacher, but if it is within grade-level expectations, a reduced load might be necessary.

Third, what role does the homework grade play in overall assessment? Some teachers and schools had a separate homework grade or an effort grade, and homework didn't count toward a class grade.

Fourth, how often should you assign homework? Sending the same homework load on a regular basis helps develop patterns of participation that become more ingrained in the family's lifestyle.

A few other questions to consider include the following:

- Should students be able to do homework at school, and what message does that send to students? How does this decision affect students of various abilities and skill levels? Is it fair?
- Is it fair to assign work that requires adult help at home? This is a tough question and is dependent on the demographics of the class and community.
- How do teachers make sure all students have the outside help or resources they need to complete their assignments and not frustrate the students' efforts? Maybe a student or parent questionnaire could be used to determine how many of your language-challenged students have access to the Internet, television, or parents able to help their children in science. The more you know, the better you will be at tailoring homework to the learning environment and not limiting student access to the resources they need.

In the study by Brock et al. (2007), teachers of students from nondominant cultures reported that 60% to 75% of their students completed their homework when the assignments were modified in some of the ways described above. The following strategies identify a few areas and ideas to use as prompts as you customize your own homework philosophies for your unique setting:

- *Activate prior knowledge.* When assigning or preteaching homework, make science links to students' lives and educational and cultural experiences. Connecting curricular concepts to their own experiences outside of the classroom will help make abstract concepts more concrete.

- *Adapt text or provide supplemental reading material.* Remember, science vocabulary is often difficult for native English speakers. The volume of new vocabulary is even more difficult for ELLs. If they are overwhelmed by the difficulty of a text (either because of linguistic complexity, the inherent difficulty of the subject matter, or a combination of both factors), they will be unable to learn the content it presents. Preview literature that will be used prior to a homework assignment lesson and adapt the science text by highlighting key vocabulary words or sentences that capture the concept to be learned. Consider a jigsaw technique as another approach—students are given a shorter passage for which they are responsible to share a summary with their peers at school. These kinds of adaptations enable ELLs to complete the homework with a goal in mind. It gives them an opportunity to contribute to group work in a less stressful manner. Text can be adapted in two ways.

o *Simplified texts.* Texts can be linguistically simplified to improve readability by substituting frequently occurring vocabulary for infrequently occurring nontechnical vocabulary, shortening sentence length, and restructuring sentences to reduce their complexity. When simplifying a text for ELLs, the purpose is to eliminate overly complex language that might prevent a student from understanding the main ideas of the text. Some publishers offer simplified textbooks.

o *Elaborated texts.* Elaborated texts aim to clarify and explain implicit information and make connections explicit. To this end, words are often added to increase comprehension. Unlike linguistic simplification, improved text coherence (or understandability) does not necessarily decrease the difficulty of a text as measured by readability formulas. Methods to improve text coherence also do not usually focus on one or two discrete text features (e.g., number of syllables or word frequency).

In practice, most text adaptations involve a combination of simplification and elaboration. For example, a teacher may simplify difficult sentences in a text while at the same time adding additional background information to make a concept clear. Be aware that there are problems (not as challenging, loss of meaning, etc.) associated with both of these strategies. Teachers will need to decide if the benefits of these adapted texts outweigh the problems.

● *Identify English language objectives.* When assigning homework, clearly identify the language objective for ELLs. Here are a few examples:

o Students will verbally identify the life cycle of an insect by responding in complete sentences.
o Students will write in complete sentences using capital letters and periods.
o Students will read their assigned section and be prepared to present a verbal summary to the group.

The sophistication of the language objective will depend on the grade, content, and English proficiency level of the students. Language objectives should be presented in a very visible manner, introduced to the individual or class, and revisited at the end of the assignment or during assessment. This is just good teaching, and language objectives can and should also be used for native English speakers.

- *Arrange for homework clubs, homework helpers, or others types of special-ized homework support.* Anytime students can be paired up or work in a group, they will have increased opportunities to develop social and acade-mic language. Small-group learning opportunities increase students' opportunities to participate in a low-risk learning environments (bilingual buddies, pair-share, cooperative learning groups, etc.).

- *Provide linguistic scaffolding.* Emphasize ways in which students can use science vocabulary in their home language and the importance of students' collaborating with others on lessons in whatever language(s) they are most comfortable. There are also clear benefits and challenges of encouraging bilingual students to assist their less English-proficient peers and allowing ELL students to write. Writing helps the students but also serves as a formative assessment technique for you. In addition, teach students how to show their learning by producing graphic materials (e.g., graphic organizers, Venn diagrams, pictures of measurement instruments, drawings of experimental setups, data tables, graphs, charts). At times, with important complex lessons, it may be a useful strategy to have students write in their home language.

While there are few studies that look at the effects of homework on achievement and learning, it's clear that homework is not going away and is an expected part of a child's school experience. With empathy and care-ful planning, the pitfalls of a lack of equal opportunity can be avoided, and students from nondominant cultures can be bolstered by academic success within the homework paradigm.

Precautions and Potential Pitfalls

⚠ Homework is a touchy subject in many schools and communi-ties. The competition for the student's time outside of your classroom is tremendous today. Families can view homework as an intrusion into family time or activities. Make sure you have a clear homework philosophy and can intelligently articulate it to colleagues, administrators, and, most important, parents, especially those who are not familiar with the American school system and the tradition of homework.

Source

Brock, C. H., Lapp, D., Flood, J., Fisher, D., & Han, K. T. (2007). Does home-work matter? An investigation of teacher perceptions about homework practices for children from nondominant backgrounds. *Urban Education,* 42(4), 349–372.

Strategy 48: Develop science standards with a multicultural perspective.

What the Research Says

Ferguson (2008) found that while "diversity" is used in various science standards, the use of the term and theme "multiculturalism" is not. Multiculturalism is the view that the various cultures in a society merit equal respect and scholarly interest. In his effort to highlight the missing multicultural elements, Ferguson researched and generated a group of literature-derived multicultural teaching standards that connect to science methods courses taught to preservice teachers. He also worked on applying those multicultural science standards in methods courses to align sample activities with his proposed standards. Ferguson's work focused on viewing the various science standards through a multicultural lens with the specific themes of equity and the transformation and assimilation of the multicultural standards into science teacher education programs.

Commenting on multiculturalism and science education, Jeffrey Weld (2000) states:

> The research literature is rife with recommendations for remediation. But many of these "cures" do more to sustain a style of science education that perpetuates cultural bias than they do to help all students achieve. As multiculturalists and as science teachers who wish to maintain fidelity to our discipline, we all want students to appreciate the scope and limitations of science, the cultural influences that have and will color it, the societal manifestations of it, and the opportunities inherent within it. But we should not abandon learning theory to "deliver" these notions when student inquiry will better provide for the construction of these meanings for each individual.

Weld feels that carefully crafted pedagogy emphasizing a science inquiry approach will help level the playing field for all students regardless of their ethnicity.

Classroom Applications

Most, if not all, current science standards lack a clear and thoughtful multicultural perspective. While diversity is mentioned, its meaning is not specific nor is it synonymous with multiculturalism. Teaching for social justice requires educators in all disciplines and content areas to engage in dialogue regarding aspects of multiculturalism.

Teachers tend to instruct the same way they were taught, and this notion especially applies to beginning teachers. Preservice teachers form their vision of good teaching from their past experiences as elementary and secondary learners, their peers and activity groups within university classrooms, their student teaching experiences, and from the view from their own particular cultural networks. These combined experiences form comfort zones, cultural and racial boundaries, and a limited assessment and reflection potential.

Few teachers think of themselves as biased toward any cultural or racial group, and while they profess student-centered idealism and beliefs, they behave in stereotypical teacher-centered ways. There is often a gap between their multicultural belief system and their classroom practice. Finally, to add to all this, there are no multicultural mandates to override a focus on the national goals of standardized assessment and "teaching to the test." Teaching to content standards seems to be mandatory. Here are a few suggestions for incorporating multiculturalism into science teaching:

• *Dialogic conversations.* Science teachers should provide, support, and facilitate opportunities for science and cultural-societal conversations. Science filters through and is critiqued by society. We are all consumers of scientific and technological knowledge. The boundaries of scientific investigation and knowledge are continually being set and reset. We all make value judgments through the lens of social justice. It is not hard to find examples of historic science readings that highlight how mainstream science has intertwined with racism, sexism, and classism. There are many examples from medical research and access to medicine and therapies that have cultural and racial elements. The availability of HIV and AIDS treatments are easy targets for examination by classes. On the cutting edge of science and social justice is the new work on race and science that seeks to understand the complex role of new sciences such as genetics in the remaking of racial classifications, identities, and politics. The genomic age has spawned whole new discussions and questions on the sociology of race, gender, and class. Ownership and exploitation of genetic information is a ripe topic for discussion. How do you study race in science without racism?

• *Authentic activities.* Ferguson (2008) uses the example of the "Burning-Peanut Lesson" to describe an authentic activity. Ferguson begins with a discussion on the possible reasons students come to school hungry. From a multicultural perspective, there might be religious or spiritual reasons (fasting) in addition to the typical reasons such as no time, late for the bus, economics, or no food at home. Students are asked to reflect on intentionally fasting as a reason. The class then performs a caloric experiment, heating water by burning the peanut and measuring the caloric-heat relationship. Discussions then move to Ramadan and the potential cultural insensitivity of performing a food lab during a time of fasting. Fetal pig dissections are prime discussion points for cultural sensitivity on many levels.

• *Transformative skill.* The science classroom should promote a cultural climate of tolerance and a continued effort to see the classroom and its multicultural component as a professional growth opportunity. All teachers need to continue to nurture an environment to better know and understand their students and meet their needs. This is especially true in the multicultural classroom. Using the topic of taboo and sacred foods, teachers can provide themselves with opportunities to discuss similarities and differences with cultural backgrounds.

- *Committed practice.* The intervention strategies advocated in much of the multiculturalist literature depart from the general principles of inquiry science. The recommendations are geared toward traditional science settings where lecture and student passivity prevail. Multiculturalism advocates implore teachers to "use examples and content from a variety of cultures, groups, and their own personal experience" to help make science more exciting (Atwater, Crockett, & Kilpatrick, 1996). Teachers are urged to cite the scientific "contributions of females and scientists of color" in their curriculum (Atwater et al., 1996), and to charge students with conducting "racism checks" of course materials (Stanley & Brickhouse, 1994). Should laboratory time arise amidst the stories, vignettes, and readings, one multiculturalism advocate cites the danger of using "complex and expensive equipment that may implicitly promote the view that science is the preserve of the rich, industrialized nations" (Hodson, 1993).

When coupled with the intervention strategies discussed earlier, the premise under which many multiculturalism advocates operate becomes clear: that "the priorities of schools with high ethnic minority populations will be significantly different from those in schools in which the student population is drawn largely from the dominant culture" (Hodson, 1993).

Precautions and Potential Pitfalls

⚠ Multiculturalists' noble intent notwithstanding, the energy expended to promote this particular collection of remedies can be seen as misspent for three reasons: (1) multicultural interventions themselves assume monocultures of minorities in classrooms, (2) the multicultural literature speaks of all members of particular ethnicities as if cut from the same mold, and (3) the foundations for an ethnically inclusive science education strategy are already at hand.

The typical teacher in a Fresno, Miami, or Chicago classroom may have as many ethnic cultures represented as there are students in the classroom (Loving, 1995). The task of validating each student's culture through citations of significant contributors to the current body of knowledge becomes a futile and patronizing practice (Stanley & Brickhouse, 1994). It can be argued that these are isolated pockets of ethnic heterogeneity; that in reality, ethnically homogeneous student groupings prevail where multicultural interventions are warranted.

Educational equity is a reachable goal, but it will come through the widespread adoption of inquiry-science practices rather than as a series of contrivances that aid and abet a pedagogical or instructional status quo.

Sources

Atwater, M. M., Crockett, D., & Kilpatrick, W. J. (1996), Constructing multicultural science classrooms: Quality science for all. In J. Rhoton & P. Bowers (Eds.), *Issues in science education* (pp. 167–176). Arlington, VA: National Science Teachers Association.

Ferguson, R. (2008). If multicultural science education standards existed, what would they look like? *Journal of Science Teacher Education, 19,* 547–564.

Hodson, D. (1993). In search of a rationale for multicultural science education. *Science Education, 77*(6), 685–711.

Loving, C. C. (1995). Comment on "multiculturalism, universalism and science education." *Science Education, 79*(3), 341–348.

Stanley, W. B., & Brickhouse, N. W. (1994). Multiculturalism, universalism and science education. *Science Education, 78*(4), 387–398.

Weld, J. (2000). Less talk, more action for multicultural science. (ERIC Document Reproduction Service No. ED442637). Retrieved February 27, 2009, from http://eric.ed.gov:80/ERICWebPortal/custom/portlets/recordDetails/detailmini.jsp?_nfpb=true&_&ERICExtSearch_SearchValue_0=ED442637&ERICExtSearch_SearchType_0=no&accno=ED442637

> ## ✓ Strategy 49: Broaden discourse opportunities to invite a diverse range of contributions.

What the Research Says

Many students do not come to class with the school's academic cultural understanding intact. When students' cultural discourse differs substantially from the discourse norms practiced in class, it is rarely gained through tacit practice. Rather, the students who already understand the rules of participation dominate classroom interactions, while those who do not fully grasp these norms are largely overlooked. How can teachers broaden classroom discourse practices and establish more equitable environments for children representing a wide range of cultural experiences? In a meta-analysis, Okhee Lee (2005) addressed many of the myths, as well as current research findings. While the roots of these recommendations come largely out of research with English language learning environments, they can be accurately applied across a range of cultural differences from normative school practices.

Classroom Applications

There is much rhetoric regarding higher-order thinking skills, the promotion of problem-based learning environments, and the establishment of learning communities where students take responsibility for their own learning. The ways to establish such goals are seldom discussed—much less with all students of every background. Such lofty goals can run counter to well-established norms of American classroom discourse. Although research and reforms embrace such progressive representations of disciplinary knowledge, schools and state assessments still largely adopt the view of content as a list of facts for a variety of reasons. Furthermore, teachers who want to make wholesale shifts in the ways they conduct class often get ahead of where diverse students can follow the implicit rules of argumentation or new ways of speaking about content.

In order to broaden the discourse of classes and invite more culturally diverse students to practice new forms of discourse (like argumentation), teachers should adopt the following strategies:

- Practice explicit instruction on academic norms and content (Lee & Fradd, 1996; Lee, 2005). This means invoking metadiscourse or *talk about the talk* when conducting authentic and meaningful tasks. Teachers should explain the structure of the conversations of the class. For example, teachers could use instructions like, "We have just completed the brainstorming part of the conversation where there were no correct answers and everyone's idea counted. We are now moving to the generation of claims about what we read and/or saw in the data. This requires that your claim needs to have backing from your data. This looks like. . . ."
- Identify students' linguistic and cultural experiences that can serve as intellectual resources for learning (Ballenger, 1997; Warren, Ballenger, Ogonowski, Rosebery, & Hudicourt-Barnes, 2001). This specific knowledge can emerge from listening in on students' sense-making in small groups and other creative spaces where intersections between students' everyday knowledge and academic practices can be identified. These intersections can be used as the basis for instructional practices.
- Utilize inquiry instruction to enhance students' communication of their understanding in a variety of formats, including written, oral, gestural, and graphic, but scaffold the transition (Lee & Fradd, 1998; Rosebery, Warren, & Conant, 1992). Students need to recognize existing structures and demands before expanding into new and uncertain discourse norms.

One way to think about creating rich discourse spaces is to consider what kinds of artifacts and experiences children bring to the table to discuss the concepts at hand. This is not the same as considering what children know. Too often, answering the question of what students know turns into a deficit-driven model of teaching. Rather, asking the question of what students *bring* to the discussion can be helpful in creating discourse opportunities. It is important to remember that discourse usually occurs in social settings, so teachers will need to figure out how to organize small groups and distribute certain expertise throughout the groups. Once these groups are formed and specific roles discussed, the students should be presented with an open-ended problem to solve or to make sense of. For example, instead of simply teaching children how to measure pH and giving them the scale to assign acid and basic properties, students could be asked to bring in examples from their refrigerator that match specific characteristics (e.g., sour, bland, salty). When students work in groups to pursue questions about pH with their peers, it gives them the opportunity to practice specific discourse like classification, while manipulating objects, exploring, and interacting with peers and the teacher. Rodriguez and Bethel (1983) demonstrated that providing these opportunities resulted in statistically significant improvement in outcomes for experimental groups in both classification and oral communication skills.

The rules of classroom discourse are largely implicit and tacit, making it difficult for students who have not learned the rules at home to figure out these rules on their own. For students who are not from the culture of power, teachers need to provide explicit instruction about that culture's rules and norms for classroom behavior. As students gradually acquire the social, academic, and cultural competencies, their opportunities grow to fully employ their native language tools, use significant cultural capital, and thrive in an environment where their discourse better matches macroculture of their lives outside the classroom (Tobin & McRobbie, 1996).

Precautions and Possible Pitfalls

Constructing more open discourse in classrooms is not without challenge, though research shows that renegotiation of classroom expectations needs to and can be accomplished. The specific skills needed for interpreting text, designing data collection, analyzing data, and discussing differing conclusions must be taught. It cannot be assumed that because a few vocal students have mastered them that all students are ready to move forward. This can be done only by expert teachers who are comfortable in promoting a new kind of classroom discourse that weaves aspects of new thinking and speaking with the old.

Changing the discourse can help all students in our increasingly diverse classrooms appropriate scientific ways of speaking, thinking, and acting. However, students who have typically been highly successful in using routine, fact-based discourse will question and perhaps even resist new norms. Parents and students alike need to buy into the changes happening in classroom discourse to minimize teacher stress. The outcomes, which will benefit all students, can include eliciting rich, cultural interpretations in class, identifying alternative conceptions, and engaging students in meaningful and authentic discourse. These reasons should be given to parents repeatedly.

Sources

Ballenger, C. (1997). Social identities, moral narratives, scientific argumentation: Science talk in a bilingual classroom. *Language and Education, 11,* 1–14.

Lee, O. (2005). Science education with English language learners: Synthesis and research agenda. *Review of Educational Research, 75*(4), 491–530.

Lee, O., & Fradd, S. H. (1996). Interactional patterns of linguistically diverse students and teachers: Insights for promoting science learning. *Linguistics and Education: An International Research Journal, 8,* 269–297.

Lee, O., & Fradd, S. H. (1998). Science for all, including students from non-English language backgrounds. *Educational Researcher, 27*(3), 12–21.

Rodriguez, I., & Bethel, L. J. (1983, April). An inquiry approach to science and language teaching. *Journal of Research in Science Teaching, 20*(4), 291–296.

Rosebery, A., Warren, B., & Conant, F. (1992). Appropriating scientific discourse: Findings from language minority classrooms. *Journal of the Learning Sciences, 2,* 61–94.

Tobin, K., & McRobbie, C. J. (1996). Significance of limited English proficiency and cultural capital to the performance in science of Chinese-Australians. *Journal of Research in Science Teaching, 33*(3), 265–282.

Warren, B., Ballenger, C., Ogonowski, M., Rosebery, A., & Hudicourt-Barnes, J. (2001). Rethinking diversity in learning science: The logic of everyday language. *Journal of Research in Science Teaching, 38*(5), 529–552.

☑ *Strategy 50: Provide diverse learning opportunities for student discourse.*

What the Research Says

 The landscape of reform and accountability has had a negative impact on diverse students' achievement and engagement in classrooms. Instruction is being driven by factual assessments, and student placement in classes and learning supports have been redefined in some cases on the basis of narrow student abilities. These same standardized tests that are driving instruction have been noted to reinforce disturbing messages about the nature of knowledge (Poole, 1994) and contribute to the deterioration of students' confidence and agency during the process of learning. While small, incremental gains have been noted in rigorous standardized environments, other studies reveal that opening up instruction to a wider array of learning opportunities can have an even greater effect for diverse students. For example, Shymansky, Hedges, and Woodworth (1990) conducted a meta-analysis of 81 research studies that contrasted the performance of students in traditional environments with those in hands-on, activity-based programs. The results favored the hands-on experience, which strongly influenced student achievement. Amaral, Garrison, and Klentschy (2002) studied rural English language learners for four years and analyzed student achievement in science, writing, reading, and mathematics. The longer the students had exposure to inquiry and hands-on instruction, the higher their scores in all areas. These studies and others like them have demonstrated that increases in achievement can be obtained by a broader array of strategies than tradition or scripted instruction.

Classroom Applications

Teachers can provide a variety of experiences that introduce students to content as they develop shared meanings for central vocabulary and concepts. This approach contrasts starkly with the approach of having students learn pertinent vocabulary *first* before being given the opportunity to apply the vocabulary in meaningful ways. Mathematical manipulatives, historical documents, science kits, and other learning artifacts should be incorporated into instruction so that students have the opportunity to build meaning and connect content to their personal experiences and understandings.

Amaral, Garrison, and Klentschy (2002) have offered a variety of ways to rethink classroom interactions to use hands-on and minds-on approaches to improve achievement. These include the following:

1. *Take time to build the context for learning.* Students can have a more concrete understanding about what they can see and touch. Through exploration, teachers and students can co-construct a common understanding around these shared artifacts.

2. *Make efforts to build common experiences.* Teachers should put a limit upon the reliance of purely text-based resources that have limited impact. Particularly with English language learners, the processing demands for the content and language can be overwhelming with only text. Teachers should build in more opportunities to learn also from one another. Manipulatives offer part of that vital context for shared discourse between students, which enhances learning opportunities.

3. *Plan to build thinking skills.* Problem-solving and/or sensemaking tasks given to students can serve as a mediator for reasoning skills that teachers may claim to be aiming for but do not know how to achieve. Many teachers report that they ultimately want their students to practice "higher-level thinking," but they never change the learning context to enable students to achieve. For example, English language learners who are allowed to access both English and their native language can place a

greater focus on the concepts or ideas being explored and learned than on learning specific vocabulary first.

4. *Pay attention to students' comfort levels.* In an environment where students are actively constructing their own knowledge, they are more apt to feel comfortable about their learning when they do not know the answer to a question or a problem. Students learn through the process of exploration that their ideas are valuable and count. Students are then more likely to participate in the future when their ideas (even if wrong) can be viewed as hypotheses or tentative claims that can be publicly pursued. Furthermore, there are many times when it is appropriate not to couch the entire lesson as a pursuit for one right answer but for possible multiple answers.

5. *Create positive attitudes toward learning.* When a student realizes that she or he has had some success in discovering something, there is an attitude developed where the student believes that there is no reason why the next thing cannot be figured out as well. Students should be encouraged to learn by "figuring it out" with some prompting and guidance from the teacher. This confidence builds to enthusiasm for the next challenge.

In addition, Rosebery, Warren, and Conant (1992) argue that classrooms can and should create opportunities for cooperative learning. This can take on a variety of facets and arrangements for learning. Students can work as partners, in small groups, or in teams where their experiences, skills, and shared knowledge transcend their specific language development. As students work collaboratively, discussions and interactions take on a higher level of sophistication than single word "fill-in-the-blank" answers encouraged by other classroom arrangements. Discussion helps to develop expressive skills and builds vocabulary in a social context— both enabling successful application of concepts to social contexts. Students may also feel less targeted as deficient as peers walk them through a procedure during a hands-on activity, rather than having a teacher guiding every aspect of a lesson. Instead of stopping the teacher during a lesson to ask a question, they may feel freer to ask questions of their peers who are not responsible to lead the whole class. Peers can also at times serve to translate from one language to another, making the learning process a team effort and thus not bringing public attention to any individual who is unable to explain his or her thinking in English.

Precautions and Possible Pitfalls

Many teachers assume that if students are going to be spending half the class period working in small groups, they only have to plan half as much. In fact, the opposite is true. Having students use collaborative time effectively takes *more* planning, not less. Teachers need to consider multiple ways students can interpret the more sophisticated task using manipulatives. Teachers need to consider what an acceptable answer would look like from a variety of student backgrounds. Rules for interacting in small groups are different than those in whole-class discussion, and these must be taught and practiced. In addition, using collaborative learning environments can seem chaotic to teachers at first glance. Teachers must use strategies that are comfortable to them, but they must also balance the notion that there is always more than one way to achieve success.

The older students become and the more socialized they are to traditional means of teaching, the more they can be alienated from the process of learning because of the strict adherence to a narrow interpretation of school success. No matter how marginalized youth may seem from academic tasks or environments, inquiry can serve to help students and teachers negotiate meaning and expectations for the betterment of the entire school community (Yerrick, 1998). Teachers can operate with even largely alienated youth if they engage students in authentic inquiry instead of just factually-based, watered-down information and basic skills. It is important for educators who are teaching students marginalized by traditional strategies to seek the help of others to think outside the constraints and ideologies that have brought them to an impasse with their students. Many schools and administrators are willing to provide the required support to make it happen.

Sources

Amaral, O. M., Garrison, L., & Klentschy, M. (2002). Helping English learners increase achievement through inquiry-based science instruction. *Bilingual Research Journal, 26*(2), 213–239.

Poole, D. (1994). Routine testing practices and the linguistic construction of knowledge. *Cognition and Instruction, 12,* 125–150.

Rosebery, A., Warren, B., & Conant, F. (1992). Appropriating scientific discourse: Findings from language minority classrooms. *Journal of the Learning Sciences, 2,* 61–94.

Shymansky, J. A., Hedges, L. V., & Woodworth, G. (1990, February). A reassessment of the effects of inquiry-based science curricula of the 60s. *Journal of Research in Science Teaching, 27*(2), 127–44.

Yerrick, R. (1998). Reconstructing classroom facts: Transforming lower track science classrooms. *Journal of Science Teacher Education, 9,* 241–270.

Strategy 51: *Manage and change your students' misconceptions.*

What the Research Says

Students do not come into your science class as "blank slates." They come with often complex views of science topics, some valid and some questionable. Numerous studies have shown that many students have "naive theories"—misinformation, preconceptions, and misconceptions—about science content, process, and reasoning. Misconceptions are faulty ideas that are based on false, incomplete information, limited experience, assumptions, or misinterpretations. It is often very difficult to teach for in-depth understanding when students enter your room with these misconceptions, many of which can interfere with learning (Finley & Jensen, 1997; Hamza & Wickman, 2007). The best and most high-profile example of this concern is the biological topic of evolution and natural selection.

Hamza and Wickman (2007) felt that the role of misconceptions in learning science was poorly understood and examined. They used the results of a classroom study to analyze to what extent nonscientific views and ideas in electrochemistry, reported by students in interviews, entered into their learning. Hamza and Wickman found that nonscientific ideas and misconceptions did not constrain the development of students' reasoning. Rather, their reasoning developed in response to the contingencies of the specific situations. When misconceptions were encountered, they appeared as alternatives and questions not actively defended. Sometimes these encounters facilitated students' reasoning. They felt that their results demonstrated that misconceptions in interviews did not impact their thinking enough to assume that they interfere with learning. In their introduction and literature search, they found that most authors agreed that identified nonscientific ideas have consequences for the learning of science, but there has been little agreement on what part they play in that learning. One interesting finding in the Hamza and Wickman research was that the same common misconceptions in electrochemistry occurred among students in three different countries.

Classroom Applications

 Misconceptions are formed and come from a variety of sources and factors:

1. Daily language can cause misconceptions. For example, students may have seen their parents buy or administer "plant food" and so believe that plants need food to grow.

2. Lack of direct and visible evidence leads students to form mistaken impressions. Because students cannot see germs or microscopic organic materials without a microscope, they may not grasp the concept.

3. Everyday discourse, biased or misinformed media reports, and speculation all produce doubt and skepticism and spread misconceptions. Students may believe that the atmosphere acts like a greenhouse because this idea is conveyed in newspapers, in adult conversations, and on the Internet.

4. Occasionally, you and your students will find misconceptions or grossly oversimplified science concepts in textbooks. Sad but true.

Confusion over science concepts can create wrong impressions and misconceptions. The discrepant conclusions concerning the role of misconceptions for learning between the different studies merits additional research. However, common sense tells us that misconceptions can play various roles in certain situations and contexts, some negative and some positive. Consequently, most teachers want some advice on how best to deal with nonscientific ideas and misconceptions. Assessing prior learning and understanding is the first step for many topics. It's a respectful strategy and will help begin a nonconfrontational dialogue. If developed well, it will reveal a range of student views and attitudes toward many science concepts. This is just good teaching.

The Understanding Science website (http://undsci.berkeley.edu/teaching/misconceptions.php) includes a long list of common misconceptions. The site was produced by the UC Museum of Paleontology of the University of California at Berkeley, in collaboration with a diverse group of scientists and teachers, and was funded by the National Science Foundation. The mission of Understanding Science is to provide a fun, accessible, and free resource that accurately communicates what science is and how it really works. The website offers teachers, both experienced and novice, clear definitions and explanations focused on each identified misconception. The site also provides teachers a resource to help add clarity to the many misconceptions in science.

Precautions and Potential Pitfalls

Simply correcting a mistaken impression by assuming the role of teacher-as-expert often may not work. This is especially true with older students. Often, these misconceptions come from family members or friends. Tread lightly and try to resist the temptation to go to battle over every misconception. Some misconceptions are deeply entrenched in family history, and you don't want to get into a power struggle. Be respectful and don't burn bridges with students. In many cases, you will have multiple opportunities to work your magic.

Sources

Finley, F. N., & Jensen, M. S. (1997). Teaching evolution using a historically rich curriculum and a paired problem solving instructional strategy. *American Biology Teacher, 55*, 208–212.

Hamza, K. M., & Wickman, P. (2007). Describing and analyzing learning in action: An empirical study of the importance of misconceptions in learning science. *Science Education, 92*, 141–164.

> ## Strategy 52: Guide students to choose authentic problems to solve.

What the Research Says

SocioTransformative Constructivism (sTc) is a theoretical orientation to teaching and learning that affirms that knowledge is socially constructed and mediated by cultural, historical, and institutional contexts (Rodriguez, 1998, 2002; Rodriguez & Kitchen, 2005). It is a special branch of constructivism with roots in equity and diversity studies and is geared toward transforming classrooms by engaging children in solving authentic problems of interest to them and the community at large. It reaches beyond simply teaching with inquiry methods by creating and invoking strategies that are intended to level the playing field for marginalized populations by empowering them with data, decisions, and local impact. It has proved to be an effective tool with Latina/Latino learners in the Southwest (Zozakiewicz & Rodriguez, 2007), Hawaiian science students (Chinn, 2002), and English language learners as well (Lee, 2004). Through these strategies, children improve their academic performance, attend school and school functions more frequently, and use the learning of content as a venue for social change.

Classroom Applications

Rodriguez is not only a theorist, but he is also an activist who works alongside teachers in the classroom to establish equitable environments. With Dr. Rodriguez in their classroom and at special community service outreach projects, teachers and researchers together are acting as change agents who are able to engage in collaborative and mutually beneficial transformative practice. Below are some of the examples from the classroom.

In a Southern California community where tourism was an important economic concern, millions of dollars were spent annually importing sand. Where was all of the sand going? Beach sand was being redistributed up and down the coast because of currents, human-made structures like piers and levees, and other local development factors. A sixth-grade class invited a local expert to come and speak to them about what could be done. Once the local geologist taught them some basic principles concerning levees by taking them to a local beachfront construction, students documented the changes over time using digital photography and surveying equipment. It was estimated that millions of dollars were being wasted on redistributing sand to maintain local tourism, but no one had collected the necessary data to make informed decisions about investing in or tearing down local structures to solve the problem. With their newly acquired mapping skills and technology, students went to work documenting the problem. Students collected data and analyzed the factors contributing to local erosion and have invited local officials to review their findings.[1]

Working with a teacher involved in the Sea Grant initiative (Sea Grant National at http://www.seagrant.noaa.gov/), students were made aware of a local disruption in the food web as the sand crab population was dropping. Protecting the ecosystem requires balance as primary and secondary predators like birds, which feed on the sand crabs, also can also be affected. Children went to work and were trained on the sampling techniques, sand crab morphology, and issues impacting this species. One of the theories for declining sand crabs and beach bird populations is a parasitic invasion. Because sand crab parasites are visible to the naked eye, students were are able to collect data regarding the frequency of parasites among sand crabs, as well as data regarding the number of sexually mature females and health of populations at different sites. The Sea Grant made it possible to share their data with that of scientists studying this same species in other locations along the California coastline.

Another example involved a lesson on nutrition. One student asked the teacher, "If french fries are so full of fat and salt, then how come we serve them every day in the cafeteria?" This one question led to a schoolwide investigation by students simply examining the menu items and polling children regarding what they *chose* from the menus to eat during lunch. The findings were shared with parents and subsequently the school board, and substantive changes were made to the menu offering to provide students with better choices that are meant to improve the health of children.

These classroom applications and countless other examples are activities in which students became change agents in their own communities because of the strategies that teachers used to choose a problem that had the potential for transformation. While these strategies favor a science orientation, many other social issues in other content areas are ripe for such lessons. Voting, recycling, bullying, immigration, and other social studies issues are perfect venues for applying this strategy.

Precautions and Possible Pitfalls

⚠ SocioTransformative Constructivism is not to be equated with multicultural efforts to simply eat different foods, show photos of successful diverse professionals, or share in the celebrations of different cultures. It is an approach that is meant to empower children. Unless the orientation is toward change and transformation

---

[1]Excerpts from this strategy were provided by a project sponsored the National Science Foundation (Grant #0306156).

to benefit community, the level of engagement for marginalized students will be minimal. To carry these strategies off successfully often requires having local experts or online resources to provide additional expertise that lies outside the classroom. It is also important for the teacher not to assume that she or he knows all the local issues, but to open up a discussion identifying the issues with children and adults from the community.

Sources

Chinn, P. (2002). Asian and Pacific Islander women scientists and engineers: A narrative exploration of model minority, gender, and racial stereotypes. *Journal of Research in Science Teaching, 39*, 302–323.

Lee, O. (2004). Teacher change in beliefs and practices in science and literacy instruction with English language learners. *Journal of Research in Science Teaching, 41*, 65–93.

Rodriguez, A. J. (1998). Strategies for counterresistance: Toward sociotransformative constructivism and learning to teach science for diversity and for understanding. *Journal of Research in Science Teaching, 35*(6), 589–622.

Rodriguez, A. J. (2002). Using sociotransformative constructivism to teach for understanding in diverse classrooms: A beginning teacher's journey. *American Educational Research Journal, 39*(4), 1017–1045.

Rodriguez, A. J., & Kitchen, R. (2005). *Preparing prospective mathematics and science teachers to teach for diversity: Promising strategies for transformative pedagogy.* Mahwah, NJ: Lawrence Erlbaum.

Zozakiewicz, C., & Rodriguez, A. J. (2007). Using sociotransformative constructivism to create multicultural and gender inclusive classrooms: An intervention project for teacher professional development. *Educational Policy, 21*(2), 397–425.

Web Resources

I2TechSciE: Sand Crab Ecosystem Study: http://edweb.sdsu.edu/i2techscie/sandcrabs.htm

I2TechSciE: Mars Rover Simulations: http://edweb.sdsu.edu/i2techscie/Mars.htm

Mars WebQuest: http://questgarden.com/author/create/preview.php?u=&l=68552-080721201643&a=&p=introduction&pt=student

 Strategy 53: Utilize meaningful cues with your English language learners.

What the Research Says

 Gagnon and Abell (2009) review the literature that supports their strategies to help ELLs bridge the gap between school science

and the academic language of school with the students' everyday language. They describe the challenges ELLs face while learning science, how ELLs develop scientific understanding through science talk, how ELLs can benefit from inquiry-based instruction, and what strategies are most helpful in developing the language of school science.

Also, focusing on ELLs, Siegel (2006) examined ways to improve written assessments for advanced English learners in two science courses in two California schools. These techniques were developed through teacher research and tested and validated with English only and advanced English learners. Both groups scored significantly better on modified classroom assessments.

Classroom Applications

Teachers strive for techniques to give all students equal access to the classroom teaching and learning environment. Toward that goal, there are a number of adaptations in instruction that science teachers can make for linguistic minority students:

- *Emphasize visual literacy.* Picture books are some of the first literature that children are exposed to when beginning their journey toward literacy. Movies and television are nothing more than moving picture books. If you take the voices and sounds away from these forms of media, it is likely that most of us would have an idea of what's happening. Regardless of linguistic background, visual literacy, or the ability to evaluate, apply, or create conceptual visual representation, can be relatively independent of text and language and is therefore invaluable to learning science and English simultaneously.

- *Utilize graphic organizers.* Concept maps in the form of graphic organizers are a means of introducing, organizing, and assessing concepts and ideas in a manner that scaffolds and encourages meaningful cognitive organization (see Strategies 3 and 9). They can require minimal language and are therefore helpful tools when teaching science to ELLs. They can be used by teachers in presentations or can be constructed by students as a learning activity.

- *Use charts, graphs, and figures.* These devices compress raw or complex data into visual representations that are more easily understood and explained by all of us. All of these visual tools can communicate concepts with minimal use of spoken or written language. Keep in mind that these visual tools can also be made complex, and teachers should focus on communicating the message as clearly as possible.

- *Preview multimedia control and preteaching.* Many programs introduce new concepts and vocabulary that linguistically challenged students may not remember or recognize. Preview any multimedia or software programs you plan on using. Look for new terms or concepts you can preteach before students view them. Don't forget to use the pause button to explain concepts and terms.

• *Encourage participation and questioning.* Many linguistic minority learners come from countries in which teacher-student interaction and student participation are not part of their classroom behavior. They may be reluctant to speak not only because of their lack of proficiency in English, but also because of their discomfort in their new learning environment. A positive and supportive environment has a significant influence on student anxiety level, participation, and a feeling of instructional responsibility. Requiring ELLs to speak in front of class may be counterproductive and cause great anxiety. Rather, encourage them to express themselves in small groups first (see Strategy 54).

• *Develop road maps to science.* "Coverage" maps can help linguistic minorities keep track of where they are in the curriculum, where they have been, and where they are going. On a smaller scale, provide students with a copy of your lecture and/or discussion outline. This will help all students, not just linguistic minorities, know where you are and where you are going with your instructions.

• *Connect spoken with written words.* Speak slowly and distinctly and write down key terms or hand out a vocabulary list. Use closed captioning when showing CDs or videos.

• *Relate to prior knowledge with mental visuals.* Find concept examples within the students' own prior knowledge. Delve into and discover what your students already know about a given topic and build upon this knowledge.

• *Offer a pictorial guide.* Provide a visual reference to glassware and other materials used in experiments and activities. Review safety symbols and post them in the classroom and laboratory.

• *Use analogies.* Mental visual analogies relate new concepts to prior knowledge and previously learned concepts.

• *Introduce pictorial flash cards.* A picture of a concept is on one side of a card, while the term (in the language to be learned) is on the reverse. The student learns to correlate concepts directly with words, eliminating the need for translation. This technique is one of the best ways to learn the vocabulary of a new language.

• *Create a word wall.* Post new vocabulary terms on the wall in an organized, grouped manner. For example, you may wish to post new biology terms in columns according to the level of organization (cell, tissue, organ, etc.).

With regard to assessments for ELLs, Siegel (2006) recommends the following linguistic and visual modifications to tests:

- Linguistic simplification of vocabulary and syntax
- Replacement sentences with bulleted lists
- Reduction of words
- Addition of visual supports
- Careful matching of the language of the assessment with the language of instruction and of the text
- Reduction of nonessential information
- Use of bold type for emphasis
- Addition of graphic organizers to test questions
- Division of questions into smaller units

Precautions and Potential Pitfalls

The type of adaptations and scaffolding required to enable ELLs to succeed in science classes can be time-consuming for teachers. However, many of the strategies can improve learning for all students, not only linguistic minorities.

Sources

Gagnon, M., & Abell, S. K. (2009). ELLs and the language of school science. *Science and Children, 46*(5), 50–51.

Siegel, M. A. (2006). Striving for equitable classroom assessments for linguistic minorities: Strategies for and effects of revising life science items. *Journal of Research in Science Teaching, 44*(6), 864–881.

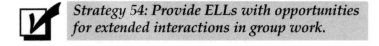

Strategy 54: Provide ELLs with opportunities for extended interactions in group work.

What the Research Says

Anderson, Thomas, and Nashon (2008) reported on an investigation that utilized meta-cognitive and social cognitive theoretical frameworks to explore and identify student perceptions of their cognitive roles and the processes that they considered affected their learning in small groups. The focus was on their interactions, perceptions of learning tasks, and their learning techniques as expressed during a field trip to a nature center. The researchers also gathered the students' descriptive accounts of their biology learning experiences, as communicated through their recollections and reflections.

Students are highly aware of their social status. Anderson et al. (2008) concluded that even among the student groups labeled as highly effectual by their teacher, there existed metasocial and metacognitive factors that influenced and shaped cognition in ways detrimental to the effective learning of science.

Classroom Applications

In planning cooperative or group learning pedagogy, teachers take on several roles. First, teachers make pre-instructional decisions about grouping students and assigning appropriate tasks. Teachers must be able to define and explain the academic task, the type of discourse, the cooperative group structure, and the tasks and expected outcomes and standards, and then must monitor and intervene when necessary. Finally, the teacher is also the one who is responsible for evaluating student learning and the effectiveness of each group's work (see also Strategies 22 and 23).

Where do we find cooperative models to emulate? Science has long been a process practiced with interaction that is considered argumentative. Peer review at all levels of science, from lab meetings to published journal articles read by peers, thrives on collaborative and respectful debate on contentious matters. Teachers need to look no further than the world of science to find models of appropriate interaction that should be taught to science students. The world of art has a similar language of critique that becomes part of every college or university art class when assessing art in general and student-created art.

Anderson et al. (2008) propose that there is a need for teachers to focus on the students' development of content knowledge and conceptual understanding.

Students might make decisions to maintain friendships and the associated social capital rather than engage in argumentative discourse and discussion to enhance their science learning. Many student groups are good at following procedures, but their thinking or scientific reasoning rarely progresses into what could be called "peer review."

Many feel that pairing ELLs with native English speakers is a good strategy. However, according to Goldenberg (2008), more typically, English speakers cut the interactions short in order to finish the assignment, as did the student who said, "Just write that down. Who cares? Let's finish up." Studies reviewed by Goldenberg suggest at least two important points about grouping English speakers with ELLs. First, English speakers must be grouped with ELLs who are not so lacking in English skills that meaningful communication and task engagement become problematic. Second, the tasks in which students engage must be carefully designed to be instructionally meaningful and provide suitable opportunities for students to participate at their functional levels. Simply pairing or grouping students together and encouraging them to interact or help each other is not sufficient.

Finally, it is suggested that the most important strategy is to take the time to develop clear guidelines for group interactions and outcomes. Teachers can insert themselves into student groups to model the types of interactions expected. Let others in the class see how group communication should work. Develop clearly expected work products that exhibit mastery of the content in addition to the communication and involvement desired. Try to build in accountability for the participation of all group members.

Precautions and Potential Pitfalls

First, parents sometimes have a problem accepting activity grades for their child's efforts that rely on the contribution and production of other students within a group. They don't think it's fair that the work of others influences their student's grade. It may be a good idea to add something to a parent information packet or syllabus that addresses the nature of cooperative learning and group work and your philosophy on assessment and grading. Also, discuss these points on back to school night. Science is routinely conducted in teams, and many people within a team contribute. Team skills are important and part of every job interview. From this point, it is easy to justify structured collegial relationships within instruction.

Second, one fear teachers have about using cooperative learning is that low-status or low-performing students will not participate and/or that high-status students (usually dominant males) will take over the group. If cooperative learning is to work, teachers must create balanced groups that are equitable and have the abilities to work "smart" so that all students participate fully and use multiple-ability strategies. Teachers also need to convince students of four things: (1) that different cognitive abilities and skill sets are required in cooperative-group learning; (2) that no one student has all of the abilities, skills, and time needed; (3) that each member of the group will have abilities and skills to contribute to the overall goals of the collaboration; and (4) that all members will need to contribute to a satisfactory outcome.

Third, it's great when students can manage their own group interaction and work products. However, in some classroom situations and with some student groups, teachers will need to be more aggressive in structuring outcomes for all of the students in the groups.

Fourth, the need to scaffold collaborative group work derives from student reliance on the teacher for the "right" way to things. Ultimately, what you want are groups of students who are totally responsible for facilitating group interactions, establishing a productive group, setting standards, and meeting instructional goals. The methods to accomplish this type of collaboration need to be taught and supported, but ultimately, the teacher needs to pull away the supports slowly, as the students' skills improve, until the students can manage their own interactions independently.

Finally, group learning strategies can yield mixed results. Every class is different, and teachers will need to always consider the benefits versus the costs of group work. In some cases, it just might not be the answer.

Sources

Anderson, D., Thomas, G. P., & Nashon, S. M. (2008). Social barriers to meaningful engagement in biology field trip group work. *Science Education, 93*(3), 511–534.

Goldenberg, C. (2008). Teaching English language learners: What the research does—and does not—say. *American Educator, 32*(2), 8–23, 42–44.

7

The Complex Nature of the Gender Gap in Science

> **Strategy 55: Examine the evolving nature of gender issues in science classrooms.**

What the Research Says

There are a number of perspectives in which to look at gender differences in science classroom, regarding achievement, performance and long-term impacts. One perspective looks at the gender issues during the post-secondary school years and in career choices. It also examines gender through a socioeconomic lens once graduates enter the work force. A second perspective deals directly with learning, achievement, and the secondary school classroom. Much of the information on this perspective comes from the U.S. Department of Education's (NCES, 2004) fast facts that frame how U.S. students relate to students from other nations.

York (2008) examined whether male and female valedictorians, who appear academically equal in reaching the top of their class, also have equivalent career and higher education plans. The work indirectly examined performance in the science classroom and career choices in the sciences once leaving school. York studied a special group of gifted high school valedictorians to determine if their college and career aspirations fell along sociologically traditional gender lines. York prefaced her work by examining a human capital model that ties investments in education and training to later rewards and returns in the form of higher wages. She felt that as long as the present value of the returns is greater than the costs, then the model assumes that a rational individual would pursue more education. York found that there were a number of variables that mitigated these decisions based on the gender profiles of 92 female valedictorians. This study took place in the Research Triangle of central North Carolina and was based on data from profiles of the 2003, 2004, and 2005 graduating classes. Here is a summary of some of York's findings:

- Among the sample group, there were no gender differences in mean weighted GPA or in the mean of high school average SAT scores (p. 589).
- Female valedictorians were equally likely to intend to major in fields in the humanities and social sciences (p. 579).
- Female valedictorians were less likely to intend to major in mathematics, computer science, or engineering and were planning careers in lower-paying occupations (p. 579).
- Majoring in a science or health field was very popular for both males and females, and no statistically significant differences in interest were found (p. 594).
- The differences cited above mimic the current gender gap in pay equity. Also, often due to caregiver needs, women tend to average fewer years in the labor market and tend to receive a lower return on their investment and to invest in less education.
- The female valedictorians were also, on average, planning to attend less-selective colleges (p. 579).

Addressing what has been called a new gender divide, Wilson (2007) found that the proportion of females pursuing postsecondary education has increased, and females now outnumber males on most college campuses. She cited the U.S. Education's Department's statistics that women now make up 58% of undergraduates nationwide. Wilson also cited the American Council on Education paper published last year that concluded girls are more likely than boys to take college-prep courses in high school, more likely to enroll in college directly out of high school, and more likely to earn a bachelor's degree. Wilson also found that the gender gap is greatest among low-income students of all races and disappears among students whose families are at the top of the socioeconomic scale. She goes on to say that boys have improved their performance, but girls have improved their performance even more.

Classroom Applications

Between 1970 and 2001, women went from being the minority to the majority of the U.S. undergraduate population, increasing their representation from 42% to 56% of undergraduates (Freeman, 2004). Wilson's (2007) statistics show that currently 58% of undergraduates are women. Consistent within these enrollment changes, women surpassed their male peers in educational expectations and degree attainment over the last 30 years (Freeman, 2004). However, the York (2008) investigation focuses not on high school performance but on more fundamental questions.

The K–12 establishment needs to do a better job in setting expectations for how successful high school students fare in their college and university choices, their selection of a major, and, ultimately, their career choices and incomes. First, for counselors and teachers interested in how students and parents select colleges and universities, based on York's research, the selection process merits attention and possibly requires updating. Second, counselors and teachers should not only encourage females to pursue interests in math and in the sciences, but also encourage male students to look at the humanities for potential careers.

The results of the York (2008) study really reinforce the need for gifted and high-achieving students to receive specialized career counseling that will help them think beyond the boundaries of the traditional gender roles found in York's research. High-achieving students could gain admission to nearly any college or university they want to attend. It is not easy to define the gender-specific forces that drive their decisions and why girls tend to gravitate to less-selective colleges and universities.

The National Science Teachers Association (2003) offers a position statement regarding gender. It is the best source of guidance for addressing gender neutral strategies that stress a robust and diverse teaching style with many avenues for success respecting all learning modalities.

Precautions and Potential Pitfalls

Keep in mind that teachers and counselors are only one element in college and university choice, college or university major selection, or career choice. Often, family finances or the experiences of a parent, brother, or sister trump a teacher's advice. In diverse communities, different cultures often have different expectations for both boys and girls that become a large factor in these decisions. A teacher or counselor may need to draw boundaries on how persuasive and persistent she or he should be.

Teachers can have significant influence on older high school students. A positive experience in your classes can set a student's course and direction. Don't underestimate the power that encouragement and positive reinforcement can have. Teachers should make their best effort to let students know what they are capable of and the options that the students have.

Sources

Freeman, C. E. (2004). Trends in educational equity of girls & women: 2004 (NCES 2005–016). *U.S. Department of Education, National Center for Education Statistics.* Washington, DC: U.S. Government Printing Office.

National Science Teachers Association. (2003). Gender equity in science education. Retrieved March 3, 2009, from http://www.nsta.org/pdfs/PositionStatement GenderEquity.pdf

National Center for Education Statistics of the U.S. Department of Education's Institute of Educational Science. (2004). *Trends in educational equity of girls and women.* Retrieved March 3, 2009, from http://nces.ed.gov/pubs2005/equity/ Section4.asp

Wilson, R. (2007, January 26). The new gender divide. *Chronicle of Higher Education.* Retrieved March 20, 2009, from http://chronicle.com/weekly/v53/i21/ 21a03601.htm

York, A. E. (2008). Gender differences in the college and career aspirations of high school valedictorians. *Journal of Advanced Academics, 19*(4), 578–600.

> **Strategy 56: Change the opportunities and experiences of girls in the science classroom.**

What the Research Says

 A number of "gaps" exist in the education field, all with potentially important implications for the outcomes of our students. The gender gap in science impacts approximately 50% of the population of the United States. Despite progress over the past 30 to 40 years, girls and women continue to be underrepresented in science, technology, engineering, and mathematics (STEM) fields (AAUW, 1998). The attrition of girls in STEM fields begins early, with interest beginning to decline in middle school.

Carol Gilligan's (1982) seminal work brought into the educational discussion the idea that women place a larger emphasis on relationships and connections between ideas, events, and people than do men. One can certainly argue that each of us, regardless of gender, interprets our experiences in a completely individual way based on our previous experiences. However, feminist theory posits, " . . . the difference in the social experience of men and women gives them different ways of looking at life and interpreting events" (Roychoudhury, Tippins, & Nichols, 1995, p. 898).

Research over the past decade or so has helped to inform us about how girls learn. Girls interact in ways that are different from boys: they are more cooperative and less competitive. Relationships matter to girls, and they act in ways to develop and maintain those relationships (Alexopoulou & Driver, 1997). An earlier study conducted by Ridley and Novak (1983) suggested that girls engage more frequently in rote learning in science than do boys and this contributes to girls' lack of perseverance in science. However, Meece and Jones (1996) found that girls were as likely, or more likely depending on ability level, to use what they referred to as meaningful learning strategies. They found that boys in all ability groups were more likely than the girls to utilize strategies designed to reduce effort. This research supports the idea that girls prefer to take the time to understand science on a conceptual level and to connect to a broader whole (Burkam, Lee, & Smerdon, 1997; Cavallo & Laubach, 2001; Lee & Burkam, 1996).

Brotman and Moore (2008) identified several issues that emerged from their detailed analysis of the studies of girls and science published between 1995 and 2006. In particular, they noted the following:

1. Girls more frequently chose the biological sciences over the physical sciences. Boys chose the physical sciences over the biological sciences or seemed to have a broader range of preferences.

2. Both young boys and girls hold stereotypical views about who engages in what kind of science activities. The idea that physical science activities were more for boys and biological activities were more for girls were more strongly held by boys than by girls.

3. Girls tend to have fewer extracurricular experiences in science, particularly in the physical sciences.

4. Interest in science by girls declines after elementary school.

This research advocates changing curriculum and pedagogy in such a way that aligns with the reform movement in science education (AAAS, 1993; NRC, 1996). What is helpful is that there is consistency in what we are learning about effective science teaching, regardless of the sub-group. Instruction that is more inquiry based appears to have better outcomes for all students. What we see in curriculum and pedagogy that works for both girls and boys is that which draws upon experiences and interests of the students we teach, incorporates the preconceptions our students bring with them to the classroom, and provides opportunities for our students to explore and interact with materials and collect data, generate explanations based on the data they have collected, and represent and communicate their ideas—all within a cooperative, supportive environment (NRC, 1996). It isn't necessary to provide "girls" science and "boys" science.

Classroom Applications

This research speaks to what we ask students to learn and the way in which we ask them to learn it—curriculum and pedagogy. While we may not have an extraordinary amount of control over the content our students must learn because of local and state standards, we may have some control over the ways in which we present the content to our students. Getting away from lecture-format presentations with fast-paced question-and-answer sessions is a start. This type of format often favors boys who tend to be more aggressive and respond well in this environment. Girls and less-aggressive students often disengage and become nonresponsive. It is difficult for a teacher to know what is going on in the head of a student who is not talking.

Recognize that the participation pattern of the girls in class may differ from that of the boys. The boys may be much more aggressive in calling out both questions and answers, which may serve to silence the girls. This effectively changes the type of experiences girls have in class when compared to that of boys. The boys simply get more attention because their actions demand it. Find a way to give the girls a voice. It may mean initially monitoring who is called on. Do a count or tally or have someone else do this for you. Record the type of questions that get asked of girls and of boys. Are both girls and boys asked high-level questions? Are both girls and boys asked for follow-up responses to the questions? Adding wait-time improves the quality of responses for both girls and boys as well as for students with special needs and English language learners. Keep in mind the proportion of girls to boys you have in class. You might be surprised who gets your attention on a daily basis.

Creating opportunities for students to work collaboratively is important. The work in which the students collaboratively engage should be meaningful and should provide the opportunity for substantive talk—not something like, "What is the symbol for calcium?" It is helpful to have something real for the students to talk about, such as data that they have collected on a particular phenomenon. This creates the structure and goal for the discussion. It is *not* open-ended in the sense that you don't know what end you have in mind, and it is not without purpose.

Find a way to ensure that all students have a voice. Girls and other students who may be quiet, less aggressive, or less confident may be reluctant to put themselves out there in whole-class discussions. However, it is important for you to hear from all students. Small-group work will generate more opportunities for students to have a voice and to get their ideas heard and valued, and for you to get a sense of what they are thinking. Give some thought to how you decide on grouping students and how you decide to assign tasks. Productivity always improves when the teacher assigns the group, and thought should be given to group membership based on both strengths and areas of academic, social, and behavioral needs of group members. Gender may also come into play in this equation when manipulation of materials is important. If you observe that the boys assume control over equipment and the girls are always the recorders, you may want to intercede. You can assign roles, having boys become the recorders and girls the materials managers. You can also assess all students on their ability to manipulate equipment, thereby building in more incentive into tasks to have students interact and practice with equipment. You might also decide to use single-gender groups on occasion. This configuration is often seen in middle schools where social interactions may be an issue. All of these strategies can encourage the girls to assume more responsibility for playing with the "stuff" of science, thereby creating more equitable opportunities.

Teachers often have little control over the textbooks they use. When using texts perceived to demonstrate bias of any kind (gender, racial, ethnic, cultural, etc.), you may want to discuss the limitations of the text with your students. Furthermore, talk about why, for historical reasons, much of the science students learn in high school came from the research of the "dead white guys." It's hard to make it multicultural. It just isn't. But students can learn the reason for this. The breakthroughs by women and persons of color are important to discuss. Representations of all types of individuals should be present in materials used in class—text, video, and Internet. Look materials over carefully before using them with your students to eliminate any bias that you can, or discuss what bias might be present and how that might impact how individuals might interact with the information.

Precautions and Potential Pitfalls

You might also want to explain to your students about some of the equity you are trying to provide in the classroom. Explain the concept of wait-time and what the advantages are to the students. Explain why you want them to raise their hands so that the boys aren't just yelling out the answers and so that the girls never get to answer. It's okay to make your teaching practices transparent to your students. It will help them to better understand the things that you do to help them to learn.

Think carefully about the tasks you design for your students. Are they as gender neutral as you can make them? Are the topics that appeal to boys more prevalent than those that appeal to girls? Include examples and experiences to which girls can relate. While some girls are into sports, others are not, so use sports analogies carefully. Provide opportunities for students to connect what they are learning to experiences they have already have.

Constantly changing groupings of students can be time-consuming, and students can complain. Once you have a sense of who has what strengths and areas of need, effective groups can be established. Groups may need to be changed as they are fine-tuned. Several configurations of different sizes generally work (twos, threes, and fours). One suggestion is to use a numbering system for groups and locations around the room. The group number and student membership would be put on the overhead projector. Students would get together with their group members and move to their appropriate location. Starting this practice early in the year and *never* allowing students to choose their own groups will likely eliminate much of the complaining. Once you allow students to choose their own groups, they will always want to do this. Students will choose to work with others for reasons that likely will not match yours. The ideal situation is a smoothly running classroom in which students meet learning goals and objectives. Students will quickly learn that you run the classroom and that they do not.

Sources

Alexopoulou, E., & Driver, R. (1997). Gender difference in small group discussion in physics. *International Journal of Science Education, 19,* 393–406.

American Association for the Advancement of Science. (1993). *Benchmarks for science literacy: Project 2061.* New York: Oxford University Press.

American Association of University Women. (1998). *Gender gaps: Where schools still fail our children.* Washington, DC: AAUW Educational Foundation.

Brotman. J. S., & Moore, F. M. (2008). Girls and science: A review of four themes in the science education literature. *Journal of Research in Science Teaching, 45*(9), 971–1002.

Burkam, D. T., Lee, V. E., & Smerdon, B. A. (1997). Gender and science learning early in high school: Subject matter and laboratory experiences. *American Educational Research Journal, 34,* 297–331.

Cavallo, A. M. L., & Laubach, T. A. (2001). Students' science perceptions and enrollment decisions in different learning cycle classrooms. *Journal of Research in Science Teaching, 38*(9), 1029–1062.

Gilligan, C. (1982). *In a different voice.* Cambridge, MA: Harvard University Press.

Lee, V. E., & Burkam, D. T. (1996). Gender differences in middle school science achievement: Subject domain, ability level, and course emphasis. *Science Education, 80*(6), 613–650.

Meece, J. L., & Jones, M. G. (1996). Gender differences in motivation and strategy use in science: Are girls rote learners? *Journal of Research in Science Teaching, 33*(4), 393–406.

National Research Council, (1996). *National science education standards.* Washington, DC: National Academy Press.

Ridley, D., & Novak, J. (1983). Sex-related differences in high school science and mathematics enrollments: Do they give males a critical head start toward science- and math-related careers? *Alberta Journal of Educational Research, 29,* 308–318.

Roychoudhury, A., Tippins, D. J., & Nichols, S. E. (1995). Gender-inclusive science teaching: A feminist-constructivist approach. *Journal of Research in Science Teaching, 32*(9), 897–924.

Strategy 57: Represent science in ways that encourage girls to stay interested.

What the Research Says

Many of us are familiar with the test designed by Chambers (1983) in which students are asked to "Draw-a-Scientist." The images drawn by children were originally evaluated by comparing them to seven standard images. Later versions of the test expanded these to eleven images (Mason, Kahle, & Gardner, 1991). It probably isn't surprising that students from around the globe of varying ages (from very young onward) draw amazingly similar depictions of a scientist—a white male in a lab coat, balding, holding physical science equipment, looking slightly like Bill Nye (Matthews, 1996; Newton & Newton, 1998). This image has maintained itself over time although the Matthews (1996) study did reveal less gender bias than previous studies. However, a fairly strong message seems to persist as to who can be and is a scientist. It also suggests a bit about what the life of this scientist in particular might be like. It is, of course, a very narrow representation of the broad range of folks who engage in science and the type of science they do.

Along with the idea that those who do science are men (and old, unattractive men at that), is the idea that science is hard. Carlone (2004) found that even in a physics classroom characterized as "reform-based," female students resisted participating in the ways required by the reform curriculum. Perhaps being required to step out of the familiar typical participation structure that involved taking notes and solving problems was a risky space that was too uncomfortable for some girls. Some girls reported a preference for paying attention and taking notes, as opposed to engaging in hands-on activities. One girl's response to enrolling in the reform-based physics class was, "It has been a living hell." This same student responded that she did not want to "think beyond what equation to use" (Carlone, 2004, p. 403). Other students enthusiastically preferred the more hands-on version of the physics course even if they perceived the course as more work. Both of these apparently conflicting attitudes held by girls are necessary to overcome. It would appear that no matter the approach, science can be viewed as a difficult subject.

An additional consideration is one linked to our understanding, or misunderstanding, of one of the facets of the nature of science—that of science as a creative endeavor. Science in schools is often portrayed as a very linear, constrained, formulaic process with little room for error or creativity. Science, as actually practiced, is a wonderfully creative process filled with countless examples of "accidental" discoveries. The "final form" science to which most students are exposed in schools provides few opportunities for students to experience or investigate the lives of real working scientists (past or present). Viewing science as strictly objective and without emotion places it squarely in a masculine domain, perhaps making it less appealing to girls (Brickhouse, 2001). Providing opportunities for students to see science in a more robust, accurate form contributes to a better understanding of the scientific process not only for girls, but for all students.

Classroom Applications

First, we need to address the issue that science is seen as something that is difficult and boring. For example, in a social setting that does not include other teachers, when you indicate that you teach science, you can expect responses like, "I *hated* chemistry." A rejoinder is, "You had the wrong teacher." Not that teaching or learning stoichiometry is a picnic, but you can still manage to introduce some fun into your science classes. Your students can learn to balance equations using snowflake parts and gumdrops. They can learn limiting reagents by building paper versions of Big Macs. Pull into your repertoire strategies that are more likely to actively engage all of your students by drawing on their experiences and interests. Find ways to demonstrate that learning science is something of which they are capable.

Let students know that you are there to help them learn and will do whatever it takes. Often, the impression is that once the "smart kids" get it, the class moves on. Become one of those teachers who is known for helping all students learn and who won't move on until everyone in the class understands the topic. Make each student's learning your personal responsibility. Your students will feel your passion for their learning and will respond. They will know that their success is important to you. A lot of students truly believe that their teachers don't care whether they are successful. The tough part can be selling the approach to reluctant students. The good news is that student motivation increases with active engagement in learning.

Provide opportunities for students to see that science includes a broad array of individual subdisciplines that may not be represented by those they see in school science. Opportunities for career exploration can be eye-opening for students. Often, students hear a title for a career but have little knowledge of what a person with that career might actually do or what education and training it might take to have that career. Using what students are interested in can be a starting point. Music, dance, sports, and fashion can all be used as entrees into science. It is important for students to be able to see themselves, or someone like themselves, in a particular job or career. It does help to have role models. This is one of the reasons why young people want to be professional athletes and rap artists—there are lots of role models.

Precautions and Potential Pitfalls

⚠ Providing opportunities for students to explore beyond the curriculum can be problematic with an already tightly packed school year. Having students investigate the workings of a real-life laboratory or researching the progress and set-backs of a previous scientific discovery (the work of Marie Curie or Barbara McClintock might be good examples) can take much more time than allotted by scripted curriculum. But there are wonderful things that both girls and boys can learn about the scientific process by engaging in such tasks.

Sources

Brickhouse, N. (2001). Embodying science: A feminist perspective on learning. *Journal of Research in Science Teaching, 38*(3), 282–295.

Carlone, H. B. (2004). The cultural production of science in reform-based physics: Girls' access, participation, and resistance. *Journal of Research in Science Teaching, 41*(4), 392–414.

Chambers, D. W. (1983). Stereotypic images of the scientist: The draw-a-scientist-test. *Science Education, 67,* 255–265.

Mason, C. L., Kahle, J. B., & Gardner, A. L. (1991). Draw-a-scientist-test: Future implications. *School Science and Mathematics, 91*(5), 193–198.

Matthews, B. (1996). Drawing scientists. *Gender and Education, 8*(2), 231–244.

Newton, L. D., & Newton, D. P. (1998). Primary children's conceptions of science and the scientist: Is the impact of a national curriculum breaking down the stereotype? *International Journal of Science Education, 20*(9), 1137–1149.

☑ **Strategy 58: Improve attitudes toward science through STS approaches.**

What the Research Says

 In an article reviewing the research literature on the science, technology, and society (STS) approach, Bennett, Lubben, and Hogarth (2007) report on 17 published studies that focused on high school students' understanding of science concepts and their attitudes toward science. Specifically, the authors sought to answer the question, "What evidence is there that teaching approaches that emphasize placing science in context and promote links between STS improve the understanding of science and the attitudes to science of 11- to 18-year-old students?" (p. 351).

What is the STS approach? Bennett et al. (2007) provide the following definition:

Context-based approaches are approaches adopted in science teaching where contexts and applications of science are used as the starting point for the development of scientific ideas. This contrasts with more traditional approaches that cover scientific ideas first, before looking at applications. (p. 348)

The authors examined 12 studies that investigated students' understanding of science ideas in context-based and STS courses. Just over half of the studies led to scientific understanding comparable to that of more traditional courses, four studies found that students in STS and context courses developed better scientific understanding than students in conventional courses, and two studies indicated lower performances or performances that were dependent on the types of assessment.

Seven of the nine studies examined by the authors reported evidence of more positive attitudes toward science from students in context-based and STS courses when compared to students in more traditional courses. These studies asked students about their attitudes about school science, including individual disciplines, and also about science generally. Bennett et al. (2007) also looked at several studies that examined students' attitudes in elective science courses. Data from these studies were mixed; however, the trend of student preference toward STS- and context-based courses seemed to hold with students choosing this option in high school, electing to take science courses in their post-secondary education. This pattern was further supported in a study conducted by Reid and Skryabina (2002), who found interest in science-related careers is tied to context-based and STS learning approaches.

Another finding is that of the reduction in the gender-gap effects in attitude. Generally, the interest level in science of girls decreases as they continue through school. Bennett et al. (2007) found moderate evidence to support the suggestion that context-based and STS approaches to science instruction not only promoted positive attitudes among both boys and girls but also helped to reduce the gap in attitude differences between boys and girls. In addition, one study found more positive outcomes with lower-track students both in academic achievement and attitude with this approach when compared to a more traditional approach.

Classroom Applications

Individual classroom teachers do not always have a lot of control over the curriculum they will teach. Often, that is determined for them, and there may not be a great deal of flexibility for implementing a context-based and/or STS approach. The problem-based curriculum and literature that are available may be one way to implement some of this in smaller pieces.

An example of a mass-produced curriculum with which teachers might be familiar is ChemCom. For those who want to move toward project-based learning, lots of resources are available. The University of Delaware hosts the Problem-Based Learning (PBL) Clearinghouse website, which is limited to educators who register (free) via an online application. This website then provides access to problems and articles that have been reviewed by PBL experts. An additional resource, PBL Online (www.pbl-online.org), provides free information on designing projects, access to projects designed by others, as well as research about problem-based learning. Utilizing these types of resources will allow teachers with limited time and resources to implement a context-based and/or STS approach as time and opportunity permit.

Precautions and Potential Pitfalls

Carving out time in an already full academic year to revise and implement changes in the curriculum may be problematic. Think about choosing a problem that will incorporate as many standards as possible and link your instruction to those standards. In the lower grades, you might think about something that is cross-curricular, involving reading, writing, mathematics, and perhaps research skills. This will provide students with the opportunity to work on a larger project while integrating a variety of academic skills.

Sources

Bennett, J., Lubben, F., & Hogarth, S. (2007). Bringing science to life: A synthesis of the research evidence on the effects of context-based and STS approaches to science teaching. *Science Education, 91,* 347–370.

Reid, N., & Skryabina, E. (2002). Attitudes toward physics. *Research in Science and Technology Education, 20*(10), 67–81.

8

Science and Literacy

Strategy 59: Address the three key elements of reading fluency in science instruction.

What the Research Says

Hudson, Lane, and Pullen (2005) have done a wonderful job of dissecting and defining the most important elements of reading fluency. They explain the concepts of accuracy in word decoding of connected text, automaticity in recognizing words (plain old word identification), and appropriate use of prosody (expressive reading characteristics) or the use of oral expression in reading aloud. As reading fluency is one of the defining characteristics of good readers, the researchers also link these skills as reliable indicators and predictors of comprehension problems. They go on to explore the links between reading accuracy and proficiency, reading rate and reading proficiency, and prosody and reading proficiency. Furthermore, they explore various assessment techniques for accuracy, rate, prosody, and overall fluency. Finally, they examine the various instructional methods.

Rasinski (2006) critiques the work of Hudson et al. (2005) by validating much of what they had to say but expressing some concerns about instructional priorities implied in their article. Hasbrouck and Tindal (2006) simply examine the use of oral frequency reading norms as an assessment tool for reading teachers. They feel that everyone associated with schools today needs to be aware of the increasing requirements for number- or data-driven student performance accountability. They go on to examine the use of assessments in oral reading fluency and its various components.

Classroom Applications

Learning about new science words and being able to incorporate them into writing and discourse is a key element in overall science literacy. Accuracy in word decoding, automaticity in recognizing words, and appropriate use of prosody or meaningful oral expression is the pathway to science content comprehension. If these skills are mastered, the students' limited intellectual or cognitive resources can be used for greater comprehension, which is the higher order thinking goal of fluency. Rasinski (2006) takes issue with teaching these three skills separately and feels that this type of instruction requires precious extra time out of the instructional day. He feels that some of the activities focus only on gains in reading rates or reading faster for the sake of just reading faster, and indicates that classroom practice needs to unify accuracy, automaticity, and prosodic reading methods.

So where does that leave teachers? You might be able to clinically engage younger students in separate instructional activities to strengthen these elements of fluency, but you pay a price for it. Students lose their motivation and incentive as you take the comprehension and meaning out of science reading. Repeated reading is a common strategy for increasing fluency. However, the older the student, the less likely she or he will be motivated to read using this method. Would you want to improve your reading rate and fluency by using a repeated reading strategy? These isolated strategies would not be very motivating for adult literacy classes either. It's like doing basketball or soccer drills in isolation and never engaging in a motivating, authentic game.

Rasinski (2006) makes some good suggestions for fluency instruction. It is best described as authentic instruction and fits well in the content areas. He suggests engaging students in performance of passages that combine all three instructional goals. Any type of performance requires repeated reading, practice, or rehearsal. He goes on to say that if performance is the incentive to practice, then what kind of texts lend themselves to expressive oral performance? Many types of texts are important yet offer a limited number of opportunities for expressive interpretations. As he points out, there are a specific number of texts meant to be performed and can be considered easy to perform. Songs, poetry, lyrics, plays, scripts (theater, movie, TV), monologues, and other types of oral presentations work well for expressive oral reading and mastery of meaning. These strategies expose students to a wider range of reading material and also motivate them to master the elements of fluency and comprehension. Unfortunately, these strategies don't lend themselves to science textbook reading. This is where science teachers can get creative.

In addition to textbooks, there are many books that feature first person narrative. If you can find dialogue from noted scientists, students can be asked to role-play using the reading to describe and discuss the work of these famous scientists whose ideas contributed to current textbooks. There are many role-play activities that can be used to apply Rasinski's (2006) ideas on reading expression.

Rasinski (2006) states that his purpose was to reinforce the recommendations of Hudson et al. (2005) that repeated reading was a key instructional strategy. To this notion, he adds that it should also be meaningful and motivating and provide expressive oral potential. We should be looking for text and activities that bring these ideas together to keep reading motivating and important in the students' lives and also serve to cement meaningful and important ideas enhancing retention of science concepts.

Finally, you should recognize that fiction dominates much of what students are asked to read and write in secondary schools. Science reading and writing is very different, and it would be a mistake for science teachers not to stress reading and writing skills in their own content area. Make reading and writing skills part of your grading, and develop point values for these skills to help motivate students. Teachers are always tempted to teach science around poor reading and writing skills, thinking that just transferring science content is more important, especially in this era of high-stakes testing. However, you should value reading and writing skills and weight your assessment accordingly. This practice will let students know that you recognize how reading and writing skills will affect them after they leave your class. College and university placement tests, including the SAT, are high-stakes sorting devices that separate those with good reading skills from those without those skills.

Precautions and Possible Pitfalls

In regard to Rasinski's (2006) recommendations for reading performance, keep in mind that a teacher first has to create a safe environment and a trusting relationship with his or her students. Many students with reading problems simply won't want to risk the social consequences of a public performance. While Rasinski touted the success of reading performance as an instructional tool, he failed to talk about the social factors involved in this type of activity. An empathetic teacher will need to use all of his or her skills to build an environment where students are willing to take very personal risks.

Sources

Hasbrouck, J., & Tindal, G. A. (2006). Oral reading fluency norms: A valuable assessment tool for reading teachers. *The Reading Teacher, 59*(7), 636–644.

Hudson, R. F., Lane, H. B., & Pullen, P. C. (2005). Reading fluency assessment and instruction: What, why, and how? *The Reading Teacher, 58*(8), 702–714.

Rasinski, T. (2006). Reading fluency instruction: Moving beyond accuracy, automaticity, and prosody. *The Reading Teacher, 59*(7), 704–706.

> ☑ *Strategy 60: Use scaffolding to improve science reading comprehension.*

What the Research Says

Kathleen Clark and Michael Graves (2005) maintain that scaffolding plays a vital role in developing a student's reading comprehension. They define scaffolding as a temporary supportive structure teachers create to assist students in accomplishing a task they probably could not have completed alone, and it is grounded in Vygotsky's (1978) social constructivist view of learning in which a child's development first appears in collaboration with an adult. According to Clark and Graves (2005), what makes scaffolding an effective teaching technique is that it helps keep a task whole, while students learn to understand and manage the individual parts, without being too overwhelmed by the whole.

Classroom Applications

Clark and Graves (2005) describe different types of scaffolding that may be useful for reading teachers. Dissecting and learning this type of instruction strategy can be very useful in the science classroom and also serve as formative assessment. Two examples are detailed below:

Moment-to-Moment Verbal Scaffolding

Here, the teacher prompts his or her students by asking probing questions. According to Clark and Graves (2005), teachers must consider two things while scaffolding in such a manner:

- How their instructional talk moves students closer to the goal, and
- How they can use students' responses to make them more aware of the mental processes in which they are engaged.

Instructional Frameworks That Foster Content Learning

These frameworks are used to guide and improve students' understanding as they read and may or may not include moment-to-moment verbal scaffolding. Here, teachers use the strategy of questioning the author. For example, Clark and Graves (2005) suggest that teachers could ask students the following questions:

- What do you think the textbook author means by that?
- How does that connect with what the author has already told us?
- How did the textbook author work that out for us?
- Did the textbook author explain it clearly?
- What's missing or should be elaborated on?
- What more do we need to find out to fully understand?
- Is the content of the reading evidence based, or does it come across as opinion or anecdotal?
- How could the author improved the credibility of the writing?

In science, authors routinely infer a level of validity or confidence in their writing. Students often assign high validity to text just because something is in print. It's always a good idea to help students develop a range of analytical skills to assess the validity of a variety of print material and digital text. Such instructional strategies are especially important in high school, where students read a range of science writing from primary science literature to secondary science writing, from trade magazines to the science sections of newspapers. The Internet also provides a variety of science writing, with mixed credibility. Students need to learn to ask," Is the writer credible, or is bias built into the reading?" Reading and writing in science are very different from reading and writing creatively. Students need to know the difference, and science teachers are in the best position to help them learn it.

Precautions and Potential Pitfalls

Teachers should be aware that, during the planning phase of scaffolding, they must consider all of their students' strengths and weaknesses and who will be doing the reading, the reading selection itself, and the purpose of the reading. It is important that the teacher create some prereading, during-reading, and post-reading specialized activities designed to help students in reaching those purposes; otherwise, the activity may not be as effective as it could be. In addition, teachers should be able to provide enough support for students to succeed but not so much that the teachers do all the work—not an easy balance to maintain.

Also, it is common to be working with students with so little reading confidence that your probing turns into a lecture. It is important to facilitate reading success and to keep the students focused on making sense of the text themselves, rather than having you do it for them.

Sources

Clark, K., & Graves, M. (2005). Scaffolding students' comprehension of text. *The Reading Teacher, 58*, 570–580.

Vygotsky, L. S. (1978). *Mind in society: The development of higher mental processes.* Cambridge, MA: Harvard University Press.

Strategy 61: Consider reading as inquiry with primary literature.

What the Research Says

The May 2009 issue of the *Journal of Research in Science Education* is completely devoted to the idea that the language of school science and the language of science, as it is practiced, are widely divergent. This can be traced back, in a general sense, to a simple and generic view of reading, writing, and discourse that prevails in science and other content areas. This issue is devoted to an effort to elevate communication, especially science reading into the realm of inquiry, communicating, and generally thinking and reasoning like a scientist.

For example, Phillips and Norris (2009) explain, "Our position is simple to state: When scientists read, they are doing inquiry. Reading as inquiry should be part of school science instruction." Based on the importance of language in science and the role of language in capturing and communicating the essence of the nature of scientific reasoning, they recommend the use of adapted primary literature as curriculum and instruction. In this way, they feel science teachers can illustrate the notion of reading as inquiry and also more closely align the communication and critical thinking elements of the everyday lives of scientists. Phillips and Norris consider reading a constructive process and hold that meaning must be inferred from the text by forging links between the reader's background knowledge and the text.

In the same issue, Osborne (2009) and Ford (2009) both welcome the challenges to the established notions of what it means to learn science and see the value of adapted primary literature, but are more critical of the potential of its use as an instructional strategy. They discuss the strategy's potential pitfalls and precautions for teachers and students.

Classroom Applications

The basic assumption presented by the researchers referenced for this strategy is that the concept of using appropriate, adapted primary science literature during science instruction is a good idea. Doing so adds a level of argumentation and authentic inquiry writing and discourse found in the practice and art of science. The researchers felt that the nature of scientific reasoning and inquiry are missing from science textbooks, classroom instruction, and communication. Below is some of the logic and reasoning for a potential or partial switch to structuring adaptive primary literature for your students.

Before delving into the potential merits of adapted primary literature, let's look at the types of communication activities in which scientists engage. Tenopir and King (2004) found that scientists read during 23% of their total work time and that number increases for the most high-achieving scientists. When the activities of writing and speaking are included, scientists are active in communication activities 58% of their total work time. Scientists also rated reading as essential to their work and creative stimulation. While the "hands-on" movement is valid and much of science is hands-on, lab-based, and field-based, it is also conceptual and more concerned with ideas than data gathering. The minds-on activities of reading, writing, and speaking are just as important.

Now let's turn to the way students interact with science reading, writing, and communicating in the classroom. Most science textbooks frame science in an expository style, rarely provide proof for their content, present statements as accredited facts with no hedging or discussions, and provide no argumentative function resembling how science is conducted. They are basically nonfiction accounts of factual information. Any tentativeness or uncertainly would be hard to discern in most textbooks, and the process of scientific knowledge generation is represented as a linear procedure rather than reasoning from evidence. The argumentation that is so much a part of science is removed, and the messy road to discovery is sanitized to a point where the true science is unrecognizable. The science behind the knowledge is missing. Furthermore, much of what goes on in science classroom instruction and activities today also looks and sounds like the language within the textbook. Finally, discourse and writing in the science classroom also tend to be a regurgitation of passages from textbooks students have found or committed to memory. These activities are often confined to reinforcing textbook concepts and vocabulary.

In contrast, let's consider the language of primary literature. The following types of information are most commonly found in primary research reports or the literature:

- The motivation for the research and usually a clear thesis statement or question(s)
- Reported past relevant results

- Reported limitation of past research
- A description of what was done
- Methods and an argument for the suitability of the techniques or experimental designed used
- Explained observations and results
- Conjecture of what might be happening
- A summary of challenged or alternative interpretations
- Conclusions, limitations, and the potential for further research

In its totality, an entire research paper is a series of arguments for the following:

- Conducting the research
- The methods used that made other possible designs implausible
- Supporting the interpretation of the results and findings the authors and researchers favored

Arguments are shaped in science papers to support given conclusions. Most argumentation in primary literature is not presented as absolute truth. Peer review opinion and response could range from true or probable to uncertain or false. Not all statements have the same implied truth status.

We can see that reading, writing, and speaking about science are essential to science. However, as teachers, we need to look at the quality of those activities and try to build a more clear alignment between the classroom and the way science is practiced. Many students and parents hold on to a simple view of reading focused on word recognition and concept identification. All of the researchers cited here agree that in the science classroom, reading, writing, and discourse should aspire to be best thought of as an inquiry process. Science teachers need to begin to consider the notion of reading as inquiry within their curriculum. Adapted primary literature, written or rewritten so as to be understandable by secondary school students, is more like the language of science than the language of the typical school science classroom. It is authentic and engages students in the critical thinking and inquiry, reasoning, and rhetorical practices of science. It provides a more balanced image of the practices in which science practitioners engage. It also allows teachers to scaffold students' thinking as they interact with the uncertainty, messiness, strengths, and weaknesses of research, scientific claims, and the development of new information.

Where can science teachers find primary literature? Colleges and universities now provide access to e-journals. Most subscribe to hundreds of journals in many disciplines. Creative teachers can begin there. Also, a quick Internet search using the key words "classic science papers" yielded "Profiles in Sciences" at the National Library of Medicine featuring all of the classic papers from many scientists and selected classic papers from the history of chemistry and horticulture science. A search through the

Francis Crick link produced all his classic papers from the 1950s regarding the development of the modern view of DNA. Searching this way helps teachers find the real classic and important papers from the history of science. Also, another quick search of Amazon.com produced books with collections of classic papers in selected disciplines.

Potential Precautions and Pitfalls

The difficulty of adapting and utilizing written text from primary research journals still needs to be researched. It is also not clear if all science disciplines offer the same opportunity to adapt primary literature. Within very sophisticated papers, adoption may be beyond the realm of the content expectations of the national standards. Teachers are the most important factor in the adoption of these types of strategies, and they must understand all facets of instruction in order to scaffold pedagogy and help students recognize the components of inquiry and argumentation and content. Finally, and most important, reading these papers needs to fit within the overall instruction commonly found in the science classroom.

Sources

Ford, D. J. (2009). Promises and challenges for the use of adapted primary literature in science curricula: commentary. *Journal of Research in Science Education, 39,* 385–390.

Osborne, J. (2009). The potential of adapted primary literature (APL) for learning: A response. *Journal of Research in Science Education, 39,* 397–403.

Phillips, L. M., & Norris, S. P. (2009). Bridging the gap between the language of science and the language of school science through the use of adapted primary literature. *Journal of Research in Science Education, 39,* 313–319.

Tenopir, C., & King, D. (2004). *Communication patterns of engineers.* Hoboken, NY: Wiley.

> ☑ **Strategy 62: Focus on developing scientific literacy and student reasoning.**

What the Research Says

 Lee, Lewis, Adaamson, Maeerten-Rivera, and Secada (2007) investigated urban elementary teachers' knowledge and practices regarding the teaching of science to English language learners (ELLs). Within a larger five-year research project, 38 third-grade teachers were involved in the first-year implementation of a professional development intervention that involved curriculum units and teacher workshops. The research and the intervention focused and examined four instructional areas:

- Teacher knowledge of science content
- Teaching science for understanding
- Teaching science for inquiry
- Teacher support for English language learner development

This study used questionnaires, classroom observations, and post-observation interviews to measure performance in these areas. The results suggested the following:

- The teachers' science content knowledge was generally accurate within the boundaries of the curriculum content.
- Teachers taught to promote scientific understanding, and students were engaged in deep understanding of some science concepts.
- Teachers reported teaching science integrating scientific inquiry, yet students rarely engaged in the process of science beyond basic skills or tool use.
- Teachers did not generally reflect on their practices involving scientific inquiry.
- Teachers often confused "hands-on" as scientific inquiry and didn't engage students in more "minds-on" activities. While teachers highlighted "hands-on" activities, students were less likely to engage in the intellectual work of data collection, analysis, or looking for explanations based on evidence.
- Teachers in this study serving ELLs generally supported the goals of English for Speakers of Other Languages (ESOL) instruction, English language acquisition, and support strategies.

In another article, Medina-Jerez, Clark, Medina, and Ramirez-Marin (2007) cite a rich bank of research supporting the notion that native English speaking and linguistically diverse students are equally capable of learning scientific concepts and processes.

Classroom Applications

The tension between providing preservice science teachers with appropriate content knowledge in addition to pedagogical knowledge is an ongoing problem. Because of the No Child Left Behind Act (NCLB) and the many forms of standardized testing and accountability, science is often taught as a body of facts with curriculum and instructional methods that focus on breadth of coverage rather than on a deeper knowledge and understanding of important concepts. Also, despite reform efforts to develop students' knowledge of inquiry practices, science is still experienced as knowledge that comes from a book rather than through inquiry. This was very evident in the cited research and is the premise of this strategy.

The following are three specific ideas supporting scientific inquiry. Keep in mind that true open-ended scientific inquiry features true unknowns with results and outcomes that may be ambiguous and suspect. Teachers need to know and be comfortable with the process of authentic inquiry.

- Use more open-ended science projects as a vehicle for developing practice-based scientific literacy. This fosters scientific curiosity and helps students begin to question the validity of situations and information they encounter and experience throughout life.
- If you need help creating structure for students to engage in more authentic inquiry, consider seeking out scientists and mentors or other outreach science programs to help you with engaging your students. You can also orchestrate outside experiences that incorporate community-based professionals.
- Incorporate and model in carefully planned ways the processes of science in the lessons you teach.

A simple activity to help students of many ages begin to understand how science works is to involve students in the process of asking questions. Take a walk with them and ask them to start writing questions down about anything that comes to mind. Older students can usually compile a larger number of questions than younger students. Teachers then have a bank of questions to explore with their students. It's hard to predict the questions; however, it is likely that some of them would make good science questions. A good science question is one that can be turned into a hypothesis and investigated through observation or experimentation. Other questions might not make good science questions. Some questions can't be answered utilizing science processes. Some questions exhibit potential answers that might be faith based. Other questions might require a much more complex investigation and can't be done within the class. However, there usually are a few questions that can be answered in the class context. Once good science questions are identified, students can be engaged in thinking about how they could construct a model for answering the questions and validating or disproving their hypothesis.

Precautions and Possible Pitfalls

Inquiry teaching can be challenging at all age levels and can take more work and time than doing a simple chapter march through a book. This is especially true for those just beginning to use inquiry as a way to structure instruction. Students usually need to be out of their seats, there is usually more setup and cleanup time, and all students want your individual attention. Don't give up! We want students to adopt critical thinking skills and a strong knowledge base, but we also want students to be curious and motivated to engage in the scientific process and understand how scientific knowledge is generated and validated.

Sources

Lee, O., Lewis, S., Adaamson, K., Maeerten-Rivera, J., & Secada, W. G. (2007). Urban elementary school teachers' knowledge and practices in teaching science to English language learners. *Science Education, 92*, 733–758.

Medina-Jerez, W., Clark, D., Medina, A., & Ramirez-Marin, F. (2007). Science for all ELLs: Rethinking our approach. *The Science Teacher, 74*(3), 52–56.

Strategy 63: Use paraphrasing to promote reading comprehension in science textbooks.

What the Research Says

Contrary to some opinions that the word *paraphrasing* implies students copying from encyclopedias and changing only a few words to write a report, Candace Fisk and Beth Hurst (2003) maintain that the technique can be used to promote reading comprehension. This is because paraphrasing reinforces such reading skills as identifying the main idea and finding supporting details, while integrating such forms of communication as reading, writing, listening, and speaking. Therefore, Fisk and Hurst suggest that when teachers first introduce the concept of paraphrasing to students, they should clearly explain what it means and why it is useful in promoting reading comprehension. Students must be told that paraphrasing is a general rewriting in their own words that maintains the original meaning. Students must therefore be able to keep the voice of the original author (comical, serious, sarcastic), and this process helps students identify characters in the reading.

Classroom Applications

Fisk and Hurst (2003) offer the following four steps for using paraphrasing to promote reading comprehension:

1. The students read a text silently and after vocabulary problems are clarified, they are asked to identify the main idea of the text. They can also be asked specific questions related to the text's tone and style.

2. After they have become familiar with the main idea of the text, students read it again to take notes, this time looking for main ideas and supporting details but avoiding using the same vocabulary as in the text.

3. When they have finished taking notes, they turn in copies of the actual text they were reading, so they have to rely only on their own words but are instructed to retain the original voice in writing a paraphrase.

4. When they have finished their paraphrase, students form pairs and share their writing. They address the following questions: How are the paraphrases similar? How are they different? How is the author's voice communicated in the two paraphrases?

This approach takes reading to a level that could be considered formative assessment. It also integrates reading into the day-to-day science curriculum well beyond just assigning pages or chapters to read, and it ensures that most students utilize the textbook content.

Precautions and Potential Pitfalls

Although Fisk and Hurst (2003) point out that paraphrasing can be used with upper elementary, middle, and high school students, teachers should be cautious about using the technique before students are ready. It may overload their processing systems because it involves all four modes of communication: reading, writing, speaking, and listening. Teachers must be aware of their students' developmental levels in reading before using paraphrasing, and when they do incorporate it, they should do so only along with other strategies to promote comprehension.

Source

Fisk, C., & Hurst, B. (2003). Paraphrasing for comprehension. *The Reading Teacher,* 57(2), 182–185.

 Strategy 64: Utilize think-alouds to reveal students' thought processes while reading.

What the Research Says

 Think-alouds (thinking out loud strategy) remove the cloak of mystery surrounding the comprehension process as teachers and students verbalize their own thoughts while reading orally.

Think-alouds require a student to stop an activity periodically, reflect on how a text is being processed and understood, and relate orally what reading strategies are being employed or not being employed.

Baumann, Jones, and Seifert-Kessell (1993) conducted research with fourth-grade students to determine if thinking-aloud techniques are an effective tool for helping students learn to monitor their comprehension. Results from a series of quantitative assessments and in-depth, individual student interviews led the researchers to conclude that think-aloud instruction was highly effective in helping students acquire a broad range of strategies (typical of highly effective readers) to enhance understanding of text and to deal with comprehension difficulties. Their research found that using think-alouds helped students develop an ability to monitor their reading comprehension and employ fix-up strategies when they detected comprehension difficulties. The researchers also recommend that students participate in the social construction of think-alouds, either as part of the lessons or within lessons (see also Sainbury, 2003).

Classroom Applications

As the phrase implies, "thinking aloud" is a great strategy to use to slow down the instructional process and let students get a good look and feel for how skilled readers construct meaning from a text, especially a complex science book and other activities. Teachers model thinking aloud to explain the strategies they use as they read. Students think out loud to show each other how to understand what is read or happening in the instructional activity. Thinking aloud by the teacher and more capable students provides novice learners with a way to observe "expert thinking," which is usually hidden. Many self-directed students developed comprehension skills implicitly by simply doing a lot of reading of all sorts of texts or paying attention to the details of an assignment or activity. Therefore, when we teach at the elementary and secondary levels, we must take what we know and do *implicitly* and make it *explicit* for students, especially for struggling students in all cognitive modalities. Teachers and students use the think-aloud strategy to monitor and improve comprehension and share the secrets of reading and learning for meaning and understanding. The think-aloud, by its very nature, is a great formative assessment tool.

Below is a beginning list of what skilled readers do implicitly; we need to help our science students learn and apply these skills and strategies on a regular basis to improve their interactions with text, especially expository reading.

1. *Explore a student's prior knowledge.* Whenever effective students and readers approach new media, text, or other information, they consciously (or unconsciously) summon any information or background they have to

relate to the topic, idea, people or characters, setting, historical context, author, similar events, and so forth. This process provides a foundation for the reading; it helps us to make sense of the new media. Teachers should help explore this and model it for their students. It will help you assess their cognitive level of understanding about any given topic.

2. *Develop goals and objectives for activities and especially reading.* Establishing what they expect to get out of reading is another common step for skilled readers. Depending on the purpose, skilled readers adjust their reading to meet the chosen goal. Making students aware of the reason, purpose, or goal for the reading is a crucial initial step in helping them successfully interact with any media, directions, or their own writing. Again, this is something in which teachers can model and engage their students by guiding them to learning the technique.

3. *Decode the media into meanings and words.* These are the basic reading skills that our children *begin* to learn at the elementary level, but secondary teachers must continue to work on them as the texts and multimedia become more varied and sophisticated. Decoding text into words and meaning can also involve using strategies to define unfamiliar words with the help of context clues or word parts (e.g., prefixes, suffixes, roots).

4. *Identify, engage, and connect with the media and its context.* As skilled and effective readers move through a text and other media, they constantly compare and contrast their knowledge and experience with what is presented and revealed in the text. This process of personal reflection on the media improves the reader's comprehension and understanding. Skillful readers often ask themselves (consciously or unconsciously) the following questions as they read: How is this piece of media like or unlike something I know or have experienced? How can I relate the ideas here to other texts or experiences I have read? How is this media (and the ideas presented in it) useful or relevant to me? These are all good questions to share with your students.

5. *Engage intellectually and make predictions.* From the moment skilled readers pick up a text or other form of media, they start making predictions about it. They look at all the parts of the text—the title, table of contents, dedication, number of pages, font size, photographs, commentary on the back or book jacket, and so on—and they begin to engage in making predictions regarding the text. As their thinking progresses, they continue to alter their view in response to new information. They make assumptions about its usefulness and how relevant and interesting it will be for them, and decide how they are going to engage the reading.

6. *Visualize what you read.* One of the most powerful tools that skilled readers develop is their ability to imagine and visualize what they are reading. Mental pictures and intellectual role-playing create the setting and characters, in short, they visually immerse the reader in the world of

the story. In an abstract nonfiction text, the reader may create a mindset that helps him or her to keep track of the information and organize it.

7. *Engage in self-questioning and mental exploration and challenges.* Good readers view the writer as the other half of a good conversation. They make a habit of asking all types of questions as they react to reading. They question the media, their own responses, the opinions, and other reactions to the reading. These may be questions that probe for a deeper understanding or simply questions that voice their internal confusion and need for clarity. When explicitly taught, this is a skill that often shocks some of your less-skilled students; they often think it is time to stop reading or thinking when they are frustrated or confused, assuming that good readers rarely have these problems. It is a great lesson to see others dig for understanding.

8. *Monitor understanding and summarize.* Successful students collect significant points as they navigate the media. Along the way, they drop certain facts and mental constructs into memory that help them make sense of the assignment or activity. If something doesn't make sense, they may decide to let it go, hoping it will become clear later or pause and take a closer look. They may take a step back to clarify and understand before moving on.

9. *Use or apply what has been read.* Both during and after the reading, skillful readers are constantly asking themselves how the information relates to their lives or how could it be used. This goes back to a reader's goals and objectives. When students are reading a text or other form of media to fulfill the demands of a goal or objective, they may consider how they will apply information from the text to complete an assigned task or fill other intellectual needs. Discovering how reading applies to our lives and how readers identify with the information is essential for engaging students in text and dialogue. Students often need help discovering the ways in which they can reflect on how the reading relates to them. Teachers really need to help science students here. Connecting the topics to their lives takes skill.

The goal here is to build these points into all instruction routinely and set them in the student's mind as expectations for all reading and thinking assignments.

Precautions and Potential Pitfalls

It is very important to decide how to use the information in this strategy. The ability and reading and skill levels of your class will determine how much or which parts of this strategy you want to use. If you have too many skilled students and readers, you will lose them with a simple or boring text or activity. On the other hand, many times students want to share and discuss their experiences. Skilled and success-ful students usually like to exchange ideas regarding a provocative activ-ity, book, or bit of text. Ultimately, teachers will need to decide the role and nature of this strategy with each individual class.

It also may be a good time to help students develop guidelines for classroom discussion and discourse. Often, the least-skilled students need help finding their voice and confidence in classroom discussions. You don't want the aggressive students to overpower their voices.

Sources

Baumann, J. F., Jones, L. A., & Seifert-Kessell, N. (1993). Using think alouds to enhance children's comprehension monitoring abilities. *The Reading Teacher* 47(3), 188–193.

Sainbury, M. (2003). Thinking aloud: Children's interactions with text. *Reading, Literacy, and Language*, 37(3), 131–135.

 Strategy 65: Select commercial reading programs that can improve scientific literacy.

What the Research Says

 Norris and colleagues (2007) examined a wide-ranging set of studies designed to assess the potential of commercially avail-able reading programs to help teach science literacy in the ele-mentary context. Specifically, the investigation focused on these areas:

- The proportion of selections in the programs that contained science content and the amount and accuracy of science content that is in those selections
- The overall context of the science that is portrayed, the areas and the major concepts of science covered, the text and visual features used to communicate the science
- The pedagogy and assessment techniques recommended within the programs

The authors found a variety of scientific genres and content in about one-fifth of the selections, and they determined that the content was gen-erally accurate. Their conclusions support the notion that commercial reading programs have changed and are no longer dominated by literary-related texts and references that contain very little science text, references, and science-related curriculum. This investigation concluded that there is considerable potential in commercial reading programs to foster science literacy and meet science instruction goals; however, the findings also show that the recommended instructional strategies and assessment techniques packaged with the programs do little to help realize this potential. The major complaint centered on instruction and assessment techniques that are better suited to literary genres and not the expository writing and reading techniques found in the science realm.

Classroom Applications

For those of you that focus on specific science content mandates in your curriculum, here are a few thoughts on the role literacy plays in the real world of science (Norris & Phillips, 2003). Scientists do lots of reading. Tenopir and King (2004) reported data that show scientists spending two-thirds of their informational input time engaged in reading activities rather than in other forms of transfer of knowledge. The same study found that scientists read during 23% of their work time. When you add speaking, listening, and writing to the mix, they spend 58% of their time in communication activities. Tenopir and King (2004) go on to state that these numbers have changed little over the last 60 years. Furthermore, they report that scientists rate reading as essential to their research and rate reading as their primary source of creative stimulation. It's important that teachers at all levels take this information to heart. We are all responsible for teaching content-appropriate reading and writing skills within our own specific content discipline.

Often, teachers are so focused on their specific content curriculum and mandates that they forget how important it is to stress reading and writing skills as curriculum in a discipline-appropriate way within their instructional planning. The overriding premise here for teachers is that science literacy is a very important specialty within all areas of science and needs to be taught and learned in all grade levels. Content literacy includes reading and writing specific to the discipline of science. Teachers should consider the cited statistics as guidelines in deciding the proportion literacy activities should play in their instructional planning.

Here is the problem: High school and middle school teachers often make the assumption that their students come with the ability to read and comprehend scientific and other expository text without specific mentoring. Content teachers also make assumptions regarding the students' ability to write in an expository style and structure as opposed to a more literary style of expression. These teachers also often believe that their students have learned to read and write in elementary school and their job is to "assign" reading and writing, not to teach it.

A basic tip is as follows: If you have a choice or input in selecting a commercial reading program for your school or class, see it as an opportunity to strengthen your elementary science program. For those of you who are disappointed that we have not included the program recommendations from the research, keep in mind that the investigation cited was published in 2007 and the research was done earlier. By the time you read this strategy, the reviewed programs could be over five years old, outdated, or out of print. Your major job is to be a more informed consumer when evaluating and assessing what's out there when and where you shop for commercial programs. You want to find programs that balance informational or nonliterary text with fictional narrative in the early elementary grades. You also want the evaluation and assessment strategies in the programs to reflect informational text and content, along with the fictional literary side.

We want students to read science critically and learn to avoid personal bias and opinion that is not based on the text content. There are also those who believe that because a student can simply read a body of text that he or she will comprehend it. Science in text form also needs to make sense to the students. The acts of constructing, interpreting, selecting, and critiquing text are as much a part of science as collecting, interpreting, and challenging data. The idea is to identify what scientists do when they read and teach students to learn those skills. Scientists take into account all relevant information, develop and apply criteria for judging the adequacy of interpretations and determining whether alternative interpretations are inconsistent with know facts, and finally whether the proposed interpretation is plausible. This is defined as reading inquiry, and therefore, reading is inquiry and is composed of analyzing, critiquing, and interpreting text. The reader infers meaning by integrating the text information with relevant background or content knowledge before drawing inferences and conclusions.

If involving students in inquiry is important and inquiry is a huge part of scientific literacy (which it is), then reading and writing in a science context are important and need to become part of the science curriculum at all grade levels. Being able to read when the text and the content is science is what is required to engage intellectually in public discourse and debate, as important science and technology issues filter through the media and society in general.

These are all arguments you can take to the table when deciding on any commercial reading program. The teacher is key to fully developing the potential offered by any reading program and scientific material!

Precautions and Possible Pitfalls

Ongoing dialogue between literacy specialists or reading teachers and science educators is needed to fully clarify the value of integrating the types of content embedded in any reading program. According to the research, commercial reading programs may have flaws and exhibit little usefulness in developing scientific literacy even when scientific material is included. Reading specialists may not recognize whether the material is beneficial. Science educators and teachers responsible for science instruction need to be proactive in assessing the usefulness of any commercial program. They need to realize that just because there is science content in a commercial program, it may not be taught any better than within a stand-alone science curriculum.

Sources

Norris, S. P., & Phillips, L. M. (2003). How literacy in its fundamental sense is central to scientific literacy. *Science Education, 87,* 224–240.

Norris, S. P., Phillips, L. M., Smith, M. L., Guilbert, S. M., Stange, D. M., Baker, J. J., & Weber, A. C. (2007). Learning to read scientific text: do elementary school commercial reading programs help? *Science Education, 92*(5), 765–798.

Tenopir, C., & King, D. W. (2004). *Communication patterns of engineers.* New York: IEEE Press and John Wiley & Sons.

Strategy 66: Use a variety of print materials to inspire student reading and writing.

What the Research Says

 Bracey (2001) discusses the findings of Nell Duke from Michigan State University in her research analysis of how reading is taught differently in low-socioeconomic status (SES) and high-SES first-grade classrooms. The most significant difference was the variety of extended texts and activities that relate meaningfully to those texts. Although the research indicated little difference in the time spent on reading between the two groups, the variety of print material presented in the high-SES setting was substantial. In the high-SES classrooms, magazines, newspaper articles, and text materials were displayed prominently with student-authored work on specific topics. In the low-SES classrooms, worksheets were the primary form of print material, and few examples of extended student writing were present. Bracey also noted that low-SES school libraries had 40% fewer books available and seldom added to their numbers during the school year.

Classroom Applications

Chances are that the only science reading students do is conducted in the context of your science class and involves the textbook only. Science filters through society and culture through media outlets including magazines, newspapers, and the Internet. There are writers that make their living keeping tabs on the scientific community. Many times, this type of contemporary writing includes historical, moral, and ethical factors that students might not find in textbooks. Also, much of the time, this type of writing is inherently more interesting and motivating for students to read.

Teachers need to ensure that the opportunity for reading a variety of print materials is available for their students regardless of grade level or content area. Research indicates that the more students read, the better their skills develop, and yet reading the standard classroom text often leaves students bored and unengaged, particularly if the text is outdated by student standards. Teachers need to work with school librarians, the Internet, other teachers, parents, community members, and the students themselves to provide a wide range of print material beyond the basic textbook.

Many local newspapers have programs for free newspaper delivery to local classrooms. Often included with these papers are curricular activities that teachers can use or adapt to their own curricular needs. Many newspaper articles are short and provide a more motivating context for class content. Content and its relevant "real-world" applications will be more easily accessible for the struggling reader. Even comics and editorial cartoons provide opportunities for students to derive meaning from printed material.

Grinell Smith (2008) wrote about how he asks his preservice teachers to select a book to read from a list of science-related books with only one request: that they enjoy the book they select. The list Smith found was put together by Boyce Rensberger, Director of the Knight Fellowships. Rensberger admits the list is more offhand than authoritative or exhaustive and considers his list a work in progress. Smith goes on to state that there is something for everyone regardless of their level or background in science.

Teachers may find these books useful for professional pleasure reading and also as supplemental reading material for their classes. Of course, each suggested book comes with a different level of complexity, and teachers will need to evaluate how appropriate individual books are for their students. The original list can be found at http://web.mit.edu/knight-science/resources/science_books.html. It should also be noted that the National Science Teachers Association offers an annual list of outstanding science books at http://www.nsta.org/publications/ostb/.

Precautions and Potential Pitfalls

Many of the items listed above and each of the books on Rensberger's list can be used to supplement chapters in a range of science textbooks and science disciplines. Instead of just adding to the amount of content to be taught or text to be read by students, teachers might consider these nontextbooks as a replacement for some sections in a traditional textbook. Viewing them as replacements for parts of a textbook is less intimidating for young readers. Generally, the textbook content within these suggested books is placed in a more interesting and motivating context. If this is true, your students might find them more interesting and motivating than the textbook.

It is important that teachers remain mindful of school and district policy regarding materials that can be used in the classroom. Some districts allow anything, and others have strict guidelines. Some districts have well-defined boundaries for acceptability of materials. It is very important that teachers make themselves aware of these policies prior to introducing controversial materials to their classrooms. Teachers should screen the materials they bring to the classroom to ensure they are appropriate for the students and the curriculum.

You will also have to decide how you can provide these books to students. With tight budgets, there are no easy answers as to which books to consider or how to afford them.

Sources

Bracey, G. W. (2001). Does higher tech require higher skills? *Phi Delta Kappan, 82*(9), 715–717.

Smith, G. (2008). Science books for professional pleasure reading. *Science and Children, 45*(9), 40–43.

Strategy 67: Expand vocabulary instruction to improve comprehension and motivation.

What the Research Says

In the larger scheme of literacy instruction, the vocabulary research done by Joshi (2005) and Harmon, Hedrick, and Wood (2005) stand out. Both Joshi and Harmon et al. explored vocabulary, revisiting its role within the literacy paradigm. Both feel that vocabulary development and the role it plays in reading-skills acquisition have received much less attention than decoding and comprehension strategies. Joshi goes on to state that there is a close relationship between vocabulary and comprehension; hence individuals with poor vocabulary have difficulty understanding written text. Carrying the idea further, students with poor vocabulary knowledge tend to read easier material and fewer books, and consequently, their vocabularies grow at a slower pace. In contrast, students with bigger vocabularies read more, comprehend better, and thus read still more, increasing their vocabularies (the Matthew effect). Joshi states that to prevent the Matthew effect from taking hold, vocabulary assessment and instruction need to be important components of reading programs, especially for the struggling readers.

A review of the literature on vocabulary instruction and its role within other literacy components is found in Rupley and Nichols (2005) and Yopp and Yopp (2006). They also explore the ebb and flow of vocabulary instruction in classrooms over the years as it has fallen in and out of favor.

Classroom Applications

Vocabulary instruction is a common activity in many science classrooms. We often question how effective and useful is it and how can we do it more effectively. A common theme underlying the cited research states that vocabulary instruction is important but an ignored teaching skill. The researchers go on to argue about the important relationship between vocabulary (the amount of words children are exposed to from very early years) and the many other instructional concepts related to literacy.

Joshi (2005) talks about the discrepancy between oral and reading vocabulary. In spite of large oral vocabularies (45,000 words for an average high school graduate), reading vocabularies are drastically smaller. According to Biemiller (1999), only about 300 words are learned in a year through direct vocabulary instruction.

Currently and frequently, vocabulary is taught by asking students to do some form of glossary search or definition search in the dictionary. Dictionary-based or rote-memory vocabulary instruction is noted for short-term retention in contrast to meaning-based approaches, which results in more lasting memory and better overall comprehension.

Examples of meaning-based alternatives beyond dictionary-based approaches (Joshi, 2005) are as follows:

- Instructors can embed targeted words in sentences and draw the student's attention to the context. Sentences with missing words could be utilized to have students find words from the context of the sentence supplied to them.
- If it fits your teaching style, the use of antonyms and synonyms can also make words meaningful.
- Again, if it fits your style and knowledge background, common morphemic roots can provide students with insights into word meanings. For example, if you know the meaning of "rupt" (to break), you can begin to give students the tools to unlock meaning with words such as *abrupt, interrupt, corrupt,* and *erupt.*
- Word origin, or etymology, also can offer paths to meaning-based strategies. The fact that words have a history you can share with students provides a context and a "hook" to begin to mentally attach a word to an authentic context. Old English or Anglo-Saxon words are common in elementary reading materials. These are high-frequency words, which comprise 15% of the English language and are acquired easily. The Greeks also gave us about 15% of English words and these tend to be specialized words found in the sciences. About 60% of English words come from Latin and are found everywhere and in every content area. Relating the stories behind the words helps give the words a "presence."

- A variety of word or concept mapping or webbing activities can be used to support the active processing of new words. Students can expand their vocabularies and begin to understand the concepts between words and context ideas. These activities and strategies can be used as part of a prereading activity, a during-reading activity, or a post-reading activity. In a prereading context, as a visual display, they serve to activate and begin to construct important concept ideas before the reading begins. These activities between the development of vocabulary and reading comprehension reinforce the connection between the two concepts. (See also Yopp and Yopp [2006] for a three-step process to help engage students in attacking and learning vocabulary in its correct context.)

Once you train yourself to teach from these strategies, you will offer your students a richer experience and a stronger "glue" for retaining the use of vocabulary words. Because fluent reading is largely determined by a reader's stock of sight words, it is logical to believe that stronger vocabulary knowledge will yield greater fluency in reading.

The common goal in these strategies is drawing the student's attention to word meanings. Words meaningful to students are more easily learned and retained than if they are only memorized. Knowing there is a gap between a student's receptive and expressive vocabulary, keep in mind that using words is more important than just knowing them. Teachers need to encourage their students to use as much of their receptive vocabulary as possible to help solidify the words in their memories.

For more strategies, information, and instructional tips on vocabulary, visit the Education Development Center's Literacy Matters website (http://www.literacymatters.org/). It is one of the largest collections of vocabulary-based teaching ideas on the Internet. There is also a "Learning Strategies Database" at http://www.muskingum.edu/~cal/database/content/genscience6.html that has activities and guidelines for teaching vocabulary in the sciences.

Precautions and Potential Pitfalls

Creating arbitrary vocabulary lists that have little to do with other learning in the class is not a good idea. If students are not actively engaged in individual use and discussion of words, you're working against students encountering words in a meaningful way. Teaching words and vocabulary strategies that are functionally important within a specific context, and in the context of their science textbooks, fosters vocabulary development and long-term retention.

Sources

Biemiller, A. (1999). *Language and reading success*. Cambridge, MA: Brookline Books.

Harmon, J. M., Hedrick, W. B., & Wood, K. D. (2005). Research in vocabulary instruction in the content areas: Implications for the struggling reader. *Reading & Writing Quarterly, 21,* 261–280.

Joshi, R. M. (2005). Vocabulary: A critical component of comprehension. *Reading & Writing Quarterly, 21,* 209–212.

Rupley, W. H., & Nichols, W. D. (2005). Vocabulary instruction for the struggling reader. *Reading & Writing Quarterly, 21,* 239–260.

Yopp, H. K., & Yopp, R. H. (2006). Primary students & informational texts. *Science and Children, 44*(3), 22–25.

Strategy 68: Use students' native languages in science literacy instruction.

What the Research Says

When reviewing research on the role that literacy in one's native language plays in literacy development, Klaudia Rivera (1999) found that instructional approaches to literacy should incorporate the learners' native language into instruction. Rivera suggests that learners may benefit from developing their native language literacy skills because they can transfer basic skills (e.g., in reading) from their first to their second language. She further suggests that literacy teachers should, in fact, promote bi-literacy in their classes.

Classroom Applications

Teachers who use the learners' native language as a positive influence on literacy acquisition must place their native language and cultural background and experiences at the center of the program. Teachers can achieve this by involving the students in generating materials for use in class and having them connect the literacy activities to their oral language, culture, and prior experiences. For example, teachers could develop a science theme within their discipline for the literacy curriculum and ask the learners to contribute to the theme by developing and producing a video documenting their views, experiences, and research on that theme. Teachers can use the learners' native language in beginning-level language classes as a means of helping students with basic vocabulary related to the project's theme. In this way, literacy in their native language and English are taught together, usually by a bilingual teacher. There are other ways in which young literacy learners can be instructed, such as keeping the learners in their native language literacy classes until they reach a proficient level of reading and then transferring them to ELL classes. The second method emphasizes literacy development first in the child's native language, which in turn can help literacy acquisition in English (Rivera, 1999).

Precautions and Potential Pitfalls

Because the learners' native language is used at the beginning literacy levels, the classes may need to be team taught with a bilingual teacher, so it is important to coordinate such lessons carefully by planning ahead and even practicing together before the lesson takes place. Depending on their level of English literacy proficiency, learners may need to stay in their native literacy classes until they have reached sufficient proficiency in reading and writing in English. Teachers must also be aware of what they are trying to achieve by using the learners' native language as a source of instruction: to develop literacy in both languages or literacy only in English.

Source

Rivera, K. (1999). From developing one's voice to making oneself heard: Affecting language policy from the bottom up. In T. Huebner & K. Davis (Eds.), *Sociopolitical perspectives on language policy and language planning in the USA* (pp. 333–346). Amsterdam: Benjamins.

9

Families and Science Instruction

Strategy 69: *Avoid the "blame game" mindset.*

What the Research Says

Thompson, Warren, and Carter (2004) looked at the impact of high school teacher attitudes and expectations on student achievement. The researchers wanted to identify the teachers in an underperforming, "urban-fringe" high school who were most likely to blame students and their parents for underachievement. Data were collected from the questionnaires of 121 teachers at a high school in southern California in 2002. Results of this study corroborate previous research about high school teachers. Sixty-four percent of the teachers agreed with the statement, "I believe that parents are largely to blame for students' low-achievement." Fifty-seven percent of the teachers agreed with the statement, "When students fail to pass a test or assignment, they are largely to blame." Also, it was found that teachers who blamed students also were the most likely to blame parents. The indications from this research are seen as a huge obstacle to reforming the relationship between home and school.

Applications

 Teachers in all disciplines size-up the demographics of their classes. One of the strengths of the Thompson et al. (2004) study is that it demonstrates that improving student achievement in underperforming schools is a challenging and complex task that must include the work of changing teachers' mindsets, beliefs, attitudes, and expectations about students and parents. When teachers become aware of the potential impact their attitudes have on student achievement, hopefully, they will do what is necessary not to communicate these messages to their students.

The results of the study suggest that there is a need for the individual teachers, administrators, professional developers, and reformers to shift from focusing solely on systemic change to considering the specific pedagogical environment of the classroom and teacher. Because teacher beliefs and expectations can become self-fulfilling prophecies, professional development would do well to focus on strengthening instructional practices and changing the deficit mindsets and negative beliefs that teachers harbor for specific students and student groups.

Attending inservices and workshops designed to increase teacher self-efficacy can be helpful, as Thompson et al. (2004) found that teachers' expectations are correlated with their sense of teaching efficacy. Many teachers in the cited study stated they had not been adequately prepared to effectively teach most of their students, especially in an urban setting. Teachers in underperforming schools are especially vulnerable to develop negative beliefs about their students, parents, and the school community.

The goal is to avoid the pitfall of the "blame game" and avoid the stereotyping, bias, and negative attitudes that subliminally are communicated to parents and students. Individual teachers can better help parents and students by being prepared to take responsibility for student achievement, which means that teachers need to revisit and redefine how they view the students in their classes.

Precautions and Potential Pitfalls

Professional development remedies to this situation are rarely found in schools. Teachers themselves need to begin to recognize the symptoms of the described phenomenon and do what they can to avoid the "blame game" pitfall. They need to see their students and parents as educational opportunities rather than classroom burdens.

Source

Thompson, G. L., Warren, S., & Carter, L. (2004). It's not my fault: Predicting high school teachers who blame parents and students for low achievement. *The High School Journal, 87*(3), 5–14.

Strategy 70: Involve low-income parents in their children's academic learning.

What the Research Says

Drummond and Stipek (2004) interviewed 234 low-income African American, Caucasian, and Latino parents about how important they rated (1) helping their second- and third-grade children in reading and math homework and (2) knowing what their children are learning. Also, parents reported whether they had taught their child in math and reading and whether they had read with their child in the past week. In addition, they responded to open-ended questions about the type of help they deemed appropriate. On questionnaires, teachers rated each student's reading and math skills and noted whether they had given a child's parent suggestions for helping with either subject.

Findings showed that parents rated the importance of helping their child with academic work very high. Parents of second graders tended to rate the importance of helping higher than did parents of third graders. Drummond and Stipek (2004) stated that, similar to past research, ratings varied systematically as a function of parents' perceptions of children's academic performance and as a function of whether teachers had offered suggestions. However, parents perceived helping with reading as more important than helping with math. Results suggest that teachers who desire more parent involvement might need to use different strategies for the two subjects.

In another study, Ingram, Wolfe, and Lieberman (2007) investigated the critical elements of parent involvement as it related to children's improved academic achievement. Survey data was collected from 220 parents whose children attended three Chicago public elementary schools. The schools serve largely minority, low-income student populations, yet score in the top third on the Illinois State Achievement Tests. The results suggest that schools struggling with unsatisfactory student achievement may benefit from focusing parent-involvement efforts on building parenting capacity and encouraging learning-at-home activities.

Applications

Veteran teachers are generally well aware of the benefits of family involvement in children's education. Parental support has always been seen as a critical component of education and, in the past, teachers assumed, accurately or not, that families supported their efforts and expectations for children's learning. In today's society, the issues surrounding parental school involvement and support are complicated by a large range of family arrangements and a wide sociocultural difference among classroom teachers, children, and families. Specifically, urban families are often marginalized from everyday school life by poverty, racism, and language and cultural differences, and the parents often perceive that public education is designed for children from middle-class, white families at the expense of others. Upper- and middle-income parents, for example, feel that they should collaborate with school efforts. But low-income families often perceive themselves as outside the school system and feel it is the school's responsibility to do the teaching.

Another factor contributing to parental involvement in their children's school is a feeling of efficacy. Parents who believe they can make a difference in their children's education are more likely to visit and participate in school activities than those who feel ineffective. Another contributing factor is the extent to which schools make parents feel comfortable and valued. Teachers and schools serving low-income, ethnically diverse neighborhoods must make greater efforts to welcome families because those are the parents who often feel excluded as a result of differences in their ethnicity, income, and culture.

There are various reasons why low-income parents, especially from diverse cultures, resist involvement in school activities, but certainly cultural and communication differences between teachers and families lie at the heart of the problem. When teachers' conversation styles match that of the community, children and families are more able and eager to participate in classroom activities. Urban teachers or teachers in schools with large numbers of low-income students often lack knowledge and respect of the ethnicities and cultures of the children they teach, and often have a limited knowledge of what parents do to help their children at home. Even the most well-meaning teachers do not always recognize the impact of family values, beliefs, and expectations about schooling. Consequently, some parent involvement projects do more harm than good because they do not build on the families' cultural capital and cultural prior knowledge.

Drummond and Stipek (2004) found that over half of the parents in their study felt that they should go to school and ask their children's teacher what they are learning. Schools and teachers need to remain committed to communicating with parents about their children's learning. Here are a few suggestions:

1. Teachers should ask parents what they are doing at home to help their children academically and reinforce the parent's interest in helping. It should also be noted that, in general, reports of giving help were higher for literacy curriculum than math. Parents need to know from the teacher what the homework is and how to help their children. Keep in mind also that parents may need more help in some content areas than others.

2. Teachers should actively develop an understanding of children's cultural backgrounds. Low-income urban parents are more likely to

participate in school activities when they feel their children are respected and their communities and heritages are valued.

3. Schools are responsible for establishing open communication with parents. However, teachers should not expect parents to communicate with the schools in middle-class ways, such as telephoning them, visiting, and writing notes. Many low-income diverse parents feel vulnerable with school authority, and they don't comfortably communicate with teachers. Many parents do not have cars and can't easily visit the school. Some speak little English, and some feel anxious about their own lack of education.

4. Low-income schools need alternative ways of connecting and communicating with parents who live in high-poverty areas. For example, the conventional "Parents Night" might be placed at a community room in the neighborhood where families live. Schools with children who are acquiring English should plan for interpreters when parents attend conferences and other school events. While some of the parents are bilingual, we know their anxiety about visiting school still blocks their ability to understand what teachers say to them.

5. Teachers must learn how to conduct effective parent conferences and break out of the "us versus them" mentality. Teachers should learn conversational strategies that focus on children's positive qualities and identify ways in which they might grow and be helped at home.

Parents who participated in the Ingram et al. (2007) study made several recommendations with implications for teachers:

- Provide families with information on homework policies and how to help their children with their schoolwork.
- Offer guidance and support for caregivers to supervise and assist children at home with homework assignments and other school learning opportunities.
- Encourage parents to become aware of the informal learning opportunities outside of school such as libraries, zoos, museums, and so on. Teachers can reinforce the importance of these activities by recognizing the efforts of the students and families in the classroom environment in a positive way.
- Aid parents in locating the community resources necessary to help them accomplish their parenting and other family goals.
- Provide training for both teachers and parents. Parenting education courses and other training opportunities can make a big difference in helping parents maximize their impact on academic achievement.

Precautions and Potential Pitfalls

There are no "one-size-fits-all" solutions to interacting with parents, especially within low-income and diverse demographics. This should always be viewed as work in progress. Rarely do teachers find themselves in a homogeneous school or classroom in an urban or suburban setting anymore. Once you shoulder the responsibility and gain some experience in dealing with parents and relationships between home and school, this becomes another part of your skill set. The rewards for helping families can be great!

Sources

Drummond, K. V., & Stipek, D. (2004). Low-income parents' beliefs about their role in children's academic learning. *The Elementary Journal, 104*(3), 197–215.

Ingram, M., Wolfe, R. B., & Lieberman, J. M. (2007). The role of parents in high-achieving schools serving low-income, at–risk populations. *Education and Urban Society, 39*(4), 479–497.

Strategy 71: *Understand how homework can present problems for students and families.*

What the Research Says

A book by John Buell and Etta Kralovec (2000) presents a unique view of the homework concept and questions the value of the practice itself. Few studies have been conducted on the subject, and while the book offers perspectives from both sides of the debate, it is clear that the homework concept needs to be examined more closely. For example, the authors cite homework as a great discriminator, as children, once leaving school, encounter a range of parental support, challenging home environments, afterschool jobs and sports, and a mix of resources available to some and not to others. Clearly, opportunities are not equal. Tired parents are held captive by the demands of their children's school, unable to develop their own priorities for family life.

The authors provide examples of communities that have tried to formalize homework policy to balance the demands of homework with extracurricular activities and the need for family time. They also point out the aspects of inequity inherent in the fact that many students lack the resources at home to compete on equal footing with those peers who have computers, Internet access, highly educated parents, and unlimited funds and other resources for homework requirements. However, homework persists despite the lack of any solid evidence that it achieves its much-touted gains. Homework is one of our most entrenched institutional practices but one of the least investigated.

The big questions explored in their research and discourse include the following:

- With single-parent households becoming more common or with both parents working, is it reasonable to accept the homework concept, as it is now practiced, as useful and valid considering the trade-offs families need to make?
- How does homework contribute to family dynamics in negative or positive ways?
- Does it unnecessarily stifle other important opportunities or create an uneven or unequal playing field for some students?

Classroom Applications

Consider the inequalities that may exist within the range of students in your classes regarding their ability to complete homework assignments. Certain students may be excluded from the opportunities for support and other resources. Think about the following questions when developing a homework philosophy or policy:

- What is homework?
- How much homework is too much?
- What are or should be the purposes of homework?
- Can different assignments be given to different students in the same class?
- Do all your students have equal opportunity to successfully complete the homework?
- Who is responsible for homework, the students or the parents?
- Do all your students have the same capacity to self-regulate?
- How are other school activities or family-based responsibilities factored in?
- What is the best and most equitable way to deal with "overachievers"?
- Is the homework load balanced between teachers?

Furthermore, consideration should be given to the following points and tips:

1. Integrate the homework activities and expectations into your curriculum planning. Ensure that the tasks are an integral element of your coursework and build the feedback from the homework into a following lesson.

2. Explain to parents and caregivers why you need their assistance. Parents and/or families need to understand why their involvement

is helpful, as some believe schools expect pupils to complete homework entirely independently. A range of approaches may be required to explain to as many parents and caregivers as possible, what you are proposing to do. This might include contact by telephone, personalized letters, specific meetings (consider venues other than the school), use of the support of other agencies and community contacts, and so on.

3. Stress that education is a "shared responsibility" between home and school. Homework can provide an ideal vehicle for establishing such a working partnership. Explain to parents that what happens out of school has a significant impact on children's performance at school—the assistance of parents and caregivers is essential to ensure that pupils perform to the best of their ability.

4. Reassure parents that no specialist knowledge is required. Assure them that it is simply the time that they give to their children and the discussion involved that are important—students take the role of the teacher and explain what's expected. This is an important learning exercise for the student.

5. Explain that it need not be the parents who help. Any trusted person (brother, sister, grandparent, neighbor) may be the source of support. It can also be a different person each day.

6. Place equal value on the contribution of all parents. It has often been found that very positive support has been forthcoming from homes where contact in the past may have been somewhat limited. Don't underestimate the contribution of any family.

7. Encourage the use of the language of the home. Homework tasks can be discussed or undertaken in any language. This should be encouraged.

8. Be realistic about how frequently you can call on the support of parents and caregivers. It is essential not to place too many demands on the goodwill of the home—it can easily be lost. Give consideration to how frequently these homework tasks should be set. Consult colleagues about the demands they place upon parents.

9. Value the responses from the home. It is important to ensure that the completion of these tasks is valued. If practicable, display the homework in a prominent place, in or out of school.

10. Evaluate the homework activities with the students and their families. This can be undertaken through the use of questionnaires, homework diaries, record sheets, or even the students' exercise books. Problems and successes need to be reviewed. A meeting can also be arranged to listen to the views of the parents and consolidate the working practices.

11. Sustain the commitment of families. Sending end-of-term thank-you letters to families can give the homework activities a high profile. Also, acknowledging the homework responses through assemblies, school newsletters, and displays can also help.

12. Share the outcome of your practice with all colleagues. It is important that all teachers are fully aware of the homework activities and the benefits that ensue.

13. Consider a training day focusing on homework. This may provide a valuable opportunity to broaden the base of support for your homework links with parents.

ED.gov at the U.S. Department of Education at http://www2.ed.gov/parents/academic/involve/homework/part.html offers information and a link to a book, Home Tips for Parents, to which you can refer students' parents.

Precautions and Potential Pitfalls

Homework is still a contested paradigm, and teachers need to have their own philosophy and be ready to engage in conversation with parents and administrators. Traditionally, homework has usually been seen as a solution to educational problems rather than the cause. It takes a little bit of acclimation time to begin to look at the homework paradigm with new eyes. Be very careful of the politics involved in any discourse regarding the homework concept.

Source

Buell, J., & Kralovec, E. (2000). *The end of homework: How homework disrupts families, overburdens children, and limits learning.* Boston: Beacon Press.

Strategy 72: Change parents' attitudes toward science to change students' attitudes.

What the Research Says

Two types of parental attitudes—parents' level of satisfaction with their children's performance in school and the importance parents place on children's academic success—were the focus of a study by McGrath and Repetti (2000). The data from 248 children, 219 mothers, and 146 fathers were consistent with the belief that parents' attitudes play a central role in shaping children's self-perceptions. Mothers' satisfaction was positively associated with both sons' and daughters' perceptions of academic competence, independent of children's actual grades in school. Fathers' satisfaction correlated with sons' self-perceptions but not when mothers' satisfaction was also included in the model. Both mothers and fathers reported being more satisfied with their daughters' grades than with their sons' grades, despite the fact that there were no actual differences between girls' and boys' academic performance. Finally, the importance fathers (but not mothers) placed on children's academic success was positively associated with girls' self-perceptions. Acherman-Chor, Aladro, and Gupta (2004) and Holt and Campbell (2004) also call attention to the importance of parental attitudes in math success and the ability and confidence to feel supported in taking academic risks by taking more difficult classes.

Applications

 Parents and students form ideas about the potential of various disciplines to become career choices when children are young. Science and math are somewhat unique disciplines in this regard. Parents can instantly devalue these disciplines by telling their child that they were not very good at science or math or that they never use science or math as adults. The application is simple. Let parents know that their attitudes about math or science carry weight with their children.

Teachers' teaching style, such as their use of cooperative rather than competitive learning and their overall expectations for females in math and science, also plays a pivotal role in girls' relationship with the disciplines. It is important that all individuals in students' lives validate the importance of science and math in their lives. Sell the importance of both disciplines. This is especially important for girls. York (2008) found that girls made career choices, post K–12, that as a group, moved away from math and science as a college or university major and as career choices. This phenomenon was not based on their lack of achievement in K–12 science and math classrooms but on other cultural factors and general attitudes toward science and math. Teachers need to be aware that in addition to teaching and learning, changing attitudes is important also!

Precautions and Potential Pitfalls

 There are no precautions or pitfalls here. The earlier a teacher is able to affect a parent's attitude, the better. Sometimes the damage is done in the younger years, and it is hard to undo.

Sources

Acherman-Chor, D., Aladro, G., & Gupta, S. D. (2004). Looking at both sides of the equation: Do student background variables explain math performance? *Journal of Hispanic Higher Education, 2*(2), 129–145.

Holt, J. K., & Campbell, C. (2004). The influence of school policy and practice on mathematics achievement during transitional periods. *Education Policy Analysis Archives, 12*(23). Retrieved June 6, 2007, from http://epaa.asu.edu/epaa/v12n23

McGrath, E. P., & Repetti, R. L. (2000). Mothers' and fathers' attitudes toward their children's academic performance and children's perceptions of their academic competence. *Youth and Adolescence, 29*(6), 713–723.

York, A. E. (2008). Gender differences in the college and career aspirations of high school valedictorians. *Journal of Advanced Academics, 19*(4), 578–600.

> ## ☑ Strategy 73: Involve community members in learning to explore home-based discourse.

What the Research Says

There are many studies that suggest that students' academic success is greatly improved when instruction is better matched with the discourse practiced outside of school or in the home (Au, 1980; Ballenger, 1997; Hogan, Pressley, & Nastasi, 1996; Roth, 1996, 1997; Warren, Rosebery, & Conant, 1989). Research on incorporating home-based discourse into teaching methods has suggested that the more connections teachers can make to the culture and community of students, the more likely the students' success. Beth Warren and her colleagues suggest that teachers work together to coteach lessons and to examine carefully through rigorous research the connections between students' culture and academic concepts. The result has been increased engagement and achievement of typically marginalized youth (Warren, Ballenger, Ogonowski, Rosebery, and Hudicourt-Barnes, 2001). Their Cheche Konnen model includes having native-speaking Haitian Creole parents working side-by-side with content teachers in the classroom, which has led to teaching and research innovations that otherwise would have gone unrecognized. Other models of cultural and community inclusion in the science teaching process were exemplified in Hammond's (2001) work with Hmong students and their families in the creation of a traditional Southeast Asian garden. Hammond demonstrated the value of using cultural discourse as a "fund of knowledge" in her successful attempts to interest students in science. The most important aspect of these and other successful projects is the connection between school and community—often by the collaboration between schools and community volunteers.

Classroom Applications

When teachers understand the cultural contributions children can bring to the classroom and the discourse they practice, the teachers are less likely to begin from a deficit model of instruction. Instead of

assuming, "My students can't (or don't) because they've never been to
_____," teachers of this orientation begin with what students *do know* and
how to incorporate it into instruction for students' success. There are many
ways in which children can become directly involved in issues in their
communities. As a first step in designing a project that would engage
children and teachers together in local community planning and development, teachers can identify issues that directly affected the community,
including local water sources, pollution and recycling, and school safety.
What follows is an example of children working together with volunteers
in the community to make an important change—namely, the changing of
speed limit signs to make the street safer for children.

Collaborating university faculty worked with teachers and students to
identify specific issues, develop a strategy for assessing the problem,
brainstorm solutions, and present children's ideas to the appropriate community leaders. One of the schools was located on a busy street, across
from an apartment building. Students were very concerned about the
speed of the cars that drove past and were aware that one student from
their school had been killed by a reckless driver. After brainstorming ideas
about the best way to bring this issue to the attention of community
leaders, it was agreed that videotaping offenders and presenting letters
and public service announcements would have the desired effect. For two
weeks, university faculty, teachers, and community volunteers, such as
police officers, integrated science instruction with mathematics, technology, and social responsibility within the literacy emphasis at the school.
Topics taught included motion, speed, school and societal rules, responsibility, and effective action while trying to provide an authentic context for
problem solving. "How fast do cars actually travel in front of our school?"
was the question they explored. Children used motion detectors to measure remote control cars, made graphs of constant and changing speeds,
and designed experiments to test a variety of phenomena.

Teachers then invited others to assist the children in more accurately
answering their question. A kind, but nonetheless imposing, police officer
from the local police department agreed to visit the classroom to discuss
speed limits, safety, and his equipment. Several officers on multiple occa-
sions came armed with radar detectors to assist children with their experiments. With notepads, graph paper, and signs in hand, students videotaped
offenders and documented the number of cars exceeding the speed limit.
Students observed some adults (a few saw their own parents) slowing
down once they realized they had been clocked, but others sped past unre-
morsefully, seemingly without noticing the legion of students and their
new friend, the police officer, with his radar detector. Officers trained
students to be keen observers of cars, speed, and safety, and suggested that
they point at speeding cars to let their drivers know they had been noticed.
When students tried this out, they found it was quite an effective tactic—
particularly when the officers found themselves pointing a mighty finger

(not the detector) at the cars. Students jumped up and down, elated by their new-found power to influence their neighbors and community.

Once all the data had been collected, students began the task of analyzing their results and compiling appropriate video clips for their public service announcements. The findings disturbed everyone. Of the 68 cars they clocked and charted, 59 were exceeding the limit. In the classroom, students chose to write letters, write and produce public service announcements, or use some other means to turn their science study into social activism. Publishing their findings in the local newspaper, posting pictures of speeding cars on local street signs, and designing more personal written pleas were some of the ways children used to make the existing laws more relevant to the community, and teachers learned to interact with parents and community members in new ways.

The teachers' efforts to make community connections caught the attention of a local television reporter, who asked the children and volunteers to repeat their study for broadcast to the larger community. Children took the opportunity to demonstrate again the classroom activities that helped them learn and showcase their video and written work. This literacy, science, and technology project taught children the power of writing in a powerful way, connected the teacher with community members of a wide diversity, and helped teachers to understand how to include home-based discourses into academic study. Children learned how writing can reach a wide audience, how it can promote change, and how it can educate adults and children.

Other examples of including community volunteers to incorporate home-based discourse could include the following:

- Inviting parents to come and share their vocations and expertise
- Beginning after school programs addressing opportunities for future work in the local area (e.g., culinary club)
- Asking for volunteers to come and help struggling student readers during reading time
- Creating assignments that require home contributions (e.g., "Who has the best recipe for the hottest salsa?")
- Asking students to interview family members for cultural knowledge about topics (e.g., "How can we keep from catching a cold?")
- Finding a common need in the community and volunteering as a class to meet the need (e.g., building a community garden)

Precautions and Possible Pitfalls

 It may seem overwhelming to open up the intended questions of study to a larger community focus or to coordinate strangers who may volunteer in the classroom. However, the payoffs for such daring teaching strategies are worth it. Teachers should choose wisely and be satisfied with small steps at first instead of taking on big challenges. The challenge for the teacher is to offer opportunities for students to populate classroom discourse in ways they do outside of school. These norms of discourse challenge the accepted beliefs of how to teach marginalized students as these strategies tend to sever teacher control from content-oriented questions. Notions like remediation and teaching "just the basics" run contrary to opening up classroom discourse to other forms of speaking, thinking, and acting. Although this approach may seem more complex or difficult, it is imperative to do so if teachers are to make changes for all students and live up to current reform visions.

Sources

Au, K. (1980). Participation structures in a reading lesson with Hawaiian children. *Anthropology and Education Quarterly, 11,* 91–115.

Ballenger, C. (1997). Social identities, moral narratives, scientific argumentation: Science talk in bilingual classrooms. *Language and Education, 11*(1), 1–14.

Hammond, L. (2001). Notes from California: An anthropological approach to urban science education for language minority families. *Journal of Research in Science Teaching, 38,* 983–999.

Hogan, K., Pressley, M., & Nastasi, B. (1996, April). Discourse patterns and scaffolding strategies that promote and inhibit student thinking during collaborative scientific inquiry. Paper presented at the annual meeting of the American Educational Research Association, New York.

Roth, W.-M. (1997). Interactional structures during a grade 4–5 open-design engineering unit. *Journal of Research in Science Teaching, 34,* 273–302.

Roth, W.-M. (1996). Teacher questioning in an open-inquiry learning environment: Interactions of context, content, and student responses. *Journal of Research in Science Teaching, 33,* 709–736.

Warren, B., Ballenger, C., Ogonowski, M., Rosebery, A., & Hudicourt-Barnes, J. (2001). Rethinking diversity in learning science: The logic of everyday sensemaking. *Journal of Research in Science Teaching, 38,* 529–552.

Warren, B., Rosebery, A., & Conant, F. (1989). Cheche Konnen: Science and literacy in language minority classrooms. BBN Technical Report No. 7305. Cambridge, MA: Bolt, Beranek and Newman, Inc.

Web Resources

Speed Limit Study:
http://gsewebvm.gse.buffalo.edu/fas/Yerrick/Taking_It_To_The_Street_How_One_Classroom_Changed_a_Community/Introduction.html
Comparing East and West Coast Estuaries: http://gsewebvm.gse.buffalo.edu/fas/Yerrick/Comparing_East_and_West_Coast_Estuaries/Introduction.html

Strategy 74: Recognize the diverse needs of language-minority students and families.

What the Research Says

Tapia (2000) conducted research in Tucson, Arizona, where 25% of the city's 400,000 member population are of Mexican descent. The city's Mexican demographic includes descendants of the original settlers of the city when it was controlled by Spain and later by Mexico. New immigrants are primarily from the Mexican state of Sonora. Many families are considered "cross-border" families because they make frequent trips across the border for jobs, family, and many other reasons.

Tapia's (2000) goal was to measure the relative weight of specific factors in shaping Mexican American students' school performance. The factors included interplay of cultural, economic, linguistic, and educational factors. Household analysis was used to illustrate how students' schooling and academic achievement was influenced by the household members' activities at home, in the community, and in the schools.

Most of the data were collected over a three-year period from 1988 to 1991. Thirty households were studied as part of a larger project; however, data were only collected from 15 households, and only four households were selected for in-depth studies. These households were visited between 15 and 23 times. The data collected gave clues and patterns to a study of economic and cultural survival, adaptation, and schooling practices.

The household analysis indicates that the level of family stability and the social and economic conditions of poor communities are the strongest factors affecting students' learning and academic achievement. The researcher argued that Mexican American students' learning and academic achievement will be better understood when seen in an accurate cultural and community context.

The four families investigated in Tapia's (2000) study had a total of 12 children among them. The majority of the children were cycling through middle school and high school. Many of the parents had attended school in Mexico, and none of the parents had attended college. While this research was more anecdotal in nature, some patterns did emerge that could be seen as unique for the community demographics studied. These patterns illustrate educational vulnerabilities that occur more frequently in Mexican American cultures. The study presented some student situations or snapshots typical of these Mexican American communities. The descriptions have been included here to help readers create an understanding and a context for any teaching strategies they might be considering or creating.

- *Family 1*. This family's children were highly influenced by several residential moves during the study period. School activities and academic performance were mitigated by unsettled living conditions. The family first came across the border and lived with grandparents. The household was full of cousins and other family members. After a year, the family moved to an apartment in another school district. The parents opted to keep the children in a bilingual program at their former address. An additional move to another house did result in a move to a new school. The change in curriculum required the children to step up to a more demanding curriculum and more homework. They had become accustomed to being with friends after school and didn't adjust well to homework demands.

- *Family 2*. This family had three school-age children that began their schooling in Mexico and then moved to the Tucson area and into a bilingual program. While learning to read and write in English, they were also encouraged to read and write in Spanish. The students did well, and the parents, although not completely understanding the curriculum, continued to help their children. One day, the father became enraged over his daughter's history assignment on the United States–Mexican War. The title was "The Mythology of the Alamo." In this assignment, Mexicans were depicted in a less-than-positive light and as troublemakers. The parents felt the teachers were teaching students using stereotypes and prejudices toward minorities, and they felt this was disrespectful. All communication from the parents stopped.

- *Family 3*. Jose, the oldest sibling of this large family, was frequently placed in highly academic classes and played on the school's soccer team. As a junior, he became a varsity player. There were high expectations for the varsity players the following year when the team would be made up of a majority of seniors. Jose found academic success although his record of completing homework was mixed. He was part of a small group of Mexican American players that formed the core of the team. Conflicts for Jose began in his senior year when he did not return from a Christmas trip to Mexico until school league play was well under way. His family's economic situation changed between his junior and senior years. Not only did he miss his winter break obligations to his soccer team, he returned to school from his trip to Mexico two weeks past the traditional winter break, which compromised his academic standing. Rather than practice soccer, Jose was asked to watch his younger brothers and sisters after school. He was demoted to junior varsity and was forced to play with younger students who were not as skillful. This placement lasted until grades came out in the middle of the season, when Jose became academically ineligible to play on any team. From then on, Jose lost all motivation for school, went to work to help support his family, and dropped out of school in his senior year. In this case, there were no calls home from any school representative, and Jose just dropped out of sight.

- *Family 4.* Seven people lived in the Sanchez household. Mr. Sanchez was born in Sonora, Mexico, where he completed 12 years in Mexican schools. He worked as a musician in Mexico and repaired cars in Tucson. Mrs. Sanchez completed nine years in Mexican schools and worked in a potato chip factory. The three oldest sons who were born in Sonora ranged in age from 14 to 18 years old. The youngest two children were born in Arizona and were four and 12 years old. The family's household survival strategies had direct and indirect effects on the students' schooling. These strategies were deemed more important than the curriculum of the school and the language of instruction. Mr. Sanchez made five trips to Mexico per week for his music contacts and practice, and his oldest son, Roberto, often went with him and finally joined the band. For Roberto, academic performance was heavily influenced by his incorporation into the band and his cross-border trips. The next youngest, Ricardo, did not take as many trips across the border. Ricardo had a close relationship with his mother, keeping her company and helping with the household chores. Staying at home allowed Ricardo to do homework in a relatively stable environment in contrast to Roberto who did his homework in the car. However, Ricardo did eventually join his father's band as well. Both found girlfriends in Nogales, further complicating their academic performance. Later in Tapia's study, all three of the oldest children graduated from high school.

Applications

 The Mexican American families and students described can be considered somewhat characteristic of the United States Mexican populations along the border. While it would be a mistake to stereotype every Mexican family based on this study, it is clear there are factors and influences in this specific demographic that are unique, and it would be a mistake not to consider them. Teachers need to place their students in an accurate context.

While there are many variations to these stories, they point out how a family's survival strategies and the structure and organization of each family's situation have direct and indirect influences on home and school connections and the students' academic success. The community's poor economic context also contributed to a less-than-ideal school-home situation. These perspectives present a more dynamic and heterogeneous view of students' learning than would a more stereotypical, uniform cultural model. There are some basic assumptions that teachers and schools can make from Tapia's research:

- Compatibility between the language of instruction and interaction with students' and parents' home language facilitates learning. Students do learn best in their native language—schools need to be aware of this, and they can help by communicating with parents in their native language. Schools and teachers need to recognize that to enlist parental support, native language use is critical. Schools can become more *user friendly* for language minority parents.

- Changes in a household's economic and survival strategies, in some contexts, are more important than the language of instruction and school in general.
- There is an increasing influence of peers and family on student behavior as the students become older. Neighborhood social relationships sometimes limit high-level academic competence. There may be few high-achieving role models. Visits to the school by minority community role models can help. One school sponsors minority trips to colleges and universities as a strategy to pique student interest and motivation beyond high school.

Of the 12 children in Tapia's study, most graduated from high school but none from a college or university. These examples illustrate that there are no easy solutions, and every family and student must be seen and dealt with as individuals. Stereotyping students in these communities will not serve a teacher well.

In this era of high-stakes testing, the academic performance of minority children has been hotly debated in the media and in academic circles. It should come as no surprise that learning and academic performance are influenced by a range of factors and interactions between family and community economics, historical inertia, cultural norms, social norms, and linguistic backgrounds. All of these factors interact with the student at home and in the community and come into the school and influence performance in the classroom.

Teachers need to consider adapting classroom instruction to these circumstances and try to accommodate the instructional program to meet the needs of the students and parents. Rigid, ultralinear programs will only frustrate students and parents. Frustration can mean that given a choice, family and personal concerns will win over school concerns, and the student may drop out.

Teachers need to make school important to students and their families, both from a student perspective and a parent perspective. Teachers may not have all the answers, but empathy can go a long way in making a student's time in school a positive and stable experience. In turn, parents who have positive experiences at their children's school and who believe that school personnel want to work with them to help their children succeed in school are more likely to initiate contact with teachers and schools.

Precautions and Potential Pitfalls

 It is understandable that teachers, who have been successful in school and highly value school themselves, may not always understand the priorities some parents have. Teachers often see students from these communities as problematic to their linear instructional agendas and programs. Rather than trying to fit students into a model of instruction that puts them at a disadvantage, teachers could try instructional models used by continuation schools and other similar programs that are designed to accommodate heterogeneous groups on different schedules and instructional paces.

Sources

Tapia, J. (2000). Schooling and learning in U.S.-Mexican families: A case study of household. *The Urban Review, 32*(1), 25–44.

Strategy 75: Consider parental responses to a child's learning disability.

What the Research Says

Ferguson and Asch (1989) reviewed the research on family reactions to having a child with a disability. As with many social phenomena, a family's interpretation of the meaning of disability cannot help but reflect to some degree the larger context of social attitudes and historical realities within which personal interpretation emerges. Ferguson and Asch (1989) tried to reflect the interpretations of families within the research orientations of the time. Ferguson (2002) found two new strands that have emerged in more recent research, and his review explores how these approaches promise more useful interpretive frames for efforts to improve linkages between families and schools. The basic two questions the researchers looked at were the following:

- What is the nature of parental reaction to having a child with a disability?
- What is the source of the reaction?

Ferguson (2002) dealt with how the answers to these questions have changed over time. Professionals have shifted their attention to how a family is affected by the birth of a child with a disability. Whether researchers preferred to use primarily attitudinal (guilt, denial, displaced anger, grief) categories or behavioral ones (role disruption, marital cohesiveness, social withdrawal), most assumed a connection that was both intrinsic and harmful. They go on to describe and characterize a range of repeated responses typical of families. The main parental categories that describe the parents' state of mind, as developed by the researchers, are as follows:

- Psychodynamic Approach: The Neurotic Parent
- Functional Approach: The Dysfunctional Parent
- Interactionist: The Powerless Parent
- The Adaptive Family
- The Supportive Family Applications

Each of these categories brings a different set of circumstances and characteristics for teachers to deal with in helping students with special needs. The research centered on analyzing the specific categories.

Applications

 First, keep in mind that the term "family" can describe and categorize a wide range of living conditions for a student, and relationships to family may have changed over time for a child. Much of the time, a disability is seen as a message telling the parents what the student can't do or accomplish or what he or she can't become in his or her life. Also, many times it's the child's teachers who deliver the messages, which can put teachers in a less-than-favorable role.

Teachers are part of a team of adults concerned about the individual students in their classes. Regardless of where one stands regarding the cultural and societal context of families and children with special needs, there is an immense variety of beliefs and practices that have undeniably powerful influences on how a specific family interprets a specific disability. Teachers will often be pulled into the mix, and it is a good idea to have some understanding of the potential structure of the family situation and how the family might choose to react. They might be apathetic or involved, angry or accepting. They might express displeasure with the providers over a supposed lack of supports, as displaced anger originally directed toward their child. Teachers may want to examine their own performance inadequacies before categorizing the parental responses as nonjustifiable anger toward the system.

On the positive side, Ferguson and Asch (1989) found there is increasing recognition that many families cope effectively and positively with the additional demands experienced in parenting a child with a disability. They found in the most recent literature that families of children with learning disabilities exhibit variability comparable to the general population with respect to important outcomes.

Some suggestions for the general education teachers are as follows:

- Read individualized education plans (IEPs) and know how the information within them manifests itself in your classes. There is nothing less professional than not being familiar with students' issues or their performance in class. Stay on top of it.

- Be prepared to deal with parents who exhibit many of the characteristics described here. Check with special education teachers or counselors who may have been working with the parents before contact.
- Discuss strategies for parental contacts with counselors and special education teachers. If you are a teacher of a first- or second-grade child, it is likely you will be part of the initial assessment and IEP process, so it is important to talk with the psychologist and case manager and relay what you know about the family and child prior to the meeting.
- Be prepared to focus on what is best for the child. When talking with parents, avoid discussing curricular or instructional needs and constraints. Parents want to know how you are going to help their child be successful.
- Remember to avoid telling parents what their child can't do. Thoughtfully prepare positive comments and strategies in advance of meeting with the parents.
- Listen carefully, as parents may provide information that will help you.

Typically, it is the academic classes, including science and math, in which students with learning disabilities struggle the most. If the parents believe you are making a sincere effort to individually work with their child, they are likely to make success in your class a priority at home. It is very rewarding to orchestrate a special education student's success in science by considering the parents' viewpoint and making the effort to involve them.

Precautions and Potential Pitfalls

Parents are primarily concerned with their children and how the school and teachers can help them. Always, in conversation, keep their child's needs as the focus and your teacher needs and school's limitations on the back burner.

Sources

Ferguson, P. M. (2002). A place in the family: An historical interpretation of research on parental reactions to having a child with a disability. *Journal of Special Education, 36*(3), 124–131.

Ferguson, P. M., & Asch, A. (1989). Lessons from life: Personal and parental perspectives on school, childhood, and disability. In D.P. Biklen, D.L. Ferguson, & A. Ford (Eds.) *Schooling and disability: Eighty-eight yearbook of the National Society for the Study of Education,* Part II (pp. 108–140). Chicago: National Society for the Study of Education.

Index